THE ETHICS OF ANTHROPOLOGY

Since the inception of their discipline, anthropologists have studied virtually every conceivable aspect of other people's morality – religion, social control, sin, virtue, evil, duty, purity and pollution. But what of the examination of anthropology itself, and of its agendas, epistemes, theories and practices? In 1991, Raymond Firth spoke of social anthropology as an essentially moral discipline. Is such a view outmoded in the postmodern era? Do anthropological ethics have to be rethought each generation as the conditions of the discipline change, and as choices collide with moral alternatives?

The Ethics of Anthropology looks at some of these crucial issues as they reflect on researcher relations, privacy, authority, secrecy and ownership of knowledge. The book combines theoretical papers and case studies from eminent scholars including Lisette Josephides, Stephen Nugent, Marilyn Silverman, Andrew Spiegel and Veronica Strang. Showing how the topic of ethics goes to the heart of anthropology, it raises the controversial question of why – and for whom – the anthropological discipline functions.

Pat Caplan is Professor of Anthropology at Goldsmiths College, University of London, and former Chair of the Association of Social Anthropologists of the UK and Commonwealth. Her books with Routledge include *Class and Gender in India* (1985), *The Cultural Construction of Sexuality* (1987), *Gendered Fields* (1993), *African Voices, African Lives* (1997) and *Food, Health and Identity* (1997).

THE ETHICS OF ANTHROPOLOGY

Debates and dilemmas

Edited by Pat Caplan

Routledge
Taylor & Francis Group

LONDON AND NEW YORK

First published 2003
by Routledge
11 New Fetter Lane, London EC4P 4EE

Simultaneously published in the USA and Canada
by Routledge
29 West 35th Street, New York, NY 10001

Routledge is an imprint of the Taylor & Francis Group

Typeset in Garamond by
Rosemount Typing Services, Thornhill, Dumfriesshire
Printed and bound in Great Britain by
MPG Books Ltd, Bodmin

British Library Cataloguing in Publication Data
A catalogue record for this book is available from the British Library

Library of Congress Cataloging in Publication Data
The ethics of anthropology / edited by Pat Caplan.
p. cm.
Includes bibliographical references and index.
1. Anthropological ethics. I. Caplan, Patricia.

GN33.6.E86 2003
174'.9309–dc21

2002045494

ISBN 0-415-29642-0 (hbk)
ISBN 0-415-29643-9 (pbk)

CONTENTS

CONTENTS

PLATES

CONTRIBUTORS

Gill Barber is a midwife and nurse as well as an anthropologist. She has a particular interest in using anthropology as a means of understanding women's health and the experience of pregnancy and birth. She worked in Senegal soon after qualifying as a midwife, and then taught for many years at the Royal College of Nursing in London. She now works independently as an anthropologist, teacher and advisor in midwifery, nursing and education and is currently involved in a safe motherhood partnership project with Kenyan and UK professional organisations. She is also about to complete her PhD thesis entitled 'The processes of childbearing in rural Malawi: an ethnographic study of knowledge, risk perception and decision making in a matrilineal community' at Goldsmiths College.

Pat Caplan is Professor of Anthropology at Goldsmiths College, University of London. She has carried out fieldwork in Tanzania, Nepal, Madras City, and in Wales, and has published a number of monographs and edited collections. From 1998 to 2000, she was seconded for three years to serve as Director of the Institute of Commonwealth Studies, School of Advanced Study in the University of London. She also served as Chair of the Association of Social Anthropologists from 1997 to 2001. Most recently, she has been working on issues of food, which has led to an interest in risk, the subject of her latest book, *Risk Revisited* (Pluto 2000), and now in ethics and morality. She currently holds a Leverhulme Research Fellowship, and is working on local understandings of modernity in Tanzania.

Nigel Eltringham is a postdoctoral researcher (funded by the ESRC) in the Department of Anthropology and Sociology, School of Oriental and African Studies, University of London. He has previously worked for a conflict resolution and development NGO in Rwanda and in rural development in Latin America. A book based on his PhD thesis is to be published by Pluto Press in 2003 (*Accounting for Horror: Post-Genocide Debates in Rwanda*).

Susan Greenwood is a Lecturer in the School of Cultural and Community Studies at the University of Sussex, an Open University Associate Lecturer, and Visiting

Fellow at Goldsmiths College, University of London. She conducted PhD research on Paganism in London in the 1990s and is currently completing a study of Pagans' attitudes to nature, to be published as *Nature Religion: Paganism, New Age, and western Shamanism*. Her recent publications include *Magic, Witchcraft and the Otherworld: An Anthropology* (Berg 2000), and *The Encyclopedia of Magic and Witchcraft* (Lorenz 2001).

Lisette Josephides has a background in philosophy as well as anthropology. Following doctoral fieldwork in the highlands of Papua New Guinea she continued to live in that country for seven years, and taught at the local university. She then taught at the London School of Economics and the University of Minnesota before moving to Queen's University, Belfast. Her first book, *The Production of Inequality*, presented an analysis of Melanesian gender relations as modelling and disguising relations of inequality. Subsequently her interests have ranged over topics such as anthropological knowledge and its production; methodological, epistemological and psychological questions in fieldwork and ethnographic writing; myth and narrative; 'biographies of social action'; the pragmatics of speaking and the strategies of everyday life. Currently she is engaged in research on ethics, morality and human rights.

Vasiliki Kravva studied history and archaeology at the Aristotle University of Thessaloniki (1990 to 1995). In 1993, she spent six months at the University of Cagliari Department of Social Anthropology in Sardinia. In 1996 she completed an MA in Social Anthropology at Goldsmiths College, University of London and in 1997 started a PhD programme at the same institution. Between October 1998 and December 2000 she carried out fieldwork among Thessalonikan Jews on the relationship between Sephardic cuisine and Jewish identity. She has recently presented her PhD thesis entitled '"Tell me what you eat and I tell you if you are Jewish": food and discourses of identity among Thessalonikan Jews'.

David Mills carried out fieldwork in Uganda and obtained his PhD from the School of Oriental and African Studies, University of London. He subsequently taught at the University of Manchester. In 1999 he was awarded a Leverhulme Special Research Fellowship to work on a political and institutional history of social anthropology in Britain in the latter half of the twentieth century. He is currently based in the Department of Cultural Studies and Sociology at the University of Birmingham, where he is also Anthropology Coordinator of the Centre for the Study of Sociology, Anthropology and Politics (C-SAP). He was co-organiser for the 2002 ASA Conference held in Arusha, Tanzania.

Stephen Nugent is Reader in Anthropology at Goldsmiths College and also an Associate Fellow of the Institute of Latin American Studies, School of Advanced Study, both in the University of London. He has carried out long-term fieldwork in the Brazilian Amazon and is the author of *Big Mouth: the Amazon Speaks* (Fourth Estate 1990) and *Amazonian Caboclo Society: an Essay on Invisibility and Peasant Economy* (Berg 1993) and co-editor (with Cris Shore) of *Anthropology and*

Cultural Studies (Pluto 1997) and *Elites and Anthropology* (Routledge 2002). He also co-edits the journal *Critique of Anthropology*.

Marilyn Silverman is Professor of Anthropology at York University, Toronto. She has carried out field research in Guyana, Ecuador and, most recently, Ireland. Her areas of interest are local-level political economy, historical anthropology, labour studies and agrarian processes. Her ethnographies include *An Irish Working Class: Explorations in Political Economy and Hegemony, 1800–1950* (University of Toronto Press, 2001); *Merchants and Shopkeepers* (with P.H. Gulliver, University of Toronto Press, 1995); and *Rich People and Rice: Factional Politics in Rural Guyana* (Leiden: E.J. Brill, 1980). She has edited several volumes, including *Approaching the Past: Historical Anthropology through Irish Case Studies* (with P.H. Gulliver; Columbia University Press, 1992) and *A House Divided? Anthropological Studies of Factionalism* (with R.F. Salisbury; Newfoundland: ISER, 1978).

Andrew Spiegel is Associate Professor and Head of the Department of Social Anthropology, University of Cape Town. His work focuses on southern Africa and has been concerned with kinship and domesticity in contexts of labour migration, urbanisation and housing policy. He has also worked on the constructedness of tradition and is at present engaged in an ethnographic study of the expansion of a Europe-based pedagogical movement into southern and east Africa.

Veronica Strang has recently become Professor and Dean of the School of Social Science at the Auckland University of Technology. Prior to that she was the Royal Anthropological Institute Fellow in Urgent Anthropology, based at Goldsmiths College London, on leave from her post as a Senior Lecturer at the University of Wales, Lampeter, and Director of the Centre for Anthropologist Australian Studies in Wales. As an environmental anthropologist, she has conducted extensive fieldwork both in northern Australia and in the UK. Research on land and resource issues in Australia has led to applied work on indigenous rights and land claims. Her book *Uncommon Ground: Cultural Landscapes and Environmental Values*, published by Berg in 1997, explores the different environmental interactions of Aboriginal communities, pastoralists and other land users in Far North Queensland, and her present work is directly concerned with representational issues and Aboriginality.

PREFACE

Four events coincided to suggest to me that the ethics of anthropological practice was a subject which might well be re-aired. The first was the decision in 1999 of the Committee of the Association of Social Anthropologists (ASA), of which I was then a member, to revise the ethical guidelines originally formulated a decade earlier. The revision was prompted in part by the remark of one member that the guidelines appeared 'somewhat dated', but also by a complaint from another that the Ethics Committee in his institution was not only demanding to scrutinise all research by academics, but that by students too. It prompted me to wonder if ethical guidelines had to be regularly revised to suit new conditions.

The second was the furore which erupted, even before it had been published, over the recent book by Patrick Tierney (2001) about anthropological research carried out over several decades on the Yanomami Indians of Venezuela, a topic which is the subject of Nugent's chapter in this book. As an office-holder of the ASA, I was jointly responsible with the Director of the Royal Anthropological Institute (RAI) for drafting a press release about the position of the two major British anthropology associations on this matter. How do such associations discuss the ethics of anthropologists who are not even their members – and is it ethical to do so?

The third was an invitation to an international meeting of European social scientists held in July 2000 with the purpose of drafting an ethical code applicable to all social science disciplines. Although the meeting lasted for two intensive days, it rapidly became apparent that the task set us was close to impossible. For anthropologists, lawyers, experimental psychologists, philosophers, sociologists from a variety of European states to find a common language, or even establish basic premises, was problematic. So are there different ethics for different disciplines? And are there different ethical traditions in different countries?

Finally, around the same time I was confronted with the necessity to make statements on the ethical implications of my own proposed research by a number of the funding bodies for social science in Britain to which I was applying. I found myself invoking the ASA guidelines, even appending copies with my application forms. Does this suggest that such codes are more for our own protection and to satisfy committees rather than ensuring that anthropologists think through the ethical implications of their research?

In the spring term of 2001, a seminar was convened at Goldsmiths College to discuss some of these issues. Ten people gave papers, of whom seven went on to contribute to this volume, while a further three (Silverman, Spiegel and Eltringham) were recruited subsequently to the project and deserve particular thanks for producing papers at short notice.

I am grateful to the staff and students of Goldsmiths Anthropology Department for their perceptive questions and comments during the course of the seminar series; to the authors for their contributions, cooperation in the editing process and forbearance during what turned out to be a somewhat lengthier time-scale than had originally been envisaged; and to the Routledge readers Bill Watson and Richard Blot for their helpful comments on the proposal. I also want to thank David Mills and Lionel Caplan for a number of useful suggestions and the latter for much assistance and encouragement.

Carole Fluehr-Lobban very kindly made available the draft introduction to the revised edition of her book *Ethics and the Profession of Anthropology*.

Pat Caplan
October 2002

1

INTRODUCTION

Anthropology and ethics

Pat Caplan

Whenever one descends from the relatively secure realm of concepts to the description of any concrete object the concepts are supposed to stand for – one finds merely a fluid collection of men and women acting at cross purposes, fraught with inner controversy and conspicuously short of the means to arbitrate between conflicting ethical positions. The moral community proves to be not so much imagined as postulated, and postulated contentiously.

(Bauman 2001: 141)

It is one of the paradoxes of the social sciences that their moral stance has not been higher than [that of] the surrounding topography.

(Appell 1978: xi)

Introduction

In the West in recent years, there has been a discursive explosion around ethics. On the political front, the newly elected Labour government in Britain in 1997 stated that it would pursue an 'ethical' foreign policy, a claim which rapidly became the butt of jokes by political commentators as being more honoured in the breach than the observance. It was reported that the 'ethical' policies of the Foreign and Commonwealth Office were regularly undermined by the Department of Trade and Industry, whose own priorities were to support British exports, while the Ministry of Defence 'promoted arms sales without adequate safeguards' (*Guardian Weekly*, 4 October 1998). Economic interests appeared largely to prevail over ethical and even, in some cases, longer-term political interests.

Ethics-talk has entered the economic arena too. A number of companies today offer their customers the option of investing their money in 'ethical' accounts. Indeed, the number of such schemes has multiplied in the last few years and they are currently growing faster than conventional investment 'products'.[1] The financial pages of the broadsheets regularly report on their progress with headlines like 'Boardrooms discover corporate ethics' (Cowe 1999), while big foundations such as Ford endorse ethical investment: 'Corporate ethics meets the bottom line: ethical behaviour is good for business – and can lead to new markets' (Lang 1999: 16). There are now 'ethical consumers', 'corporate ethics', and 'socially responsible businesses'.

The university world has not escaped these discussions. In Britain, a vociferous campaign called 'Ethics for USS' (Universities' Superannuation Scheme) called for ethical investment of the universities' pension fund.[2] After two years of hard lobbying, USS agreed that it would move to a 'socially responsible investment policy', resulting in such headlines as 'Professors' pensions are cleaned up' and 'USS strengthens its commitment to SRI (socially responsible investment)' (*Ethics for USS newsletter*, December 2001).

Academics have also been part of debates around the ethics of current academic practices, as universities have been urged by governments and forced by lack of state funding to look for income from a variety of sources. Indeed, 'Support from business and industry is regarded ... as not only necessary in the current funding climate, but as a positive good, obliging academics to engage with the real world' (*Guardian Weekly*, 24 May 1998, p. 13). Some universities have accepted money from such sources as Wellcome, Shell and British American Tobacco (BAT), leading to discussions about the need for 'guidelines'. For example, the Committee of Vice-Chancellors and Principals (CVCP) and the Cancer Research Campaign joined together in 1999 to issue protocols on universities' acceptance of funding from tobacco companies (*CVCP News*, Spring 1999: 5).[3] Yet it is the case, of course, that, as an editorial in the *Times Higher Education Supplement* put it, 'For centuries, universities have provided a socially useful way of laundering grubby money. Suppression of the monasteries, piracy, slavery, American robber barons' ruthless exploitation; all generated profits that have supported scholars and enriched academic foundations. Guilty money was washed clean' (*THES*, 23 October 1999: 14). The difference now is that such matters are perhaps more hotly debated than previously.

At the same time, universities in Britain, like their North American counterparts at an earlier date, have increasingly set up ethics committees to scrutinise the research of their academics, and even, as mentioned above, that of their students. Academics are required to make statements about the ethical implications of their work, to complete forms with checklists, and to give undertakings that all their research will be based upon principles of informed consent. While such developments are rationalised in terms of the upholding of an ethical 'gold standard' by the participants in the research, there is little doubt that universities are also increasingly concerned about the possibility of litigation, and see ethics statements and consent forms as ways of avoiding this. Clearly then, there is a politics and economics of ethics.

Anthropologists, like other social scientists (and scientists), now have not only to behave in an ethical way but also to be seen to be so doing by all parties involved: research subjects, colleagues, students, funders, ethics committees, and the public at large. For many, these aims can be achieved by adherence to a professional Code of Ethics. However, as will be seen, achieving agreement has never been easy, since such codes are often highly contested in their formulation, and agreement about interpretation is also problematic (see Mills, next chapter).

Yet the ethics of anthropology is clearly not just about obeying a set of guidelines; it actually goes to the heart of the discipline: the premises on which its practitioners operate, its epistemology, theory and praxis. In other words, *what* is anthropology for? *Who* is it for? Do its ethics need to be re-thought each generation, as the discipline's conditions of existence change? Are there different ethics for different contexts?

In an interview in 1991, Raymond Firth spoke of his view of social anthropology as essentially a *moral* discipline (Quigley 1991). Is such a view outmoded in a postmodern era? Anthropologists have, of course, studied other people's morals under various rubrics: religion, values, social control, sin, virtue, evil, reason, duties, purity and pollution; even, following Durkheim, society itself which devises moral rules for its self-perpetuation. This remains a worthwhile exercise, but so too does the examination of our own ethics and morals, as members of the tribe of anthropologists. Here is another, more reflexive sense in which morality and ethics may be studied: that of choice and conflict between choices, and the existence of moral alternatives.

Ethics and morality are frequently used interchangeably, although some see them as different. The philosopher Bernard Williams proposes that ethics is any way of answering the question 'How ought one to live?' while morality is a certain kind of answer to that question, namely one involving moral obligations such as rules, rights, duties, commands and blame (Williams 1985 in Laidlaw 2002: 316). Pocock has suggested that ethics and morality are increasingly pulling apart, and that ethics has moved in to fill a moral vacuum (1988). Is there then a sense in which we can see morality as more fundamental than ethics? Can morality have claims to truth and universal applicability while ethics is culturally and historically variable?[4] If so, what are those claims of morality and to what extent do ethics change and why? These are all questions which should inform what follows, and which will be discussed again at the end of this chapter.

While some have argued that ethics is central to the discipline, others have been less enthusiastic. Pels (1999) argues that ethics is an 'empty signifier', which can be made to mean almost anything. I prefer, however, to follow Shore's dictum, paraphrasing Lévi-Strauss, that ethics, its codes and the debates which surround them are 'good to think with' (1999: 124), since it is vital that such thinking informs our practice. That is the aim of this book.

Anthropologists writing ethics

The literature on ethics in anthropology is large,[5] and if other social sciences are included, it becomes enormous. Yet it appears that there are certain times when there are discursive explosions around the topic, and other periods which are relatively quiescent. Anthropological preoccupation with ethical matters is most vividly expressed in the numerous debates which have taken place, particularly in the USA, over ethical codes. The drafting of such codes has usually been in response to particular developments in the discipline, crises caused either by scandals such as Project Camelot[6] in the US or by the entry of its graduate students into applied work (Fluehr-Lobban 1991). I do not propose to give a history of ethical codes in British and American anthropology, since that topic is admirably covered by David Mills in the next chapter. Rather, I want here to consider *how* anthropologists have written about ethics and what circumstances might explain different ethical positions. I will thus proceed chronologically, although this chapter does not pretend to give an exhaustive survey of all the available literature.

In a recent work on the ethics of the social sciences (1997), the German philosopher Siep begins by pointing out that there is a long-standing set of differences in European philosophy. For Plato and the Stoics, the idea of the good and justice are the same for all mankind, while for Aristotle the philosopher has to reflect on the moral tradition of a particular moral community. Noting that there are variations between the ethical cultures and traditions in various European countries, Siep asks what is the relevance of this for research ethics. He wonders whether, as Europe becomes more of an entity, people may learn from each other and ethics may eventually similarly converge. But at present, he points out, there are major differences in ethical values and traditions, as a study of differing ecological movements and the varied degree of resistance to genetic engineering indicate. He argues that ethics thus need to be viewed in the historical and cultural contexts which have produced them.

For philosophers, as for anthropologists, the issue of ethics raises the hoary question of universalism versus relativism, since a comparison of different historical periods and different national disciplinary traditions suggests that the field of anthropological ethics is a shifting one. Yet, as will be seen, there is frequent invocation by some anthropologists of moral values which they hold to be universal: the intellectual search for some form of truth, the need for professional integrity, the upholding of the human dignity of their research subjects.

In what follows, I seek to place debates about anthropological ethics in their historical context over the last four decades,[7] and also to draw some comparisons between the two anthropological traditions – British and American – on which I am concentrating. I would not wish, however, to imply that there is unanimity of views within any one anthropological community; far from it. In this regard, I will explore the argument propounded by Appell several decades ago, that it is precisely at the moment when the boundaries of a discipline are redefined that ethical discourse increases. At such a point, he argues, 'the shared moral base of its members begins to deliquesce' (1978: 1). In other words, debates around the topic of ethics are part of the way in which anthropologists seek to constitute themselves as a moral community.

The 1960s: Responsibility, commitment and relevance

The 1960s were turbulent years politically: Britain, like other European colonising powers, was experiencing the end of its African empire, while the United States was engaged in a war in South-east Asia, as well as in the domestic struggles around the Civil Rights Movement. All of these issues were to have repercussions in anthropology, although it was not until the 1970s that the implications of decolonisation were tackled by British anthropology. For American academics, however, the issues were immediate since their students were liable for conscription to fight in Vietnam. A number of anthropologists became involved in the 'war on campus' and beyond; some, like Gough, even choosing to leave the United States, while other scholars, like André Gunder Frank, were forced to do so.

In 1968, under the heading of the 'Responsibility Symposium', the US journal *Current Anthropology* carried articles by Gerald Berreman, Gutorm Gjessing and Kathleen Gough. All of them were uncompromising in their critique of anthropology as it was then practised. Gough stated

> We have virtually failed to study Western imperialism as a social system, or even adequately to explore the effects of imperialism on the societies we studied ... Force, suffering and exploitation tend to disappear in these accounts of structural processes ... [we] have done little to aid understanding of the world distribution of power under imperialism or of its total system of economic relationships.
>
> (pp. 405–6)

Gough noted that anthropologists were caught between conflicting demands: demands of the people studied, colleagues and the discipline; demands of those who employ or fund anthropologists; and most recently, demands of students, 'who are now, because of their own crises, asking awkward questions about ethics, commitments and goals' (p. 405).

For Berreman, anthropologists simply *had* to get involved in such issues:

> The dogma that public issues are beyond the interests or competence of those who study and teach about man is myopic and sterile professionalism and a fear of commitment which is both irresponsible and irrelevant. Its result is to dehumanize the most humanist of the sciences.
>
> (1968: 39)

Gjessing, a Norwegian anthropologist, asked whether social scientists in general, and anthropologists in particular, were not merely 'playing an intellectual game in which nobody outside our own tiny circle is interested'. He wondered, furthermore, whether they risked developing into 'a small isolated, esoteric sect of believers … in the midst of a gigantic world revolution that threatens the annihilation of mankind' (1968: 397).

These three articles raised a number of crucial issues:

> the responsibility of social scientists, particularly anthropologists;
> the status of science and objectivity;
> anthropology as an outgrowth of colonialism;
> the relevance of anthropology to a rapidly changing world, and how it might be made more relevant;
> whether anthropological fieldwork should be carried out abroad or at home;
> the nature of the anthropologist's commitment: to the discipline, to the people studied, to students.

None of these questions has gone away in the more than three decades since they were first raised.

On the other side of the Atlantic, the topic of ethics in the social sciences was also beginning to get an airing, although more frequently by sociologists than by anthropologists (see Sjoberg 1967). The anthropologist John Barnes published his first work on the subject in the *British Journal of Sociology* in 1963, raising important questions he was to develop in two later books (1977, 1979). He asked how the social sciences differed from the natural sciences, to what extent the parameters of anthropology were changing rapidly in a de-colonising context, and also discussed issues of anonymity, informed consent, and the ethics of publication. He pointed out that by the time he was writing, some ethnographers were taking account of wider fields than the traditional tribe or village and that the subjects might be literate, even fellow citizens. Thus if the ethnographer published information about individuals which might be illegal or reprehensible, 'we run the risk of making public that which our informants would prefer to keep secret' (1967: 208).[8] Anthropologists thus needed to be aware that 'there is a significant difference between public knowledge circulating orally in a community and stories appearing in print' (1967: 205).

Barnes was also concerned about the politics of knowledge, later suggesting that it had passed from being viewed as a source of enlightenment, to an awareness of knowledge as a source of power, and then to becoming a form of property (1979: 64). Such a view of knowledge inevitably raises the issue of power and politics:

> Social research entails the possibility of destroying the privacy and autonomy of the individual, of producing more ammunition to those already in power, of laying the groundwork for an invincibly oppressive state.
>
> (1979: 22)

Barnes' style is much more measured than that of the American anthropologists quoted earlier, but in asking 'how much does the ethnographer suspend moral judgement?' his answer is equally radical: 'In some situations of conflict there are no neutral roles: an impartial social inquiry is impossible' (1967: 203). In other words, Barnes recognised that ethics cannot be divorced from politics. He saw this as an inevitable part of the anthropological enterprise, suggesting that the writing of a professional code of ethics for British social anthropologists 'might at least remind ethnographers that these problems do have to be solved and cannot be ignored' (*ibid.*: 211). It was, in fact, to be well over two decades before his advice was heeded by British social anthropology.

The 1970s: Reinventing anthropology?

By the early 1970s, versions of radical anthropology influenced by proliferating revolutionary and liberation movements, a revival of Marxism, and a continued questioning of anthropology's project had multiplied. While some anthropologists went along with the shift from function to meaning, and became increasingly interested in texts and in positing an idealist view of culture, others argued that the discipline needed to be 'reinvented' and that such reinvention must include the political dimension of anthropological practice.

During this decade a number of important books sought to grapple with these issues: from the US (Hymes 1972), from Britain (Asad 1973) and from the Netherlands (Huizer and Mannheim 1979). Mention should also be made of a book by Berreman, which, although published in 1981 under the title *The Politics of Truth*, consisted largely of articles written and published in the US in the previous decade.

Hymes' book *Reinventing Anthropology*, a collection of 16 articles to which he wrote a substantial introduction, has become something of a classic. Hymes summed up its intended audience as follows:

This book is for people for whom 'the way things are' is not reason enough for the way things are, who find fundamental questions pertinent and in need of personal answers; those for whom security, prosperity and self-interest are not sufficient reasons for choices they make; who think if an official 'study of man' does not answer to the needs of men, it ought to be changed; who ask of anthropology what they ask of themselves – responsiveness, critical awareness, ethical concern, human relevance, a clear connection between what is to be done and the interests of mankind.

(1972: 7)

Here again ethics was conflated with relevance and with a desire to link anthropology to an improvement in the well-being of humankind. For Laura Nader, this could be best achieved by anthropology reconsidering its predilection for the study of small-scale, remote societies, and instead 'studying up' and carrying out research on the powerful, the decision-makers and the wealthy. For several of Hymes' contributors, there was an awareness that 'reinventing anthropology' was a personal as well as a disciplinary project. This idea was most fully developed in Scholte's chapter on reflexivity and its relationship to critical anthropology, both topics on which he was subsequently to write a good deal more (e.g. 1986, 1987).

Gerald Berreman was one of the trio appearing in the 1968 *Current Anthropology* responsibility symposium and he also had a chapter in Hymes' book. Through the 1960s and 1970s, Berreman wrote regularly and passionately on the topic of ethics. Over and over again, he argued that social responsibility and professional ethics had become major issues in anthropology, and that anthropologists were being held increasingly accountable to those among whom they worked, as well as to their colleagues, their students and the public (1981: 23). For him such a recognition had fundamental consequences for the discipline: 'The plea for disinterested social science, for value-free research and hence for a non-political profession and a non-political professional association will be increasingly recognized as the siren song it is' (*ibid.*: 24).

Berreman's arguments rested upon twin premises. One was that of enlightened self-interest. If anthropologists failed to be accountable, 'the times will move without them, and they will find themselves ... irrelevant ... surpassed by the peoples and issues they have studied but have failed to comprehend' (*ibid.*: 28). Furthermore, they were likely to find themselves refused permission to carry out cross-cultural research by those among whom they wished to work (*ibid.*: 124).

The other was the moral duty of the anthropologist, backed by his or her conscience and professional commitment, to create a social science both honest and humane. He urged other anthropologists to demonstrate that humanity is not incompatible with science; that science without humanity is a monster and social science without humanity is a contradiction in terms as well; that we are proud to join Redfield ... in placing ourselves squarely on the side of humankind, unashamed to wish mankind well; and that we will not sell our souls for money or professional advantage to the anti-human forces in society.

(*ibid.*: 40)

Writing towards the end of this decade, George Appell suggested that radicalism had waned by that time, and his own book on ethics (1978) was concerned primarily with analyses of the ethical implications of a number of case studies. It was, however, also highly critical of American anthropology as he saw it at that period. He argued that anthropologists had become entangled in the economic reward system of American society – 'scientist as hustler' – and this had led to a subtle shift in disciplinary goals. The search for truth – 'the basic ethic' – had been forsaken for a search for profit in which 'things are loved and people are used' (*ibid.*: 2).

Asad's book, published in Britain with mainly British contributors, was somewhat different from those of Hymes and Berreman. For its contributors, the root of the malaise of anthropology was that it had not yet analysed, much less come to terms with, its encounter with colonialism, nor appreciated the extent to which this had affected the development of the discipline. Asad himself, rejecting the somewhat simplistic view that anthropology was primarily developed as an aid to colonial administration, explained it thus:

I say this ... because bourgeois consciousness, of which social anthropology is merely one fragment, has always contained within itself profound contradictions and ambiguities and therefore the potentialities for transcending itself. For these contradictions to be adequately apprehended, it is essential to turn to the historical power relationship between the West and the Third World and to examine the ways in which it has been dialectically linked to the practical conditions, the working assumptions and the intellectual product of all disciplines representing the European understanding of non-European humanity.

(1973: 18–19)

For British social anthropology, then, there was the need finally to relinquish structural functionalism and empiricism and to come to grips with ideas such as Marxism (e.g. the critiques in the *New Left Review*, ably discussed by Forster in Asad's volume). In short, if it were to gain a deeper understanding, the discipline needed to consider its past as well as its future. To this end, most of the book was taken up with a series of case studies of the relationship between colonialism and anthropology.

Even more radical voices were heard in the collection of articles edited by the Dutch anthropologist Gerhard Huizer and by Bruce Mannheim (1979), one of numerous volumes to emerge from the 1973 International Union of Anthropological and Ethnological Sciences (IUAES) Congress.[9] In his introduction Huizer noted that recent political debates in anthropology had tended to concentrate on 'the ethical question', citing such examples as Gough's view of anthropology as the 'child of imperialism' (1968b), denunciations of the Camelot Project, and the resistance of the Vietnamese. But he suggested that the question was actually more fundamental: 'In the service of whom, of what does anthropology really function? What is its purpose? What is its usefulness to the people investigated?' (Huizer 1979a: 5). Huizer proposed a 'liberation anthropology' which would draw upon the ideas of writers such as Frantz Fanon, Camilo Torres, and Gustavo Gutierrez. This would be actualised through what he termed 'action anthropology', an idea further developed in the chapter in which he analysed his work among peasants in El Salvador, Sicily and Chile. Here he advocated bringing to light basic grievances and dialogue with local people through discussions in small groups – 'the view from below' – and creating conditions for solutions using people's participation (1979b: 406).

At the same time, Huizer recognised that such an anthropology would be extremely difficult to pursue not only for political reasons – 'the elites work against it' (1979b: 412) – but also because it necessitated developing an awareness of one's own limitations and a consciousness of oneself as working with certain values. It involved the twin strategies of 'looking closely at ourselves' and 'listening carefully to voices from the Third World' (1979a: 7) as well as the 'reinvention of anthropology' in order that praxis as outlined above should inform theory.

In his view of anthropology as essentially a political activity, Huizer maintained that the anthropologist must be both partisan and *a* partisan: to show which side one is on. In short, his arguments encompassed both the practice of ethnography via fieldwork, and the theoretical premises which underlie it, including the awareness of ideology, the impossibility of value-free work and the need for reflexivity (see also Caulfield 1979).

The question of shifts in the epistemological foundations of the discipline had already been discussed by another Dutch anthropologist, Johannes Fabian, in a 1971 article in *Current Anthropology*. This was a comment on an earlier paper in the same journal by Jarvie (1969) who had proposed that the anthropologist must always remain a stranger, never a friend. Fabian was scathing of this view, indicting it as based on an 'unreflected, uncriticised, scientistic view of anthropology' and one which 'expresses a dominant positive–pragmatist bias characteristic of most Anglo-Saxon social science'. Fabian went on to suggest that the observer–data dichotomy as an ethical problem was created (not discovered) by espousing a certain philosophy of the social sciences which owed much to what he described as a 'naïve Comtean view' and which should be criticised using a 'post-Kantian epistemology'.

Like Asad *et al.*, Fabian saw the roots of this problem in the failure to deal with anthropology's past history:

> I would suggest that current concern with professional ethics in our discipline is nothing but a symptom of the failure to confront the *epistemological foundations* of anthropology in the postcolonial period … [with its] inherently domineering and exploitative attitude of a scientistic bias. (1971: 230, emphasis in the original)

For him, the way forward was the emerging recognition that the things anthropology studied were not objects and products, but rather production and processes and that the study of these was only possible through 'participation in the process of their production' (*ibid.*).

We thus find in these writings a strong awareness of the relation between ethics and politics, and of the importance of reflexivity (even if the term was not widely used at that time). For anthropology to be both a moral discipline and one which had moved with the times, it needed new ways of carrying out fieldwork, new kinds of fieldwork (including studying up), new levels of self-awareness on the part of researchers, new relations with the subjects of fieldwork, new forms of writing (including writing specially for the subjects, rather than for the academy) and new epistemological foundations which would provide the theoretical underpinnings of this praxis.

There were two other important developments in anthropological perception during the 1970s which should be mentioned briefly here. The first was that the erstwhile subjects of anthropological discourse had begun to find their own voices, and these were frequently critical of the anthropological enterprise (Banaji 1970, Magubane 1971, Mafeje 1976, Owusu 1978). Towards the end of the decade, Said's *Orientalism* (1978) appeared. This book proved highly influential, and for many, represented a significant paradigm shift, although some of his arguments had been anticipated in earlier work, including that by Asad and Barnes. Never again, however, could anthropologists afford to write about the rest of the world without considering whether they might be accused of 'orientalism', definitely not an ethical stance.

The second development was the advent of feminist critiques.[10] The new interest in looking at societies through the eyes of its female members provided a whole new take on the information that was available. Books such as Strathern 1972, Rosaldo and Lamphere 1974, Ardener 1975, Reiter 1975, Rohrlich-Leavitt 1975 and Caplan and Bujra 1978 not only critiqued existing anthropology for its male bias, but also suggested new paradigms. It is clear that for many feminist anthropologists, feminism included a particular ethical stance, and one which meant, at the very least, abandoning a view of anthropology in which 'man' stood for humankind. Their influence was to grow in the decade which followed.

The 1980s: Feminism, postmodernism and ethical compromises

Alongside the increasing impact of feminist scholarship came the rise of postmodernism, and the growing employment of anthropologists outside the academy. Given that the first two of these represented important paradigm shifts while the last signalled a shift in the institutional context in which anthropology operated, it is scarcely surprising that there was during this decade an apparent increase in the preoccupation with ethics.

Feminism and anthropology

Although feminism had become increasingly significant in anthropology during the 1970s, it was during the 1980s that it matured theoretically.[11] Feminist scholars rarely saw themselves as working within only a single discipline. Feminist scholarship, such as that represented by the American journal *Signs* or the British journals *Feminist Review* and *Women's Studies International Quarterly*, encompassed articles from a wide range of disciplines such as history, literature, philosophy, sociology, anthropology and others. Furthermore, most feminist scholars during this period were arguing for a closer link between theory and praxis – they saw themselves as activists as well as academics, and they saw feminism as a political as well as a scholarly project.

Feminists raised various ethical problems for social scientists, including the power relations between researcher and researched (Finch 1984; Roberts 1981; Jaggar 1983; Mernissi 1984). Over the course of the decade, an increasingly sophisticated series of texts discussed what came to be called 'standpoint theory' (Harding 1986; Hartsock 1987; Smith 1987; Ramazanoglu 1989). Alison Jaggar expressed it in this way:

> The concept of women's standpoint also provides an interpretation of what it is for a theory to be comprehensive. It asserts that women's social position offers them access to aspects of areas of reality that are not easily accessible to men ... The standpoint of women reveals more of the universe, human or non-human, than the standpoint of men.
>
> (1983: 384–5)

While anthropologists might take issue with the blanket assumption that women's 'position' (as it was then called) in society was subordinate to that of men, the important point was that gender made a difference. Women ethnographers could, and mostly did, do different kinds of ethnography from men. Furthermore, focusing on women or, as happened increasingly during the 1980s, on gender relations, meant that perspectives on societies were obtained which were very different from those provided by studies which took no account of them. For an increasing number of anthropologists, male as well as female, ignoring half of humanity as well as the consequences of this action, not only impoverished data, it was also deeply unethical.

However, feminist anthropology was read with a jaundiced eye by some of the subjects whom it sought to portray. Black and Asian women living in the West (as discussed, for example, in Amadiume 1987, Amos and Parmar 1984), Australian Aboriginal women (Larbalastier 1990) and subjects of research contested the notion that feminist anthropologists could represent them or the societies in which they were living, or from which they had originated. Feminist anthropology, like the discipline more generally, was forced to consider further its ethical stance.

Postmodernism

The rise of postmodernism was signalled most notably in the discipline of anthropology by Clifford and Marcus' influential book *Writing Culture* (1986). Postmodernism undermined anthropological authority by asking 'who is the author?', 'who is the audience?', and by arguing for a shift from observation and empirical methodology to a more communicative and dialogical epistemology. Kuper explains it thus:

> There could be no single, true, objective account of a cultural event or a social process. The postmodernists preferred the image of a cacophony of voices ... The ethnographic object is multifaceted, it can only be partially and fleetingly glimpsed from any one perspective, and it cannot be analysed ... Experiments in ethnographic representation were encouraged. Films, photographs and museum displays competed with books and articles and autobiographies, diaries, dialogues were preferred to orderly reviews of cultural practices ... Grand theory, ambitious historical narratives, were modernist dinosaurs ... theories were just ideologies in disguise and their day had passed ... A new era had now come to pass in which there were only local, culturally specific, temporary, partial truths. (1996: 188)

Postmodernism also demanded that ethnographers examine themselves for their own cultural baggage, and for the effect that they had on the societies they studied. It should be noted, however, that these were issues which had already been raised by feminists (Caplan 1988; Mascia-Lees, Sharpe and Cohen 1989) as well as by earlier writers on reflexivity already mentioned such as Fabian (1971), Scholte (1972) and Huizer and Mannheim (1979).

Not everyone was enamoured of the new paradigm. Some pointed out that just as oppressed groups had begun to find a voice and speak for themselves

– women, ethnic minorities, colonised peoples – they became just one more voice in a polyphonic world. Scholte (1987) noted that the postmodernist concern for 'multiple voices' undermined any notion that some might be more worth hearing than others. Keesing too criticised the postmodernists and those concerned mainly with culture and texts for ignoring power and the ways in which cultural meaning sustained privilege, noting acerbically that 'Where feminists and Marxists find oppression, symbolists find meaning' (1987: 166).

In many respects, postmodernism appeared to deny the significance or relevance of ethics, because it was essentially relativist. If there was no centre, no authoritative discourse, what was the point of debates about the ways in which we should conduct fieldwork or write it up? Yet predictably, there was another discursive explosion around the topic.

Ethics and 'Reaganethics': Anthropologists outside the academy

During the 1980s, ethics became a major issue in the social sciences, with a plethora of publications in sociology (see Bulmer 1982a and 1982b, Bulmer and Warwick 1983). In anthropology, too, books about ethical dilemmas were appearing (e.g. Rynkiewich and Spradley 1981). A number of commentators suggested that this was the result, at least in part, of a change in the profession on both sides of the Atlantic. Fewer academic jobs were available, and more anthropologists were seeking employment elsewhere in the fields of 'applied' anthropology.

In Britain, the crisis in academic employment was acute. At the beginning of the decade, universities were producing enough anthropologists to renew the profession every three years (Grillo 1996: 1). There was a move, led by Paul Stirling, to professionalise non-academic or 'applied' anthropology and make it more respectable. In 1981, Stirling had been a major moving influence behind the setting up of an applied anthropology group which became GAPP (Group for Anthropology in Policy and Practice), and which within two years had recruited over 150 members. In so doing, Stirling was ignoring a powerful current in British social anthropology which considered that 'applied anthropology' had at best a second-class status, but he argued that anthropologists should stop being 'mandarins' and instead become 'missionaries', using their disciplinary skills for the wider benefit of humankind (Mills 1999, Caplan 2001). Yet what should be the ethical practices of an anthropology which had quite as much potential to do harm as good? It was scarcely surprising that at this moment the ASA of the UK finally decided that a code of ethics was required.

In 1984, Akeroyd published a long and important review article on ethics. Drawing on both US and British material, she suggested that ethical problems had changed over time 'as the balance of power has altered between social scientist, sponsor, gatekeeper, citizens and government' (1984: 134).

The changing context in which anthropology was then being practised on both sides of the Atlantic included the institutionalisation and professionalisation of social scientific research, as well as the recognition that knowledge was a source not only of enlightenment but of power.

Akeroyd noted that:

> The adoption of a 'neutral' or 'uncommitted' stance is now seen to be no less political a position than a ' radical', 'committed' or 'antagonistic' stance. The issues cannot ... be ignored, not least because while some see a concern with ethics as a way of resolving various dilemmas afflicting anthropology and anthropologists, others see this as an evasion of the basic problem.
>
> (*ibid.*: 139)

For her, the only solution, which she admitted was very partial, was to achieve some sort of *balance* in responsibilities towards different parties: subjects of research, funders, gatekeepers and colleagues (including local scholars). She suggested, as had Appell and Barnes earlier, that ultimately anthropologists have to learn to live with compromise. Appell had proposed that the best anthropologists are those who can tolerate the moral ambiguities characterising a discipline which involves 'cross-cultural inquiry at an interface of ethical systems' (Appell 1978: 3). Barnes too had argued that 'ethical and intellectual compromise is an intrinsic characteristic of social research' (cited in Akeroyd 1984: 154) and that 'The competent fieldworker is he or she who learns to live with an uneasy conscience but continues to be worried by it' (*ibid.*).

In the US, Carolyn Fluehr-Lobban's edited volume on ethics (1991) arose out of the renewed debates of the late 1980s about the proposed revision of the AAA's Principles of Professional Responsibility (PPR). The editor argues that this major change in ethical stance in American anthropology had arisen from the lack of employment opportunities in academia and the growth in the employment of anthropologists outside the universities. Indeed, Frankel and Trend's chapter in her book suggested that American anthropology was developing two quite different cultures as a result of this situation, while another contributor, Hakken, proposed that current conceptual problems had to be located within contemporary distress over the identity of US anthropology (1991: 74). Berreman, who also contributed a chapter, agreed, arguing that the proposed changes to the PPR would result in a 'license for unfettered free-enterprise research, advising and engineering disguised as anthropology' (*ibid.*: 54); this was what he termed 'Reaganethics'.

It was scarcely surprising, then, that in an otherwise favourable review of the book, Appell noted that it was 'more useful for those attempting an ethnography of the American anthropological profession than it is for its enlightenment on the nature of ethical issues in anthropological inquiry'

(1992: 584). Perhaps we should not be surprised by this, since if we regard ethics as socially and historically constituted, they are bound to reflect paradigm shifts and changes in institutional practices within the discipline.

The 1990s: Identity politics, globalisation and the rise of audit culture

There were several important issues arising in the 1990s which had a bearing on ethics. The first was the emergence of so-called 'identity politics' in Europe (an issue which had already been significant for some time in North America) and the growing importance of a discourse of human rights. The second was the increasing pace of 'globalisation'. Finally, there were the profound changes which were taking place in institutions of higher education in the West, with the impact of the 'new managerialism' and so-called 'audit culture'.

Identity politics, conflict and human rights

With the fall of the Berlin Wall in 1989, the politics of identity became increasingly significant in Europe, often resulting in violent conflict, such as the war in Bosnia from 1991 to 1995. Ethnic differences and identity politics also played a significant role in the Rwandan genocide of 1994, in which over half a million people were killed in the space of a few weeks, the largest genocide since the Second World War (see Eltringham, this volume).

It is scarcely surprising that the discourse of human rights was increasingly invoked during this period. As Rabinow (2002) has pointed out, human rights talk has the capacity to become a 'moral vernacular' and currently has no secular competition. However, as Wilson (1997) argues, anthropology is handicapped in accepting such a discourse by its emphasis on localism and by its theoretical concern with culture, with both factors leading to a relativist stance which has placed it in opposition to universal values such as human rights. For anthropologists, the major critique of the universalism of human rights is that the discussion is lifted out of any particular context and raised to the level of the categorical imperative. Nonetheless, anthropologists who wish to position themselves ethically today cannot escape this discourse.

Furthermore, in seeking to uphold the human rights of their research subjects, anthropologists may find themselves under pressure to become advocates. Yet this is by no means a simple process. Hastrup and Elsass (1990) argue that 'the rationale for advocating a particular cause can never be anthropological. Anthropology seeks to comprehend the context of local interests, while advocacy implies the pursuit of one particular interest' (p. 301). They also argue that 'the rationale for advocacy is never ethnographic; it remains essentially moral in the broadest sense' (*ibid.*). Nonetheless, they accept that anthropologists do have moral responsibilities, and that advocacy may present itself as a 'moral imperative'.

In discussing the application of anthropology, they recognise the long-standing second-class status of applied anthropology, but also argue that 'no anthropologist can escape involvement'. Since it is widely accepted in the discipline that anthropologists themselves are part of the encounter, they are inevitably part of the material of fieldwork. Given, then, that there is no sharp distinction between self and other, the anthropologist cannot simply be an advocate for an Other. Furthermore, 'speaking for' is not the same as representation in the anthropological sense. After examining a particular case with which they became involved among the Arhuaco Indians of Colombia, the authors note that 'speaking for' raises numerous problems of exactly *whom* one is speaking for. It may involve colluding in the general pressure for minority groups to speak with one voice, but in addition it brings up the question of representativeness. Advocacy also raises all the hoary questions about the relationship between culture and development. The authors thus note that a 'consideration of advocacy rapidly leads to consideration of common anthropological problems' (p. 307). Furthermore, while anthropology involves understanding the context of interest, the pursuit of advocacy means choosing one interest within that context. They thus conclude that 'a commitment to improving the world is no substitute for understanding it' (p. 307).

Globalisation

Fluehr-Lobban (2002) has argued that since ethics and anthropology have entered the era of globalisation, professional discourse about ethics can no longer be confined to a national or domestic dialogue. Such an argument is, however, contested by Nancy Scheper-Hughes in *Current Anthropology*:

> The flight from the local in hot pursuit of a transnational, borderless anthropology implies parallel flight from local engagements, local commitments, and local accountability. Once the circuits of power are seen as capillary, diffuse, global, and difficult to trace to their sources, the idea of resistance becomes meaningless ... The idea of an anthropology without borders, although it has a progressive ring to it, ignores the very real borders that confront and oppress 'our' anthropological subjects and encroach on our liberty as well.
> (1995: 417)

Scheper-Hughes also takes a diametrically opposed stance to that of Hastrup and Elsass. For her, the role of anthropologist and that of *companheira* are not incompatible – on the contrary, she found that the more people pulled her into an activist role, 'the more my understandings of the community were enriched and my theoretical horizons expanded' (1995: 410). Scheper-Hughes contrasts the anthropology of the United States and the UK with that in other countries – Latin America, Italy and France – where anthropologists do communicate with 'the polis' and 'the public', and where therefore active and politically committed anthropology is perceived less negatively. She suggests that given 'the perilous times' in which we live, the best we can do is to compromise and practise a 'good enough' ethnography which includes seeing, listening, touching, recording and above all *recognising* our subjects. For her, anthropology should insist on an explicit ethical orientation to 'the other', it demands a 'witnessing' which is a kind of 'barefoot anthropology' (*ibid.*: 419):

> If 'observation' links anthropology to the natural sciences, 'witnessing' links anthropology to moral philosophy. Observation ... is a passive act. Witnessing ... is in the active voice and it positions the anthropologist inside human events as a responsive, reflexive and morally committed being, one who will 'take sides' and make judgements, though this flies in the face of the anthropological non-engagement with either ethics or politics. Of course, non-involvement was in itself an 'ethical' and moral position.
>
> (*ibid.*: 419)

Scheper-Hughes' article is angry, critical and passionate – a complete contrast both in style and in conclusions to the earlier one by Hastrup and Elsass. It is not surprising that whereas the latter provoked only a handful of responses, the piece by Scheper-Hughes resulted in rather more and rather longer reactions from other anthropologists.[12] Vincent Crapanzano was sceptical: 'we can never become companheiros and companheiras. We are always outsiders' (1995: 421). Marvin Harris argued that 'to claim the political-moral high ground one must have reliable knowledge' and for him, this meant scientific, objective knowledge (1995: 423). Laura Nader asked, not for the first time: 'How come, if you are interested in misery, you don't study up more, go to the source rather than the victims?' (1995: 426).

Here, then, we are back to some of the debates which first emerged in the 1960s: the basis of knowledge, the positionality of the anthropologist, and whether we should study up or down.

Audit culture in higher education

In the late 1980s, higher education in the western world began to feel the impact of what were popularly known as 'the cuts'. While, as has already been shown, this resulted in fewer jobs for anthropologists and a move into applied anthropology, it was only in the 1990s that universities themselves began to change dramatically. With the election of governments which pursued varying versions of *laissez-faire* capitalism, universities not only received proportionately less money than previously, but had to take on many more students. In Britain and elsewhere, in an apparent attempt to ensure that standards were maintained, while 'value for money' and 'transparency' were achieved, an increasingly rigorous regime of audit and inspection (quality assurance, research selectivity, reviews of teaching, etc.) was instituted (Shore and Wright 1999).

Some anthropologists have argued that this new audit culture includes ethics, since it proliferates ethics-talk, reviews and committees in the universities of the West (Pels 1999, 2000; Amit 2000; Strathern 2000). In his 1999 article, Pels considers the history of ethical codes, arguing that 'having an ethical code is a necessity in the folk epistemology of professionalism'. Anthropologists, like other professionals, developed such codes so that their relations with their employers became those of expert and client, and also so that their judgements could be considered outside political interests and thus be trusted: 'Critical to this self-image is its claim to be able to generate standards that are not culturally specific or politically partisan but founded on universal human nature … natural rights or human rights' (p. 102). For Pels, then, ethics actually *masks* politics. He suggests that ethical codes will become increasingly obsolete as the conditions of employment of anthropologists change still further.

In a later article, Pels not only repeats and embellishes his argument about ethics being part of the technology of the professional self, but also suggests that ethics are part of a *liberal* constitution of the self in which 'codes become contracts, anthropologists produce a marketable self' (2000: 146). In this process there is a move from ethics, in the sense in which people such as Berreman have argued for it, to audit: 'from a romantic primacy of the ethical to a utilitarian primacy of the economy' (*ibid.*: 148; see also Amit 2000, Strathern 2000).

As Mills points out in his chapter in this volume, there thus appears to be a paradox – from the 1960s until the end of the 1980s, support for ethical codes was seen as support for a politically radical version of anthropology, while by the 1990s, ethics had for some become a politically conservative part of audit culture. Yet much depends upon which ethics we are talking about. Sluka notes that there are two quite different kinds of ethics. He sees the new 'corporatist' ethics as dangerous, because it puts all those involved in the research on the same plane as 'stakeholders', whereas the earlier versions of ethics codes suggested that there was a hierarchy of priorities. Rather than 'professionalising' ethics codes still further, Sluka suggests that 'We need to create an alternative code of ethics that takes power into account' (1999: 126).

The turn of the millennium: The anthropologist as public intellectual?

Towards the end of 2000, news broke of the imminent publication of Patrick Tierney's book *Darkness in El Dorado* (2001). I do not propose to dwell at length on it here, since Nugent's chapter below deals in some detail with the debates around it. It is perhaps ironic that the case made by Tierney at the end of the twentieth century against Neel and Chagnon for their treatment of the Yanomami Indians has certain resonances with some of the cases at the Nuremberg trials. James Neel and Napoleon Chagnon stood accused of violating the Nuremberg Code, which insists that all research involving human subjects has to involve freely given and informed consent. Yet it is also the case, as Nugent points out in this volume, that the furore tells us more about the profession of anthropology than it does about what actually did or did not happen.

Several distinguished anthropologists commented publicly in journals on the implications of the Tierney affair or reviewed the book when it finally appeared (Sahlins 2001, Ingold 2000, Geertz 2001). For John Gledhill, 'it is not really the continuing difficulties of policing our ethical codes that is the root of our problem. That lies in our continuing failure to project a more appropriate post-colonial image of the mission of anthropology into the public sphere, and to be clear about the politics of the knowledge we should be aiming to produce' (2000: 2). Gledhill is certain that anthropology offers 'distinct perspectives on larger social dilemmas', but for such perspectives to be heard, anthropologists have to be prepared to move out of the classroom, to denounce such ills as prejudice and discrimination more loudly and to find means other than academic publishing for getting their messages across to the public. So far there has been little sign of this happening.

Secondly, and more significantly, there was 11 September 2001, the declaration of a 'war on terror', a real war in Afghanistan, and, as I write, the threat of another in Iraq. The global situation now has some curious parallels with that in the 1960s, a time when the US was also involved in defeating its enemies in faraway places. Where do anthropological ethics stand in such situations? Unfortunately, since the 1960s, with some very honourable exceptions, they have been distinguished neither by their intensity nor by their abundance. As Jonathan Benthall (1996) noted with regard to the 1991–2 Gulf War, anthropologists appear to have remained 'speechless' in the face of this cataclysmic event. Similarly, with the prospect of a new Gulf War, there have been few public comments, few teach-ins, little student protest, and virtually no ethical debates of the kind that took place in the 1960s, although of course, it is possible that these may develop.

One of the original aims in the AAA's 1971 Principles of Professional Responsibility was to exhort anthropologists to act as public intellectuals:

As people who devote their professional lives to understanding man, anthropologists bear a positive responsibility to speak out publicly, both individually and collectively, on what they know and what they believe as a result of their professional expertise gained in the study of human beings. That is, they bear a professional responsibility to contribute to an 'adequate definition of reality' upon which public opinion and public policy may be based.

(AAA 1971: clause 2d)

This is not dissimilar to the oft-quoted maxim of Chomsky that it is the responsibility of intellectuals to 'speak the truth and expose lies' (1969: 325).

In each decade, it has been a small minority of practitioners who have taken it upon themselves to ensure that the discipline examines its ethical stances. They have often done so passionately and polemically, sometimes sounding like Old Testament prophets in their condemnation not so much of ethical lapses as of indifference. In so doing, they perform an importance service to anthropology.

The contributions in this book

The book is divided into two parts. In the first part, 'Debates', David Mills discusses the history of ethical codes in Britain and the United States while Lisette Josephides considers the relationship between anthropology and philosophical notions of virtue. In Chapters 4 and 5, Stephen Nugent and Nigel Eltringham consider respectively two important issues of representation: the furore over Tierney's book *Darkness in El Dorado* and the Rwandan genocide. In the second part of the book – 'Dilemmas' – a number of case studies illuminate matters raised in the first part. Silverman deals with the differences between formal and everyday ethics in fieldwork in Ireland; Kravva discusses minority status and citizenship in Greece; Greenwood considers representations of Paganism and magic in Britain; Barber is faced with an ethical dilemma about whether to 'whistle-blow' or not in Malawi; Strang discusses the ethics of being an advocate for Aboriginal people in Australia; and Spiegel explores the ethics of an etymological exercise in the new South Africa.

Ethics, morality and virtue

How do our contributors define ethics and how do they relate it to morality? For most, the two are closely connected.

Josephides' two contexts are her field area in Papua New Guinea and the academic milieu in her university. Her primary concern is with fieldwork and she asks how she may be moral in a society whose traditions she does not share. She finds the answer first of all in the virtue of empathy which ethnographers cultivate in the field and which brings the subjects being studied ever closer 'as they respond to depictions of themselves'. Fieldwork is a 'sacred space' given over wholly to the practice of research and it has a by-product: 'a person whose empathy and commitment makes possible the ethnography as an object of knowledge'. For her, there is an inextricable link between morality and emotion. She describes how during fieldwork what she thought of as ethical became more conscious, concretised and extended as a consequence of her self-questioning moral stance derived from the maelstrom of feelings – emotions – she experienced. Using a critical reading of the work of the philosopher Alasdair MacIntyre, and particularly his work *After Virtue* (1984), she makes a strong case for the existence of a morality which does cross cultures.

Her contrasting 'field', that of the academy in Britain, does not present itself as a moral community. British anthropologists are clearly aware of this and, like other academics, use strategising techniques cynically or ironically in this space, a prime example being the Research Assessment Exercise (RAE)[13] towards which academics adopt a critical stance, while nonetheless 'playing the game'.

Silverman argues that ethics are less about big decisions than about the everyday practice of ethnography. Ethical behaviour in the field is actually about 'crafting a persona', making an identity, an idea that resonates with Josephides' stress on empathy. Using a comparison between her own statement to an ethics committee before she went to the field, and the reality of what she calls the reciprocity and confidentiality of fieldwork relations, as informants became friends, Silverman concludes that auditing actually has little to do with anthropological practice. Rather, it is the fact that ethical decisions are also moral decisions, 'in every day and with every decision', that makes anthropology a 'moral discipline'.

Strang's work is with and sometimes on behalf of Australian Aboriginal peoples. She argues that ethics necessarily draws upon the idea of human rights, which in turn are founded upon notions (and ideals) of equality, and of the commonality of human experience. Her advocacy work, especially on land cases, is an important aspect of her own ethical stance. This requires a careful balancing of objectivity with sympathy and empathy. For an 'expert witness', such as an anthropologist in a land case, to state that her data are subjective and culturally relative undermines her credibility, and therefore her usefulness to the plaintiffs whom she is seeking to assist. This is an argument against jettisoning all notions of objectivity and espousing absolute relativism, which may in any case, Strang argues, be 'devoid of any moral content'.

For Kravva too, academic knowledge should be moral knowledge, and moral knowledge is political. Her chapter shows the ways in which the Greek state and the Orthodox church construct a particular notion of citizenship which makes it very difficult for minorities such as the Thessalonikan Jews to define themselves as full members of the polity. Kravva rejects, however, a simplistic explanation of the pervasive anti-Semitism she encountered in Thessaloniki, noting that one cannot lay the blame entirely at the door of the church, but rather that it is present in the everyday reality of people's lives. She argues that it is thus the task of academics such as anthropologists to unmask this taken-for-granted discourse by listening to all parties.

Eltringham considers whether by using discourse analysis in his study of the Rwandan genocide, he risks revisionism, or even denial of genocide. He notes that the genocide is a partial, fragmented experience and that history, like anthropology, is interpretative. His analysis suggests that conflicts such as those which the genocide represents peak in a process mainly enacted in discourse and competing verbal representations. Yet there are dangers in deconstructing such an event through discourse analysis, not least that of elevating discourse over reality. Furthermore, his own writing as an anthropologist is inevitably informed by his own meta-discourse. He concludes by suggesting that his work can critique the conflicting discourses of those who hold and those who aspire to power, and that 'to understand conflict we must give voice to these disagreements and demonstrate how they are articulated'.

While all of the contributors address the question of what ethics and morals are or are not for them, few discuss ethical codes. Nugent is scathing: for him they are there simply to be invoked for the protection of anthropologists and their associates, not for the people being studied. For Barber, however, ethical codes are useful, since they are designed to highlight problems and facilitate ethical reasoning. As a practising midwife and teacher of midwifery, she was equally bound in her fieldwork in Malawi by two codes: that of midwifery and that of the Association of Social Anthropologists of the UK. Although initially she thought that she might encounter conflicts as a result, in the end, faced with a difficult decision about whether to blow the whistle on the malpractice of a traditional birth attendant, she found that the two were not so different after all.

Anthropology and representation: The question of the audience(s)

Virtually all of the chapters in this book deal with issues of representation in one way or another. Many contributors pose again the question which has already been raised many times: who is the anthropologist writing for? While it is axiomatic that anthropologists write for other anthropologists, there are other audiences too. For some of our contributors, these certainly include the subjects themselves and a number of contributors here write about how they found their writing contested by their subjects.

Kravva talks of the 'crisis of representation' and grapples with her own representations of Jewish and Orthodox Greeks in Thessaloniki. Strang asks whether anthropologists have the right to represent the other at all, who should control representations and who owns them. Both Strang and Kravva worry about negative representations of their informants: Strang is concerned about the effects of writing about social problems among Australian Aborigines, Kravva about writing on nationalist and xenophobic discourses in Greece.

The subjects of research

Strang is unequivocal about the responsibility in writing anthropology – it is first and foremost to the people concerned. She notes that she always consults them before publishing, and that some of her data are gathered primarily for the benefit of the community and remain unpublished. Eltringham, on the other hand, carried out his research on the Rwandan genocide by interviewing Rwandans who had left the country or who were members of the government; both categories used a very public analytical discourse. He argues that because he interviewed people from both sides, his work is suspect by all, and therefore cannot usefully be critiqued by those involved.

On the other hand, Silverman, who is well aware that her subjects will read and comment upon what is written, explains how in Ireland, she and her partner Philip Gulliver 'exchanged the past' with informants by sharing access to archives and other data.[14] She notes that the people of Thomastown wanted to be represented in a particular kind of way, and for this reason, it was decided that the authors' first book should be written largely as a history. Is this one way around the difficult issue of how we write up our material – to write different accounts for different audiences?

Spiegel, too, is concerned about the ethical questions raised by writing, and in particular about revealing publicly areas which are private for informants or their communities. In a careful etymological exercise around the term 'spaza', which is widely used in urban South Africa, he wonders about the right of anthropologists to expose meanings with connotations of resistance, originally to the apartheid state, but more recently perhaps even to the academic gaze. He, along with others in South Africa, is all too aware that research may 'slip ethical boundaries' and betray trust. He is also uncomfortable about appearing to write against leaders of popular culture, whose etymological explanations appeared to differ from his own. But, as he pursues his enquiry, he also becomes aware that he is being tricked, and that humour is being used as a weapon of subaltern consciousness. He thus concludes that if 'playing spaza' is just that, then exposing it is a way of celebrating such playfulness and the subaltern power it represents. For him 'the aim should be to rejoice, rather than simply record, and become part of the culturally creative and imaginative moment of modernity'.

The wider public

Another important audience is the wider public. Both Strang and Greenwood have contributed to debates in the public, legal and political arena. Strang notes some of the problems raised by having to 'represent' (in both senses of the word) Aborigines in land claims. The first has already been alluded to – it is that of needing to play the role of scientific expert. Here empathy either becomes secondary temporarily, or else it is subsumed under the requirement for the anthropologist to be authoritative, objective and factual. Strang reports that opponents of land rights have seized upon anthropological angst about authority to undermine their arguments in court.

Greenwood, who has taken advantage of the huge paradigm shifts in anthropological theory to carry out a highly experiential study of witchcraft and Paganism in Britain, notes that, when she engages with the public sphere, she needs to challenge stereotypes and preconceptions. She has acted as a consultant for children's books and appeared in court in custody cases where the grounds for dispute were the participation of one of the parents in Paganism. Greenwood notes the difficulties in 'making the leap' from the academic to the 'real' world. How is it possible to explain to a sceptical audience (the court, the public) with negative views of magic that Pagans' morality is personal, internal and determined by the individual's relation to a spiritual otherworld rather than being founded upon received views such as Christianity? What is such an audience to make of Pagans' claim to incorporate 'the dark' in their morality? And how is the anthropologist herself to decide in a court case whether the social relations of particular covens which could conceivably lead to abuse are sufficiently risky to warrant denial of child custody?

The position of the anthropologist

The politics and ethics of representation are inevitably complicated by positionality. Several of the contributors are writing in some sense about their own societies, yet none would claim to be 'native anthropologists' in the sense in which the term has been used recently (Narayan 1993, Strathern 1987). Spiegel is a white South African writing about a term used largely by black South Africans, and well aware of the implications of this in his enquiries. Kravva is an Orthodox Christian Greek citizen who is writing about her fellow citizens, both Orthodox and Jewish. She is uncomfortably aware that the former may well not like what she writes about their attitudes to minorities, and she is also mindful of the need to try to portray the Greek reality 'objectively', in other words, fairly. Strang writes with some feeling about attacks on her and other anthropologists writing about Aboriginal peoples and the ways in which they have to negotiate this minefield.

For most of the contributors to this book, then, ethics is inextricably linked to politics and particularly the politics of knowledge, to which I now turn.

Ethics and the politics of knowledge

Mills suggests that ethics are part of a broader political history of professional values, in this respect, echoing Pels' contention (2000) that they are one of the 'technologies of the self' cultivated by anthropologists. He also agrees with Pels that the language of ethics is proliferating and linked to the audit culture which increasingly shapes academic professional life. Ethics and politics are, however, widely seen as different in kind as well as in degree since ethics, like science, is viewed as 'value-neutral'. Mills contends that in fact this is not so, and shows that ethics is inextricably linked with politics and that this relationship needs to be unmasked. Through an examination of debates which have surrounded the writing of ethical codes both in the US and in Britain, Mills demonstrates that these become meaningful only at moments of crisis, when they serve an essentially political purpose.

Mills explains that for a long time, leaders of the discipline such as Evans-Pritchard and Gluckman firmly maintained that fact should be separated from value and science from application. Such contentions are an aspect of that value bifurcation in which science is seen as value-neutral and objective. However, as Mills points out, such Enlightenment principles have in their turn been questioned in contemporary theoretical debates in anthropology, especially since the rise of postmodernism.

But if some contributors are concerned about anthropology clinging to its truth claims to objectivity and scientific status, others are concerned about the implications of anthropology being entirely reflexive, interpretative and experiential.

Strang notes that the lack of any claims to objectivity undermines anthropology and its usefulness, and also undermines cross-cultural comparison, an important foundation stone of the discipline. She argues that anthropology must provide some meta-discourse if it is to have any use at all. Nugent suggests that the furore over Tierney's book is also about another political issue – the so-called 'science wars' which he interprets as being about relativist versus rationalist arguments. In the case of *Darkness in El Dorado*, he suggests, it is not difficult to show that the charges that Neel and Chagnon experimented on the Yanomami are false and equally that opinions about whether Chagnon falsified his data depend to a large extent upon views about the relevance or otherwise of (socio)biology. Nugent sees ethics and politics as being divorced from each other because ethics does not address what he sees as the 'real political issues'. In the case of Amazonia, these are less to do with whether the allegations in Tierney's book are true than with the reasons for the overall devastation of this area. For him, the real scandal is the socio-historical relation between anthropology, its subjects and public culture, since Tierney's book has provided a very bad example of how anthropology should communicate with the public.

Conclusion

I will end with four main observations about the relation between ethics and anthropology.

The first is that when we discuss ethics as anthropologists, we are actually discussing all aspects of the discipline: its epistemology, its fieldwork practices, and its institutional and wider social contexts, not some segregated, specialised interest.

The second is that it is very difficult to divorce ethics from politics, including the politics of knowledge. This suggests that ethics, like politics, is a series of processes in which power is heavily implicated. In looking at the debates on ethics and anthropology over the last four decades, the issues that recur continually are concerns about, on the one hand, the relations *between* anthropologists and the subjects of their study and, on the other, the responsibilities of anthropologists *towards* informants and others. Yet these are never purely internal matters: debates around them are products of the wider contexts – both historical and geographical – in which anthropology is practised. For this reason, while we may wish to hold on to certain moral values such as truth, integrity, empathy and human dignity, which we would like to think of as timeless and universal, we actually find ethical principles shifting over time, and different principles receiving different emphases according to the contexts in which they are invoked.

The third observation is that any discussion of ethics must of necessity be *reflexive* (Davies 1999). Sitter-Liver, a philosopher, notes that when Heidegger was asked about the possibility of an up-to-date ethics he stressed the necessity first of all to ask who we are, which is the essential Kantian query of philosophy, before asking what we ought to do (Sitter-Liver 1997: 4). This is a question which the postmodernists might claim to have raised first, but as we have seen, it is actually one which has been asked for a long time by all manner of critical anthropologists.

This brings me to my fourth observation, which is that the ethics of anthropology must be *critical*, both of ourselves and of our discipline. For this reason, those who have written passionately and polemically on the subject have done anthropology an important service in obliging us to grapple with difficult and complex issues, and to pose again the fundamental question: what's it all for?

Notes

1 In the US they currently account for 14 per cent of the value of mutual funds, although in the UK they are worth less than 1 per cent.

2 They pointed out that in 1997, the largest single investment (£300 million) was in Shell, notorious for its involvement in the Ogoni affair in Nigeria during which the activist Ken Saro-Wiwa was hanged, and that the two next largest were in British American Tobacco and British Aerospace.

3 See also 'Charities fume over tobacco funding', *Times Higher Education Supplement (THES)*, 8 December 2000.

4 Yet Leach appeared to view morality as equally relative, suggesting that 'moral rules are those which distinguish between good and bad behaviours, and ... these rules are variable. Morality is specified by culture; what you *ought* to do depends on who you are and where you are' (Leach 1968: 48).

5 For a good survey up to the mid-1980s, see Akeroyd 1984. For the period up to 1990 see Fluehr-Lobban 1991 which is shortly to be re-issued in a revised version. The topic has frequently been covered in the US journal *Current Anthropology* and in the *Newsletter of the AAA*. In Britain, the RAI journal *Anthropology Today* has frequently tackled ethical issues, and a number of relevant articles have recently been republished in Benthall 2002.

6 Project Camelot was a project proposed by the US Army's Office of the Chief of Research and Development which aimed to study 'the preconditions of internal conflict'. In effect, it was to study the problem of counterinsurgency in Latin America. The information was leaked by a Chilean academic, resulting in a furore in both Latin America and the US, and the project was finally cancelled. For further information see Sjoberg 1967, Fluehr-Lobban 1991 and Mills' chapter in the present volume.

7 Clearly the decade is largely a heuristic device since issues continue from one to another.

8 The *BJS* article was republished twice four years later (see bibliography). In this chapter I am using the page references to the version in the volume edited by Jongmans and Gutkind (1967).

9 IUAES – International Union of Anthropological and Ethnological Sciences which meets every five years in different locations.

10 Here the literature is large, but the interested reader is referred to the following useful review articles: Stack 1975, Quinn 1977, Tiffany 1978, Atkinson 1982.

11 For an excellent summary of the state of the art of feminist anthropology by the late 1980s, see Moore 1988. Her extensive bibliography also provides a very useful resource.

12 I have not dealt here with her criticism in this article of white anthropologists in South Africa, which Adam Kuper described as a 'caricature' and 'insulting' (1995: 425).

13 The Research Assessment Exercise, held every five years in Britain, scrutinises 'research performance' of each subject and department, and grades the latter on a scale of 1–5*. This has important implications for future funding, as well as for rankings in academic league tables. For an excellent critique of this and other 'disciplinary techniques' see Shore and Wright 1999.

14 The monograph on Ireland *Saints and Schizophrenics* by Nancy Scheper-Hughes produced extremely critical reactions in the Irish press. See footnote 4 to chapter by Silverman in the present volume.

Bibliography

Akeroyd, Anne (1984) 'Ethics in relation to informants, the profession and governments', in R.F. Ellen (ed.) *Ethnographic Research: A Guide to General Conduct*, London: Academic Press.

Amadiume, I. (1987) *Male Daughters, Female Husbands*. London: 2ed Press.

American Anthropological Association (1971) 'Principles of Professional Responsibility', republished in P.D. Reynolds (1982) *Ethics and Social Science Research*, Englewood Cliffs, NJ: Prentice Hall.

—— (1998) *Code of Ethics*, available on http://www. aaanet.org.

Amit, Vered (2000) 'The university as panopticon: moral claims and attacks on academic freedom', in M. Strathern (ed.) *Audit Culture*, London and New York: Routledge.

Amos, Valerie and Pratibha Parmar (1984) 'Challenging Imperial Feminism, *Feminist Review* 17: 3–20.

Anon. (1998) 'Money must be chased but with new guidelines', *Times Higher Education Supplement* Opinion column, 23 October, p. 14.

Appell, George (1978) *Ethical Dilemmas in Anthropological Inquiry: A Case Book*, Waltham, MA: Crossroads Press.

—— (1992) Review of Fluehr-Lobban (1991), *Anthropos*, 87: 584–5.

Ardener, Shirley (ed.) (1975) *Perceiving Women*, New York/Halsted: Malaby/Det.

Asad, Talal (1973) *Anthropology and the Colonial Encounter*, London: Ithaca Press.

Association of Social Anthropologists of the UK and Commonwealth (1987) *Ethical Guidelines for Good Practice*, available on http://www.asa.anthropology.ac.uk

—— (1999) *Ethical Guidelines for Good Practice* (revised version), available on http://www.asa.anthropology.ac.uk

Atkinson, Jane (1982) 'Review essay: anthropology', *Signs: Journal of Women in Culture and Society*, 8 (2).

Banaji, Jairus (1970) 'Crisis in British anthropology', *New Left Review*, 64: 71–5.

Barnes, John (1967) 'Some ethical problems in fieldwork', in D.G. Jongmans and P.C. Gutkind (eds) *Anthropologists in the Field,* Van Gorcum and Co. (originally published in the *British Journal of Sociology* 1963, 14: 11–134, and also republished in A. Epstein (ed.) *The Craft of Social Anthropology*, London: Tavistock Publications).

—— (1977) *The Ethics of Enquiry in Social Science Research*, Oxford: OUP.

—— (1979) *Who Should Know What? Social Science, Privacy and Ethics*, Harmondsworth: Penguin.

Bauman, Zygmunt (2001) 'Postmodern ethics', in S. Siedman and J.C. Alexander (eds) *The New Social Theory Reader: Contemporary Debates*, London and New York: Routledge.

Benthall, Jonathan (1996) 'End of the world: anthropologists speechless', *Anthropology Today*, 12 (5): 1–2.

—— (ed.) (2002) *The Best of Anthropology Today*, London and New York: Routledge.

Berreman, Gerald (1968) 'Is anthropology alive? Social responsibility in social anthropology', *Current Anthropology*, 9 (5): 391–7 (also reprinted in Berreman 1981).

—— (1981) *The Politics of Truth: Essays in Critical Anthropology*, New Delhi and Madras: South Asian Publishers.

Bulmer, Martin (ed.) (1982a) *Social Research Ethics: An Examination of the Merits of Covert Participant Observation*, London: Macmillan.

—— (1982b) *The Uses of Social Research: Social Investigations in Public Policy-making*, London: Allen and Unwin.

Bulmer, Martin and Warwick, D.P. (eds) (1983) *Social Research in Developing Countries: Surveys and Censuses in the Third World*, London: University College Press.

Caplan, Patricia and Bujra, Janet M. (eds) (1978) *Women United, Women Divided: Cross-cultural Perspectives on Female Solidarity*, London: Tavistock.

Caplan, Pat (1988) 'Engendering knowledge: the politics of ethnography', *Anthropology Today*, 4 (5 and 6): 8–12, 14–17.

Caulfield, Mina Davis (1979) 'Participant observation or partisan participation?,' in Gert Huizer and Bruce Mannheim (eds) *The Politics of Anthropology: From Colonialism and Sexism Toward a View from Below*, The Hague and Paris: Mouton Publishers.

Chomsky, Noam (1969) *American Power and the New Mandarins*, New York: Pantheon Books.

Clifford, James and Marcus, George (eds) (1986) *Writing Culture*, Berkeley and Los Angeles: University of California Press.

Cowe, Roger (1999) 'Boardrooms discover corporate ethics', *Guardian Weekly*, March 28: 27.

Crapanzano, Vincent (1995) 'Comment' on Nancy Scheper-Hughes, *Current Anthropology*, 36 (3): 420–1.

Davies, Charlotte A. (1999) *Reflexive Ethnography: A Guide to Researching Ourselves and Others*, London and New York: Routledge.

Fabian, Johannes (1971) 'On professional ethics and epistemological foundations', *Current Anthropology*, 12 (2), April: 230–1.

Finch, Janet (1984) 'Ethics of interviewing women', in Colin Bell (ed.) *Social Researching: Politics, Problems, Practice*, London: Routledge and Kegan Paul.

Fluehr-Lobban, Carolyn (1991) *Ethics and the Profession of Anthropology: Dialogue for a New Era*, Philadelphia: University of Pennsylvania Press.

—— (2002) 'The dialogue continues: ethics and anthropology in the 21st century: towards a new professional ethics' in revised version of book above (in press).

Forster, Peter (1973) 'A review of the New Left critique of social anthropology', in Talal Asad (ed.) *Anthropology and the Colonial Encounter*, London: Ithaca Press.

Frankel, Barbara and Trend, M.G. (1991) 'Principles, pressure and paychecks: the anthropologist as employee', in Fluehr-Lobban (1991), *Ethics and the Profession of Anthropology: Dialogue for a New Era*, Philadelphia: University of Pennsylvania Press.

Geertz, Clifford (2001) 'Life among the anthros' (review of Tierney 2001), *New York Review of Books*, 8 February: 18–22.

Gjessing, Gutorm (1968) 'The social responsibility of the social scientist', *Current Anthropology*, 9 (5): 397–403.

Gledhill, John (2000) 'Finding a new public face for anthropology', *Anthropology Today*, 16 (6): 1–3.

Gough, Kathleen (1968a) 'New proposals for anthropologists', *Current Anthropology*, 9 (5): 403–7.

—— (1968b) 'Anthropology – child of imperialism', *Monthly Review*, April, 19 (11).

Grillo, Ralph (1985) 'Applied anthropology in the 1980s: retrospect and prospect', in R. Grillo and A. Rew (eds) *Social Anthropology and Development Policy*, ASA Monograph 23, London and New York: Tavistock.

Hakken, David (1991) 'Anthropological ethics in the 1990s: a positive approach', in Fluehr-Lobban (1991) *Ethics and the Profession of Anthropology: Dialogue for a New Era*, Philadelphia: University of Pennsylvania Press.

Harding, Sandra (1986) 'The instability of the analytical categories of feminist theory', *Signs*, 11 (4): 645–64.

Harris, Marvin (1995) 'Comment' on Nancy Scheper-Hughes, 'The primacy of the ethical', *Current Anthropology*, 36 (3): 423–4.

Hartsock, Nancy (1987) 'The feminist standpoint: developing the ground for a specifically feminist historical materialism', in S. Harding (ed.) *Feminism and Materialism: Social Science Issues*, Bloomington: Indiana University Press and Oxford: Oxford University Press.

Hastrup, Kirsten and Elsass, Peter (eds) (1990) 'Anthropological advocacy: a contradiction in terms?', *Current Anthropology*, 31 (3): 301–11.

Huizer, Gert (1979a) 'Anthropology and politics: from naïveté toward liberation', in Huizer and Mannheim (1979) *The Politics of Anthropology: From Colonialism and Sexism Toward a View from Below*, The Hague and Paris: Mouton Publishers.

—— (1979b) 'Research-through-action: some practical experiences with peasant organization', in Huizer and Mannheim (1979) *The Politics of Anthropology: From Colonialism and Sexism Toward a View from Below*, The Hague and Paris: Mouton Publishers.

Huizer, Gert and Bruce Mannheim (1979) *The Politics of Anthropology: From Colonialism and Sexism Toward a View from Below*, The Hague and Paris: Mouton Publishers.

Hymes, Dell (1972) *Reinventing Anthropology*, New York: Random House.

Ingold, Tim (2000) 'Primitive laboratory', *THES*, 6 October: 16.

Jaggar, Alison (1983) *Feminist Politics and Human Nature*, Totowa, NJ: Bowman and Allanheld.

—— (1989) 'Feminist ethics: some issues for the nineties', *Journal of Social Philosophy*, XX (1 and 2) Spring/Fall: 91–107.

Jarvie, I.C. (1969) 'The problem of ethical integrity in participant observation', *Current Anthropology*, 10 (5): 505–8.

Keesing, Roger (1987) 'Anthropology: an interpretive quest', *Current Anthropology*, 2 (2).

Kuper, Adam (1995) 'Comment on Scheper-Hughes', *Current Anthropology*, 36 (3): 424–6.

—— (1996) [1973] *Anthropology and Anthropologists: The Modern British School* (3rd edn), London and New York: Routledge.

Laidlaw, James (2002) 'For an anthropology of ethics and freedom', *Journal of the Royal Anthropological Institute*, 8 (2): 311–32.

Lang, A.L.A. (1999) 'Corporate ethics meets the bottom line', in *Ford Foundation Report*, Fall: 16–17.

Larbalastier, Jan (1990) 'The politics of representation: Australian Aboriginal women and feminism', *Anthropological Forum*, 6 (2): 143–57.

Leach, Edmund (1968) 'A runaway world?', The Reith Lectures, London: BBC Publications.

MacIntyre, Alasdair (1984) *After Virtue* (2nd edn), Notre Dame, IN: Notre Dame University Press.

Mafeje, Archie (1976) 'The problem of anthropology in historical perspective: an enquiry into the growth of the social sciences', *Canadian Journal of African Studies*, X (2): 307–33.

Magubane, Bernard (1971) 'A critical look at indices used in the study of social change in colonial Africa', *Current Anthropology*, 12: 419–46.

Mascia-Lees, Frances, Sharpe, Patricia and Cohen, Colleen Ballerino (1989) 'The postmodern turn in anthropology: cautions from a feminist perspective', *Signs: Journal of Women in Culture and Society*, 15 (1): 7–33.

Mernissi, Fatima (1984) *Le Maroc Raconté par ses Femmes*, Société Marocaine des Editeurs Réunis (later translated and published as *Doing Daily Battle*, 1988. London: The Women's Press).

Mills, David (1999) *Teaching for a change: hidden histories of disciplinary 'innovation'*, National Network for Teaching and Learning Occasional Paper no. 3, Department of Cultural Studies, University of Birmingham.

Moore, Henrietta (1988) *Feminism and Anthropology*, Cambridge: Polity Press.

Nader, Laura (1973) 'Up the anthropologist: perspectives gained from studying up' in Hymes (ed.) *Reinventing Anthropology*, New York: Random House.

—— (1995) 'Comment' on Nancy Scheper-Hughes 'Proposals for a militant anthropology', *Current Anthropology*, 36 (3): 426–7.

Narayan, Kirin (1993) 'How native is a "native" anthropologist?', *American Anthropologist*, 95 (3): 671–86.

Owusu, Maxwell (1978) 'Ethnography of Africa: the usefulness of the useless', *American Anthropologist*, 80: 310–34.

Pels, Peter, (1999) 'Professions of duplexity: a prehistory of ethical codes in anthropology', *Current Anthropology*, 40 (2): 101–36.

—— (2000) 'The trickster's dilemma: ethics and the technologies of the anthropological self' in M. Strathern (ed.) *Audit Culture*, London and New York: Routledge.

Pocock, David (1988) 'Persons, texts and morality', *International Journal of Moral and Social Studies*, 3 (3): 201–16.

Quigley, Declan (1991) 'Interview with Rayond Firth', *Social Anthropology*, 1 (2): 207–22.

Quinn, Naomi (1977) 'Anthropological studies on women's status', *Annual Review of Anthropology*, 6: 181–225.

Rabinow, Paul (2002) Daryll Forde Lecture given at University College London, January.

Reiter, Rayna (1975) *Toward an Anthropology of Women*, New York and London: Monthly Review Press.

Reynolds, P. (1982) *Ethics and Social Science Research*, Englewood Cliffs, NJ: Prentice-Hall.

Roberts, Helen (1981) *Doing Feminist Research*, London and New York: Routledge.

Rohrlich-Leavitt, Ruby (ed.) (1975) *Women Cross-culturally: Change and Challenge*, The Hague: Mouton.

Rosaldo, Michelle (1980) 'The use and abuse of anthropology', *Signs: Journal of Women in Culture and Society*, 5 (3): 389–417.

Rosaldo, Michelle and Lamphere, Louise (eds) (1974) *Woman, Culture and Society*, Stanford, CA: Stanford University Press.

Rynkiewich, M.A. and Spradley, J.P. (1981) *Ethics and Anthropology: Dilemmas in Fieldwork*, Malabar, FL: R.E. Krieger Publishing Co.

Sahlins, Marshall (2001) 'Jungle fever' (review of Tierney 2001), *Guardian Weekly*, 11–17 January: 33.

Said, Edward (1978) *Orientalism*, New York: Pantheon Books.

Scheper-Hughes, Nancy (1995) 'The primacy of the ethical: propositions for a militant anthropology', *Current Anthropology*, 15: 227–83.

Scholte, Bob (1986) 'The charmed circle of Geertz's hermeneutics: a neo-marxist critique', *Critique of Anthropology*, VI (I): 5–15.

—— (1987) 'The literary turn in contemporary anthropology: a review article', *Critique of Anthropology*, VII (I): 33–47.

Shore, Cris (1999) 'Comment' on P. Pels 'Professions of duplexity', *Current Anthropology*, 40 (2): 124.

Shore, Cris and Wright, Sue (1999) 'Audit culture and anthropology: neo-liberalism in British higher education', *Journal of the Royal Anthropological Institute*, 5 (4): 557–76.

Siep, Ludwig (1997) 'Ethics and culture', in P.J.D. Drenth, Jens E. Fenstad and Jan D. Schiereck (eds) *European Science and Scientists between Freedom and Responsibility*, A conference organised by ALLEA, Amsterdam. Published by the European Commission.

Sitter-Liver, Beatt (1997) 'Responsibility of social sciences and humanities', in P.J.D. Drenth, Jens E. Fenstad and Jan D. Schiereck (eds) *European Science and Scientists between Freedom and Responsibility*, A conference organised by ALLEA, Amsterdam. Published by the European Commission.

Sjoberg, G. (ed.) (1967) *Ethics, Morals and Social Responsibility*, London: Routledge and Kegan Paul.

Sluka, Jeffrey (1999) 'Comment' on P. Pels 'Professions of duplexity', *Current Anthropology*, 40 (2): 124–6.

Smith, Dorothy (1987) *The Everyday World as Problematic: a Feminist Sociology*, Milton Keynes: Open University Press.

Stack, Carole (1975) 'Review essay: anthropology', *Signs*, 1 (1).

Stirling, Paul (1988) 'Group for Anthropology in Policy and Practice: past, present and future. Part 1 – The birth of GAPP', *BASAPP Newsletter*, 1, Autumn: 2–3.

Strathern, Marilyn (1972) *Women in Between: Female Roles in a Male World*, London: Seminar (Academic) Press.

—— (1987) 'The limits of auto-anthropology', in Anthony Hopkins (ed.) *Anthropology at Home*, ASA monographs 25, London: Tavistock.

—— (2000) *Audit Cultures: Anthropological Studies in Accountability, Ethics and the Academy*, London and New York: Routledge.

Tierney, Patrick (2000) *Darkness in El Dorado: How Scientists and Journalists Devastated the Amazon*, New York: W.W. Norton.

Tiffany, Sharon (1978) 'Anthropology and the study of women: a preliminary assessment', *Man*, 14 (1).

Wilson, Richard (ed.) (1997) *Human Rights: Culture and Context, Anthropological Perspectives*, London and Chicago: Pluto Press.

Part I

DEBATES

2

'LIKE A HORSE IN BLINKERS'?

A political history of anthropology's
research ethics

David Mills

> There are no whole truths; all truths are half-truths. It is trying to treat
> them as whole truths that plays the devil.
>
> (Alfred Whitehead 1954)

Introduction

In this chapter I present a history of anthropology's research ethics, situating
them as part of a broader political history of changing notions of scholarly
values and academic professionalism. If disciplines have shifting intellectual
and methodological concerns, they also have historically evolving
understandings of professional values. Recent commentaries have argued that
the language of ethics is proliferating, and is inexorably linked to the new
'audit culture' shaping professional life (Strathern 2000). I want to examine
this claim about the rise of 'ethics-speak' through a consideration of the
specific historical and political contexts in which British and American codes
have been written. I am intrigued by the ways in which commentators
alternately either conflate or isolate the ethical and political realms of social
scientific practice, both views over-simplifying the complex relationship
between the realms.

This chapter has journeyed through several different versions. In its first
draft I questioned the ethics of carrying out some forms of anthropological
research at all. Risking exposure on the moral high-ground, I was told to stop
worrying and finish my PhD! More recently, I have come round to the
position that 'it will never be possible to ensure that research is always
conducted in an ethical manner' (Gledhill 2000: 2). For Gledhill, 'it is not
really the continuing difficulties of policing our ethical codes that is the root
of our problem', rather it is being clear 'about the politics of the knowledge
we should be aiming to produce' (*ibid.*). But this leaves social science merely
as a player in an agonistic power game – the moral values of scholarship do

not get much of a look-in. What are the implications of talking about politics without talking about ethics, or of talking about ethics without talking about politics? MacIntyre's (1985) critique of contemporary ethical debates as merely 'emotivism' suggests that 'ethics, with its impossible conceit of impartiality, only masks politics' (Pels 1999: 103), leading to an endless oscillation between truth, ethics and politics. For Pels, 'truth and ethics are supposed to rule politics but are also always in danger of being unmasked as politically contingent' (*ibid.*: 104). I explore in this chapter both the necessity and the dangers of such 'unmasking'.

How do the realms of the ethical and the political become separated? Writing about the work of the Human Genetic Diversity Project, Whitt develops the notion of *value-bifurcation* to describe 'a well-entrenched practice within western philosophical tradition', which 'demarcates and sharply distinguishes the realm of the ethical from that of politics. The bifurcated nature of the distinction is central to it. Ethics and politics are held to differ in kind, not just in degree' (Whitt 1999: 417). Whitt is referring particularly to the way in which the ideology of value-neutrality in science restricts critique of the politics of the scientific process itself, channelling it into a narrower discussion about research ethics and informed consent. This leads to a construction of scientific ethics that is almost entirely apolitical. 'At best, particular practices are deemed morally wrong while the relations of power responsible for them – which are themselves morally reprehensible and must be challenged if such practices are to be effectively countered – are over-looked' (*ibid.*). In comparison to the natural sciences, the social sciences no longer assume value-neutrality (if they ever did), but I would argue that the notion of *value-bifurcation* helps us to understand dynamics within the social sciences today. My chapter presents the history of such values, and of value-bifurcation, within anthropology. If ethics can mask politics, then we also have to think about ways of representing politics that do not efface the moral aspects of anthropological practice.

'Like a horse in blinkers'

> Go right forward, like a horse in blinkers, neither looking to the right hand nor to the left.
> (Edmund Tylor 1885, quoted in Stocking 1996: 370)

E.B. Tylor's 1885 recommendation to students to 'go right forward, like a horse in blinkers' is an intriguing vision for the nascent science of anthropology. He makes it, according to Stocking, in an attempt to move British anthropology beyond an earlier history of moral science in the service of political reform. Tylor characterised the 1860s as a period in which anthropologists 'had taken to cultivating their science as a party-weapon in politics and religion' (quoted in Stocking 1983), a move which had been 'disastrous to its immediate position'. The reference is to the divergent politics connected with different interpretations of the evolutionary process, and to the Anthropological Institute's original roots in the Aborigines' Protection Society and its advocacy of Aboriginal rights. In this struggle, 'truth' – scientific fact – was thought to be both politically neutral and morally compelling' (Stocking 1996: 104).

If the vision of a 'blinkered' science was not a particularly flattering self-depiction, it was an important one. Stressing that the social sciences, like the natural sciences, could be value-free was a key aspect of anthropology's search for professional status and recognition. It was a refrain that Tylor himself reiterated increasingly, leaving behind his earlier commitment to anthropology as the 'reformer's science'. His commitment was to the 'scientific' process itself, and his involvement with the production of *Notes and Queries* (BAAS 1874) was part of this systematisation of knowledge collection.

More than a century later, some questions remain the same. Can science in itself determine a social good? Are scientific practice, its application and use separable realms? Where do anthropological responsibilities lie? As a researcher, is one's primary obligation to 'science', the society under research, or to one's sponsors? These are not simple questions, and neither should they be. The history of academic professionalisation during the twentieth century is also the history of moral and political debate over disciplinary values and principles.

Barnes reminds us that 'codes of practice are a symbolic attribute of professional status, and the process of professionalisation may well include the adoption of an appropriate ethical code' (1979: 159). One cannot underestimate this political symbolism, but to view such texts as simply strategic devices is to ignore the moral dimension of scholarly practice. Yet neither should the rise of debates over ethics within the social sciences during the last 20 or 30 years be viewed as a reflection of moral progress. I would argue that these changes are primarily to do with changes in our understanding of the 'values' of science and a growing scepticism of the ideology of scientific neutrality. Our own scholarly practice and professional identities are based on shifting and developing understandings of the research process, and among these changes has been the blurring of a rigid separation between truth and value.

American anthropology

North American and British anthropology have long differed in their respective size and degree of professionalisation. Many see Franz Boas' insistence on strict scientific standards as his key contribution to the early professionalisation of American anthropology. 'He seemed to personify', wrote Robert Lowie (1937: 155), 'the very spirit of science'. He played a key role in the founding of the American Anthropological Association (AAA) in 1902 as a national professional association, proposing that all prospective members have experience of teaching or publishing anthropology. He continued to make waves throughout his career. As a committed pacifist and anti-racist, he made a public protest in 1919 in *The Nation* newsletter with an editorial entitled 'Scientists as Spies' protesting about four colleagues who, 'while employed as government agents, introduced themselves to foreign governments as representatives of scientific organisations' so combining intelligence-gathering with their research. He strongly condemned their activities, suggesting that instead of dedicating their work to the 'service of truth' they had 'prostituted science by using it as a cover for their activities as spies' (Boas, quoted in Price 1998). The nationalistic sentiments of others led to Boas being publicly censured by several of the anthropological associations. The Anthropological Society of Washington called his actions 'inconsiderate to the best interests of his American colleagues', and he was removed from the council of the American Anthropological Association for bringing science into disrepute (Fluehr-Lobban 1991). Concerns were raised that the ensuing publicity would endanger the ability of others to do fieldwork. Ironically, and in a reflection of the personal rivalries on the council, he was accused of 'abuse' of his professional position for political ends.

The first move towards a formalisation of professional 'values' occurred in the context of the Second World War. Three weeks after the bombing of Pearl Harbor in 1941, the AAA placed 'itself and its resources at the disposal of the country for the successful prosecution of the war' (Fluehr-Lobban 1991). Writing just after the war, Cooper estimated that up to half of America's anthropologists contributed to the war effort in some way (Cooper 1947). Among them were a group of applied anthropologists who became involved in the administration of the ten internment camps for people of Japanese descent (two-thirds of them American citizens) in California during the Second World War. Their intention was to improve camp conditions, defuse anti-Japanese public opinion and reduce tension in the camps after a series of riots. The WRA (Wartime Relocation Authority) ethnographers saw their role as making the problems more intelligible for the administrators, and they drew on Radcliffe-Brown's theories of structural functionalism to ensure the smooth running and harmony of the internee camps. Many of them were early and active members of the Society for Applied Anthropology (SfAA), publishing articles on their research. Some, such as Elizabeth Colson, continued to study resettlement processes in other contexts. As Starn notes, their work helped to institutionalise the applied sub-field, and set an early precedent for government-contract anthropology. Yet it also legitimised and depoliticised the relocation process, promoting a 'conception of anthropology as a science of social control' (1988: 709).

In 1948, the SfAA was the first anthropological organisation to put forward a statement of anthropological research ethics. This developed out of the wartime dilemma over where one's professional responsibilities lay when working outside academia. With the caveat that 'no organisation can bind its members to specific goals or value systems', the first line of the code announced that 'the applied anthropologist must take responsibility for the effects of his recommendations never maintaining that he is merely a technician unconcerned with the ends toward which his applied skills are directed' (SfAA 1949). These ethics were inspired by functionalist theory, and the code stated that 'the specific area of responsibility of the applied anthropologist is to promote a state of dynamic equilibrium within systems of human relationships'. The code insisted that science was 'value-free', and simply noted that the 'applied anthropologist may not in any situation justify a course of action by appealing to a set of values to which he himself owes personal allegiance'. The code was later revised and shortened in 1963. This time it delineated the applied anthropologist's three primary responsibilities as being to Science, to his (*sic*) fellow men and to his clients. One's primary call was still to 'Science', and to the 'responsibility of avoiding any actions or implementations that will impede the advancement of scientific knowledge' (SfAA 1963: 237).

After the war a reorganised AAA also began to pronounce on public policy issues. Its first ever statement in 1947 was a cautious critique of the universalisms within the UN convention on human rights. This was one of the few moments where the debates on cultural relativism and human rights could meet. Yet even this ambiguous document caused outrage among its members. The response of Julian Steward and other prominent American anthropologists to it was forthright. For Steward, 'as a scientific organisation, the association has no business dealing with the rights of man' (1948: 352). Despite the SfAA guidelines and the growing demand for applied anthropology, a 1963 AAA volume on teaching anthropology (Albert 1963) makes no mention of research ethics, and values are discussed simply in terms of the importance of exposing students to ideas of cultural relativism.

Project Camelot marked the start of a very different sort of debate about anthropology's 'applications'. President Kennedy's inauguration promise to 'oppose any foe' was a very real one, exacerbating feverish worries over the spectre of communism. He poured money into any form of social science research that might have strategic uses, with Wakin (1992) estimating that between six and ten million dollars had been spent annually on counter-insurgency social science research by the end of the 1960s. For all the rumpus that surrounded Project Camelot, it was never actually carried out. Camelot was a four-million dollar study proposed by the Army Special Operations Research Office, with the aim to 'assess the potential for internal war within national societies' (Horowitz 1967). The high-ranking social scientists involved as consultants did not view it as an undercover operation, and, despite some misgivings over army involvement, most justified it on the grounds that it would influence military thinking for the better and/or enable 'applied' research to take place on a large scale (*ibid.*). The project was about to recruit Chilean academics when the plans were leaked. The Chilean press exploded with outrage: this was the same month in which United States troops had once again occupied the Dominican Republic. The ramifications of widespread Chilean protest quickly spread to the US, and within a week there was a congressional hearing. The project was cancelled.

Yet the damage had already been done. Debates began over the meaning of 'impartiality', over researchers' responsibilities to their funders, and even over the very possibility of doing research at all in the chill Cold-War climate. At the 1965 AAA meeting in Denver, Marshall Sahlins and others argued against any further involvement of anthropologists in strategic contract research. A committee of the AAA was set up to explore the issues, headed by Ralph Beals. It drew up a *Statement on the Problems of Anthropological Research and Ethics*, which was adopted by the membership in 1967 (reprinted in Wakin 1992). This statement emphasised the AAA's earlier commitment to scientific freedom, but also delineated responsibilities towards sponsors, in particular prohibiting anthropologists from clandestine government research, except in cases of declaration of war by Congress. The Camelot furore stirred up all the other social science conferences that same year. There were endless justifications and denunciations of and by those involved (Horowitz 1967). People began to recognise that 'academic authority' did not absolve one from ethical or political responsibilities.

At the AAA meeting in the following year, a resolution was proposed condemning the use of napalm and chemical defoliants in the Vietnam War. Initially the chairperson had proclaimed that the resolution was political, and hence irrelevant to the Association's stated purpose of furthering the professional interests of American anthropologists. At this point someone from the floor shouted, 'But genocide is not in the professional interests of anthropologists' (Gough 1968 quoted in Gledhill 1994: 211). The chairperson was over-ruled, but the motion was only narrowly passed. As Gough points out, anthropologists were ready to condemn mass slaughter, but not their own government. The letter pages of the AAA newsletter in the late 1960s were full of impassioned debates over the values and principles of the association. Things were not helped by the appearance of an advertisement in the *Anthropology Newsletter* for an anthropologist to work in Vietnam with the Psychological Operations Headquarters (Fluehr-Lobban 1991). To resolve the political infighting, the AAA executive agreed to set up an Ethics Committee, appointing Eric Wolf as chairperson.

A number of articles on the ethics and politics of research appeared at this time (Sjoberg *et al.* 1967, Berreman 1968, Gjessing 1968, Gough 1968), and a debate developed within anthropology (and the other social sciences) about a possible code of ethics. Gough left the US in 1967 in protest at the anti-communist witch-hunt against her, and in particular at the way the academic grades she gave to her students were being used as selection criteria by Vietnam draftboards. In her article Gough calls for a serious engagement with and study of revolutionary theorists and movements, rather than for anthropologists escaping to 'the remotest, least unstable tribe or village' they can find (1968: 405). Articles by Gjessing and Berreman, also written in the shadow of war, show an equally explicit commitment to a politicised anthropology. Berreman notes that to say nothing is not to be neutral, arguing that the notion of value-free social sciences may well have been valuable in maintaining the cohesion of the modern university, but was also a dangerous myth that could again lead to the gate of Auschwitz. These then were explicitly politicised appeals, justified by ethical principles. As Berreman (1991) remembers, it was a time when 'The virtuous and villainous were unambiguously defined no matter which side one was on, with few who were neutral or undecided.' Recent work by Price (1998) demonstrates and details the extent of US state funding of anthropological research throughout the Cold War.

The 'Thailand Controversy' (Wakin 1992) was the finale to five years of increasing professional turmoil. In early 1970, the issue of counter-insurgency reappeared when a student group sent Eric Wolf a series of leaked documents detailing the relationship between US government officials and social scientists working in South-east Asia. Eric Wolf (ironically) mishandled his position as chairperson of the Ethics Committee by publicly condemning those involved. He was accused of McCarthyite tactics and eventually forced to resign, but the AAA was still in danger of splitting down the middle. Heading a committee of inquiry, Margaret Mead exonerated those involved, declaring that the Thailand researchers were 'well within the traditional canons of acceptable behaviour for the applied anthropologist' (in Wakin 1992). Belatedly and rather half-heartedly, this report did acknowledge that a new ethical imperative had emerged from the Thailand case, but subsequently suggested that the Ethics Committee should 'confine its attention to matters of scholarly and scientific ethics'. This attempt at exoneration was later rejected by the AAA membership at their annual meeting, and the matter was left unresolved. The report's depoliticising recommendations inevitably signalled the future frame in which ethics would be discussed.

The details of this history are less important here than the relationship of ethical responsibility to political commitment. Political views are not separable from ethical principles. Yet to talk about 'ethico-political' issues is of little help, for the diversity of peoples' political commitments makes unlikely the formation of a common ground on which to base a set of anthropological research principles or ethics. One solution is to stress the importance of the *profession* of anthropology as a shared commonality, codifying a set of ethics related solely to that profession, leaving its members free to hold their own political views. Yet this professionalisation and decontextualisation of ethics reinforces the ideals of science as a politics-free zone, ideals to which its members are expected publicly to aspire (no matter what they think in private). This is the 'value-bifurcation' that Whitt (1999: 419) refers to, where 'both ethics and politics are moved out of the space of knowledge production, while a depoliticised ethics is reserved for assessing knowledge use'. It presumes an autonomous sphere for rational ethical debate, separable from any particular historical, social or political context.

The heat of the Vietnam War provided the backdrop for the final approval of the AAA code of ethics – entitled *The Principles of Professional Responsibility* – in 1971. Passions ran high over its content, and whether Wolf's Ethics Committee (which had positioned itself in opposition to the Executive) would have any adjudicatory role. The code was a powerful statement, famously declaring that 'Anthropologists' paramount responsibility is to those they study. When there is a conflict of interest, these individuals must come first' (AAA 1971). It also states that no secret research should be agreed to or carried out, insists on accountability, and includes the possibility of sanctions on those who jeopardise peoples studied or betray their professional commitment. It was these principles that anthropologists such as Berreman, Wolf and Jorgensen fought for in the early 1970s, and again protected against dilution in the mid-1980s when a watered-down modification was proposed (Berreman 1991).

One cannot dismiss the lengthy political struggle over the writing of these professional codes of ethics as the interminable 'emotivism' of MacIntyre's caricature. Yet the question of sanctions was a crucial one. The debates in the pages of *Current Anthropology* revolved around whether such a code could ever be enforceable, and what the consequences of punitive measures might be. Colin Turnbull's description of the Ik in *The Mountain People* (1972) was a test-case. Fredrik Barth condemned Turnbull in vitriolic and impassioned terms (Barth 1974), calling for sanctions to be brought against him. Turnbull was informally ostracised but never professionally sanctioned. The episode revealed the ambiguity and paradox of having an unenforceable code of ethics. In subsequent years, only a couple of cases were ever brought before the Ethics Committee, usually over accusations of plagiarism. The first principle was never invoked in order to censure individuals.

British anthropology

Is there an equivalent history of conflicting political loyalties and ethical dilemmas within British anthropology? Marginality and size meant that the distinct professional identity of British social anthropologists developed more slowly, though as L'Estoile notes, 'social anthropology's strategic importance for the colonial project of social transformation thus appears to have been an essential factor in the autonomisation of the discipline' (L'Estoile 1997: 366).

The process of value-bifurcation is again evident throughout this history, with individuals separating fact from value, science from application. While Malinowski championed the idea of a 'practical anthropology' that would study the problems of culture change, he also insisted on concentrating study on 'the facts and processes', in such a way that 'all political activities are eliminated from its activities' (Malinowski 1929: 23). After one of his students was denied a visa on the grounds of membership of the Communist Party of Great Britain, Malinowski insisted to his students that they must choose between 'radical politics and scientific anthropology' (Stocking 1996: 412).

The possibility of conflicts of interest increased dramatically in the period after the Second World War, when the Colonial Social Science Research Council (CSSRC) provided the first significant government funding for anthropological research (Feuchtwang 1973). Elaborate postwar reconstruction and development plans were drawn up for Britain's Asian and African dependencies, and social science research was a priority. However, the Council's sponsors, primarily Lord Hailey, emphasised its remit as the pursuit of scientific 'truth'. The council was made up almost entirely of academics, and as the first Annual Report notes, 'the committee should not confine itself to examining proposals put to it by Colonial Governments ... it conceives it as its duty to study the whole field of scientific inquiry' (CSSRC 1944: 2).

In relation to this period of British colonialism, Stocking comments that 'important groups within the world of colonial administration had shown themselves willing to accept the scientific status and the utilitarian promissory note of social anthropology' (1996: 420). Yet if anthropologists strategically manipulated this pure–applied opposition, so too did the Research Council. At one moment Richards describes the CSSRC as 'do-gooders trying to organise research which would increase the knowledge we felt to be helpful for "welfare and development"'. At the next she emphasises the irrelevance of this work, noting how young anthropologists involved in detailed studies 'were learning their jobs ... and had not the competence to pronounce on the problems of the colony as a whole' (Richards 1977: 178).

There were fewer misgivings in Britain of the kind that American anthropologists felt over maintaining one's research independence (Beals 1969). One of the reasons for this was the enforcement of the fact–value distinction. Evans-Pritchard made it very clear that scientific research was 'bound to exclude moral values because they are methodologically irrelevant' (1946: 92). For him, moral values were the subject of his work. At another moment he declared that 'he who sups with the administration should sup with a long spoon' (quoted in Barnes 1979). Yet he also bemoaned the fact that he had never been consulted by the Sudanese Government for his expertise, concluding one lecture by saying that, if anthropologists were to be employed by colonial administrations, it should at least be on decent terms! In his 1945 presentation to the Oxford Anthropological Society on 'Applied

Anthropology', he distinguished very clearly between value-free scientific work and the 'common-sense' practical advice anthropologists could offer. 'We are not social cobblers and plumbers but men of science on whom rests the responsibility of our time to record what cannot be recorded after us' (Evans-Pritchard 1946: 94).

The small size of the discipline in Britain ensured that conflicts rarely spilt over into a public arena. Yet political opinions and personal differences were never far below the surface. A number of Gluckman's students were highly critical of the colonial authorities, but in order to ensure funding for the Rhodes-Livingstone Institute from the Northern Rhodesian government, Gluckman too insisted on individuals bracketing off their academic research from their personal political views. Although by the end of the 1960s there were a number of leftist critiques coming from inside and outside the discipline (Banaji 1970, Goddard 1969), these critiques did not precipitate the kind of ethico-political debate that had divided the AAA. The discipline was largely overtaken by events, for by this stage decolonisation was well under way.

In comparison, the British Sociological Association came under pressure to establish a set of ethical principles in the 1960s. The increasing amounts of empirical contract research being carried out, especially in surveys, led to concern about the ethical issues which such work could raise, especially when done by inexperienced researchers. A BSA working party on ethics was set up in 1967, and its report was adopted as a 'Statement of Ethical Principles and their Application to Sociological Practice'.

This history serves two purposes: a reminder that anthropology has long negotiated the politics and morality of the use and abuse of knowledge, and a recognition that our understanding of the values of 'science' itself is constantly changing. Any heyday of supposed scientific neutrality has passed. We must once again accept that value and fact are difficult to separate.

The Association of Social Anthropologists' ethical guidelines

The ASA has its own ethical guidelines, first published in 1987. As with all such codes, they are best read in the context of the political situation facing the discipline at the end of the 1970s. The new Conservative government, at the behest of the education secretary Sir Keith Joseph, imposed major funding cuts on the Higher Education sector, and for a while the very existence of funding for social science research was in doubt. The joke at the 1983 ASA conference was that new PhDs had more chance of being run over by a bus than of getting an academic job. Peter Riviere calculated that, at that point, there were more than 100 unemployed anthropology PhDs. With very little chance of finding jobs in the discipline, they increasingly sought consultancy and policy work in the health and development fields. Whereas American anthropologists had long been employed by federal authorities and other state agencies, this was a relatively new situation for British anthropologists. A major conference was jointly hosted by the ASA and the Social Science Research Council (SSRC) in 1981 on the training and employment of anthropologists (Akeroyd *et al.* 1980). At the ASA 'Anthropology at Home' conference in 1984, there was lengthy discussion of the particular problems faced by working in one's own country, and of being employed outside the university sector. Judith Okely described her fears about ensuring the confidentiality of her research data and field-notes on gypsy communities, once the government unit funding her research was closed down. There was also a real fear of 'unscrupulous employers' – this was Tamara Dragadze's description – who would not respect the concept of academic freedom and might demand to see field-notes. These different factors, combined with a concern over the legal issues surrounding the Data Protection Act, led to the setting up of an ASA sub-committee on Legal and Ethical Issues to 'look at the feasibility of drawing up a code of professional ethics'.

The committee first met in the summer of 1985. Anne Akeroyd argued for the need for such a code, both to remind social anthropologists of potential ethical problems, and to protect anthropologists from employers, should the need arise. Recognising that guidance on how 'anthropologists should act' and the 'legal provisions that they ought to be aware of' were two rather different matters, the sub-committee agreed that it 'would not be in a position' to deal with conflicts with employers. Anne Akeroyd was asked to draft 'guidelines broad enough for there to be general agreement with them in the profession'. The ASA committee minutes that autumn note that 'it had been decided that a precise code of practice was to be avoided, but that common-sense guidelines would be drawn up instead'.[1] In her work, Akeroyd drew particularly on the code of the Social Research Association – an organisation of contract researchers.

The preamble to the *ASA Guidelines* suggested that professional codes could be divided into three types: 'regulatory, aspirational and educational' (ASA 1987). In Akeroyd's view, the ASA code differed from that of the AAA in that instead of being a regulatory document, it was to tell employees 'what they can expect of us'. It was explicitly designed to take an uncontentious and educational stance, acting pragmatically as a 'protective device for anthropologists' rather than 'to protect the profession against the undesirable behaviour of colleagues'.[2] Yet the Guidelines do make strong statements. The text adopts (in a subjunctive tense) the strong initial line of the 1971 AAA statement, where 'most anthropologists would maintain that their paramount obligation should be to their research participants'. In discussing the vulnerability of certain groups, particularly ethnic or religious minorities, it suggests that 'In certain political contexts ... it may be necessary to withhold data from publication or even to refrain from studying them at all.' Equally strongly worded is a discussion of 'undue intrusion': 'Like other social researchers, they have no special entitlement to study all phenomena, and the advancement of knowledge and the pursuit of information are not in themselves sufficient justification for overriding the values and ignoring the interests of those studied' (*ibid*.: 2).

As Akeroyd recently acknowleged, the ASA code is an 'uneasy mix of the aspirational and down-to-earth advice ... I was trying to say "think about it", but often the prescriptive language came out a little pompous.'[3] She went on to suggest that, in the case of British anthropology, the absence of scandals and a strong sense of collegiality made regulatory codes and their accompanying sanctions committees unnecessary. The draft guidelines provoked remarkably little comment – just one letter and a couple of questions at the ASA annual business meeting.

Pocock (1988: 201) made one of the few critiques of the Guidelines, arguing that the focus on competing obligations was presented as a 'new development in the world and ... the product of a heightened sensibility in anthropologists themselves'. As well as critiquing the aspiration to professionalism, he viewed it as further evidence that the 'terms ethical and moral are pulling apart, and we increasingly hear of ethical guidelines exactly when there is no moral agreement'. Instead he argued that the notion that 'anthropology finds its moral justification in application is a misguided one', and that 'anthropology is intrinsically moral knowledge because of the reflexivity of the anthropological experience' (*ibid*.). Pocock is right to recognise that the symbolic politics of professionalisation is well served by codes and guidelines, but his one-dimensional reading of the complex context of the code's formation once again relies on the logic of 'value-bifurcation', assuming that disciplinary practice could be moral without ever being political.

Waiving the rules? The status of professional ethical guidelines today

How are ethical issues viewed within the anthropological profession today? Compared with – or perhaps because of – the contentious debates over anthropological politics, debates over ethics have mostly been marginalised on both sides of the Atlantic. Contemporary theoretical debates have questioned 'Enlightenment' principles and the belief that ethical codes could act as a restraining guide to moral conduct in research. The political context of their writing no longer seems to matter. In spite of the fact that the guidelines were often hesitant, they appeared to smack of universalising regulations. There is the increasing recognition that the invocation of abstract moral principles is inadequate for the analysis of complex, sometimes intractable questions.

Have the codes been put to use? The militancy exhibited in the struggle over the initial AAA code of ethics soon dissipated, and the Ethics Committee ended up adjudicating on petty conflicts between colleagues. The code, further and further removed from first context, seemed less like a set of hard-won principles and more like an episode of liberal hand-wringing. The statement in the 1971 Principles that 'Anthropologists must do everything in their power to protect the physical, social and psychological welfare and to honour the dignity and privacy of those studied' began to look increasingly paternalistic and unrealistic. Which subjects were being invoked? Were their interests the same? How did one deal with a conflict of interests?

Such disillusionment lay behind the AAA's mid-1990s decision to renounce its original commitment to adjudicate breaches of the 1971 code (Fluehr-Lobban 1996), and to prioritise instead the modest aim of 'ethics education'. This is the second time the code has been revisited, the first being the 1984 revision criticised by Berreman (1991) as reflecting the new 'Reaganethics' of the association. As Price (1998) pointed out, this first revision watered down the original commitment to 'no secret research, no secret reports or debriefings' to a mere statement that anthropologists were 'under no professional obligation to provide reports, unless they have individually and explicitly agreed to do so in the terms of employment'. The most recent initiative merely emphasises the importance of socialisation, discussion and education. A set of guidelines is provided on the AAA website, together with a series of case-studies through which to think about the issues. This has left the curious paradox of an American anthropology (or rather those anthropologists interested in such debates), which once fought to compose ethical codes in order to demonstrate its collective political commitment, subsequently weakening them in the name of a more individualised politics. Part of this comes from a change in the conception of the 'political' to include every aspect of human life. A scepticism of universalising regulations has left adjudication of ethical breaches to seem increasingly inappropriate (AAA 1996). Since the Chagnon–Yanomami affair (see Nugent, this volume), the tide has turned once again, and attention has come back to the role of the professional association in regulating its members' conduct. A new, detailed and authoritative set of briefing papers on the 1971 code has been placed on the AAA web-site (http://www.aaanet.org/committees/ethics/bp.htm), evidence again of the located-ness of such codes, and the intertwining of political and ethical issues.

The postmodern moment ensured that there was also resistance at the European Association of Social Anthropologists (EASA) meeting in 1996 to any attempt at drawing up a similar set of guidelines. Pels advocated the promotion of a new 'ethics network' to discuss these issues. Yet he also points out the duplicity of ethnography, given the long history of anthropologists' divided loyalties (Pels 1999). On the whole the topic attracted little interest. Yet while people might not be talking about ethics, there is still great interest in questions of value and agency. The importance of 'revealing multiple voices' and 'acknowledging people's agency' is widely accepted in contemporary texts. Such principled positions are another way of talking about ethics. The current mood in anthropology encourages a concern with responsibility, partiality and reflexivity, but these are seen as more individualised concerns for researchers, rather than for any larger grouping or community.

In 1999 the ASA consulted its members and revised its own ethical guidelines. In contrast to the US trend, this new draft, written by Richard Wilson, tightens up some of the ambiguities and contradictions in the original document. Again there was relatively little response. As Richard Wilson comments (personal communication): 'Mostly my influences were from Sociology and Oral History. They work in industrialised countries and treat their informants with greater respect than anthropologists who work in Africa, Asia etc. I wanted to bring us into line with developments in other qualitative disciplines. The Oral History Society guidelines are much more stringent than anything the ASA has produced.' In doing the revision Wilson returns to the international precedent set by the Nuremberg trials, and their strong endorsement of the principles of voluntary participation and informed consent of subjects. Wilson criticises the previous guidelines for attempting to justify seeking consent *post hoc*. The new guidelines state that 'consent made after the research is completed is not meaningful consent at all'. Coming out strongly against deception and covert research, they also attempt to spell out the process of gaining consent more fully, recognising that 'consent in research is a process, not a one-off event, and may require renegotiation over time; it is an issue to which the anthropologist should return periodically'. The document also includes a section on copyright law, stating that 'Interviewers must obtain a statement in writing of the interviewees' wishes concerning future copyright ownership.' Yet the guidelines again avoid the issue of adjudication, and reiterate their role as being 'informative and descriptive rather than authoritarian or prescriptive'.

Ethical proliferation?

This chapter has sought to disentangle the important ethical, moral and political threads that make up the history of social science research ethics. I have shown how the writing of guidelines, whether in the 1940s or 1990s, has been carried out with a close attention to *both* ethical and political questions. These histories serve to challenge Pels' broader argument that 'professional ethics ... exemplifies the liberal tendency to neutralise and depoliticise political relationships by constituting the self from the political interactions in which it necessarily has to operate' (Pels 2000: 156). The evidence from both the American and British contexts is that they only become important and meaningful at moments of crisis, at moments in which they serve a political purpose. I do not think that one could argue that anthropological selves have been 'constituted' as a result of, say, the ASA guidelines. If anything, such guidelines have been largely ignored, serving primarily a symbolic and public relations purpose.

There is now a new set of codes and procedures to grapple with. Universities in the UK are following the lead of regional health care authorities in setting up ethical review committees at an institutional level. An increasing fear of litigation has also led universities to establish ethics committees to protect their employees and students. Such review boards have existed in American universities since the 1960s. How should we view and respond to these developments? For Rose, the 'proliferation of the language of ethics' (Rose 1999: 191) makes an analysis urgent and complex. Shore and Wright (2000) talk of the 'rapid and relentless spread of coercive technologies', and Strathern notes the 'recent developments ... in rituals of verification' (2000: 3). Recent anthropological commentaries suggest that the proliferation of 'audit regimes' and ethics-talk are connected. Strathern suggests that 'audit and ethics ricochet off each other' and goes further to suggest that 'ethics, especially when it is codified (ethical codes) could be thought of as an enlarged or magnified version of audit, it specifically relates "good practice" to individual conduct' (2000: 292).

In evidence, Strathern gives the example of institutions adopting accountable and transparent practices. She notes that 'the more people fulfil them, the more visibly an institution is seen to be ethical'. This is somewhat slippery logic – the research ethics expected of individual academics are not simply transposed or equated to procedures expected at an institutional level. Certainly there is a moralising tone to the language of institutional 'good practice' or 'transparency', but this is of a rather different valency to that of disciplinary professionalism. Both are undergoing codification, but this is not enough to equate the two processes.

My concern is with the way in which the politics of audit and the ethics of research are collapsed together in some critical analyses of audit culture. In yet another manifestation of value-bifurcation, a discussion of the changing moral expectations made on social science research is effaced underneath a general critique of forms of contemporary bureaucratic power. As Giri notes, 'with the articulation of professional ethics, it is politics which has mattered most rather than devotion to ethical ideals per se' (Giri 2000: 187). Giri insists that anthropologists 'treat morality as an end in itself, not simply as a means to some ulterior motives' (ibid.: 187).

Audit and ethics may well be linked, but an analysis of this new moment has to disentangle the range of factors shaping these new developments and explore their implications for academic practice. Rather than simply seeing 'ethics-talk' as the performativity demanded of the new audit regime, I suggest that we need to take both the moral and the political realm seriously. What are the implications of such developments for the future of disciplinary professionalism? A key issue is the bio-medical ethical paradigm that lies behind many of these developments. This may rub uneasily against anthropological understandings of the research process, but it has developed out of an important history of ethical dialogue and debate dating back to the Nuremberg trials. These guidelines are increasingly applied to social researchers in the health sciences, requiring researchers to justify why they do not need to gain written consent from their research 'subjects'. External review bodies such as ethics committees are now looking at anthropological research proposals (Pels 1999, Amit 2000, Murphy and Johannsen 1990), often with uncomfortable consequences. Their interpretations challenge the methodological habitus of ethnographic research. For Strathern, this emphasis on the research 'subject' rewrites the way in which all sides understand the process of anthropological research, and for Amit, this leads to an 'explicit intolerance for open-ended research procedures' (2000: 231). Yet as well as critiquing these developments, they provide an opportunity for anthropologists to redefine, debate and develop disciplinary methodologies. One can make a strong case for a genre of ethnographic research and writing that does not reduce the complexity of the research relationship to the extraction of information from research 'subjects'. But it is a case that does need to be made.

Anthropologists are not outside the value-bifurcation process. We are equally able to view ethics-talk as a political discourse, and politics as a matter for ethical deliberation. The risk of uncritically celebrating our discipline's political reflexivity is that we avoid analysing our own conditions of work and the moral demands it places on us – we turn the gaze externally, rather than on ourselves. This leaves our own sense of professional values unexamined. I doubt one could ever define what counts as 'ethical' research. But this does not validate a *laissez-faire* ethical relativism. Should we not want an ongoing dialogue about the politics and ethics of our research methods?

Notes

1   ASA archives, box RP69, ASA minutes 827.
2   Anne Akeroyd, letter to George Stocking, 9 February 1993.
3   Phone interview with Anne Akeroyd, 11 January 2001.

Bibliography

Akeroyd, A. *et al.* (1980) 'Training and employment of social anthropologists', *RAIN*, 41: 5–7.

Albert, E. (1963) 'Value aspects of teaching anthropology', in D. Mandelbaum, G. Lasker and E. Albert (eds) *The Teaching of Anthropology*, Berkeley: University of California Press.

American Anthropological Association (1947) 'Statement on human rights', *American Anthropologist*, 40: 539–43.

—— (1971) *Principles of Professional Responsibility*, Washington, DC: AAA.

Amit, V. (2000) 'The university as panopticon: moral claims and attacks on academic freedom', in M. Strathern (ed.) *Audit Cultures: Anthropological Studies in Accountability, Ethics and the Academy*, London: Routledge.

Association of Social Anthropologists of the Commonwealth (1987) *Ethical Guidelines for Good Practice*, London: ASA.

—— (1999) *Ethical Guidelines for Good Practice* (2nd edn), London: ASA.

BAAS (British Association for the Advancement of Science) (1874) *Notes and Queries on Anthropology, for the Use of Travellers and Residents in Uncivilised Lands*, London: E. Stanford.

Banaji, J. (1970) 'The crisis of British anthropology', *New Left Review*, 64: 71–85.

Barnes, J. (1979) *Who Should Know What? Social Science, Privacy and Ethics*, Harmondsworth: Penguin.

Barth, F. (1974) 'On responsibility and humanity: calling a colleague to account', *Current Anthropology*, 15: 1.

Beals, R. (1969) *Politics of Research: an Inquiry into the Ethics and Responsibilities of Social Scientists*, Chicago: Aldine.

Berreman, G. D. (1968) 'Is anthropology alive? Social responsibility in social anthropology', *Current Anthropology*, 9(5): 391–6.

—— (1991) 'Ethics versus "realism" in anthropology', in C. Fluehr-Lobban (ed.) *Ethics and the Profession of Anthropology: Dialogue for a New Era*, Philadelphia: University of Pennsylvania Press.

Colonial Social Science Research Council (1944) *First Annual Report of the Colonial Research Committee*, 1943–4, Cmnd 6535.

Commission to Review the AAA Statement on Ethics (1996) 'Draft AAA code of ethics', *Anthropology Newsletter*, 37 (4): 15–16.

Cooper, J. M. (1947) 'Anthropology in the United States during 1939–1945', *Société des Americanistes de Paris*, Journal, 36: 1–14.

Evans-Pritchard, E. E. (1946) 'Applied anthropology: the uses of knowledge', *Africa*, 16: 92–8.

Feuchtwang, S. (1973) 'The discipline and its sponsors', in Talal Asad (ed.) *Anthropology and the Colonial Encounter*, London: Ithaca Press.

Fluehr-Lobban, C. (1991) 'Ethics and professionalism: a review of issues and principles within anthropology', in C. Fluehr-Lobban (ed.) *Ethics and the Profession of Anthropology: Dialogue for a New Era*, Philadelphia: University of Pennsylvania Press.

—— (1996) 'Developing the New AAA Code of Ethics', *AAA Newsletter*, 37(4): 17.

Giri, A. (2000) 'Audited accountability and the imperative of responsibility: beyond the primacy of the political', in M. Strathern (ed.) *Audit Cultures: Anthropological Studies in Accountability, Ethics and the Academy*, London: Routledge.

Gjessing, G. (1968) 'The social responsibility of the social scientist', *Current Anthropology*, 9: 397–402.

Gledhill, J. (1994) *Power and Its Disguises: Anthropological Reflections on Politics*, London: Pluto Press.

—— (2000) 'Finding a new public face for anthropology', *Anthropology Today*, 16(6): 1–3.

Goddard, D. (1969) 'Limits of British anthropology', *New Left Review*, 58: 79–89.

Gough, K. (1968) 'New proposals for anthropologists', *Current Anthropology*, 9(5): 403–35.

Horowitz, I. (ed.) (1967) *The Rise and Fall of Project Camelot: Studies in the Relationship Between Social Science and Practical Politics*, Cambridge, MA: MIT Press.

L'Estoile, B. (1997) 'The "natural preserve of anthropologists": social anthropology, scientific planning and development', *Social Science Information*, 36(2): 343–76.

Lowie, R. (1937) *The History of Ethnological Theory*, New York: Holt, Rhinehart and Winston.

MacIntyre, A. (1985) *After Virtue: A Study in Moral Theory*, London: Duckworth.

Malinowski, B. (1929) 'Practical anthropology', *Africa*, 2: 22–38.

Murphy, M. and Agneta, J. (1990) 'Ethical obligations and federal regulations in ethnographic research and anthropological education', *Human Organization*, 49(2): 127–33.

Pels, P. (1999) 'Professions of duplexity: a prehistory of ethical codes in anthropology', *Current Anthropology*, 40(2): 101–37.

—— (2000) 'The trickster's dilemma: ethics and the technologies of the anthropological self', in M. Strathern (ed.) *Audit Cultures: Anthropological Studies in Ethics, Accountability and the Academy*, London: Routledge.

Pocock, D. F. (1988) 'Persons, texts and morality', *International Journal of Moral and Social Studies*, 3(3): 201–16.

Price, D. (1998) 'Cold War anthropology: collaborators and victims of the national security state', *Identities*, 4(3/4): 389–430.

Richards, A. (1977) 'The Colonial Office and the organisation of social research', *Anthropological Forum*, 4: 168–89.

Rose, N. S. (1999) *Powers of Freedom: Reframing Political Thought*, Cambridge: Cambridge University Press.

Shore, C. and Wright, S. (1999) 'Audit culture and anthropology: neo-liberalism in British higher education', *Journal of the Royal Anthropological Institute*, 5: 557–75.

Sjoberg, G. (1967) 'Project Camelot: selected reactions and personal reflections', in G. Sjoberg (ed.) *Ethics, Politics and Social Research*, London: Routledge and Kegan Paul.

Society for Applied Anthropology (1949) 'Report of the committee on ethics', *Human Organization*, 8(2): 20–1.

—— (1963) 'Statement on Ethics of the Society for Applied Anthropology', 22(4): 237.

Starn, O. (1988) 'Engineering internment: anthropologists and the war relocation authority', *American Ethnologist*, 133: 701–17.

Stocking, G. W. (1983) 'The ethnographer's magic: fieldwork in British anthropology from Tylor to Malinowski' in G. Stocking (ed.) *Observer Observed: Essays on Ethnographic Fieldwork*, *History of Anthropology*, vol. 1, Madison, WI: University of Wisconsin Press.

—— (1987) *Victorian Anthropology*, New York: Free Press and London: Collier Macmillan.

—— (1996) *After Tylor: British Social Anthropology 1888–1951*, London: Athlone.

Strathern, M. (2000) 'Afterword: accountability ... and ethnography', in M. Strathern (ed.) *Audit Cultures: Anthropological Studies in Accountability, Ethics and the Academy*, London: Routledge.

—— (2000) *Audit Cultures: Anthropological Studies in Accountability, Ethics and the Academy*, London: Routledge.

Turnbull, C. (1972) *The Mountain People*, London: Jonathan Cape.

Wakin, E. (1992) *Anthropology Goes to War: Professional Ethics and Counterinsurgency in Thailand*, Madison: University of Wisconsin, Centre for South-east Asian Studies.

Whitehead, A. E. (1954) Dialogue of Alfred North Whitehead, recorded by Lucien Price, London: M. Reinhardt.

Whitt, L. A. (1999) 'Value-bifurcation in bioscience: the rhetoric of research justification', *Perspectives on Science*, 7(4): 413–46.

3

'BEING THERE'

The magic of presence or the metaphysics of morality?

Lisette Josephides

Introduction

I begin with a dream, recorded after the first time I left my fieldsite in Papua New Guinea.

> I dreamt we returned to our highland Kewa village, to find it built
> up out of all recognition. There was a supermarket and a department
> store, and scores of brightly-clad Europeans ambled about leisurely.
> It looked to our shocked eyes like a scene from The Village in *The
> Prisoner*, the 1970s cult television programme, with the same aura of
> unreality about it. Our old house was completely run down, dwarfed
> by a luxurious mansion that Rimbu, my Kewa patron and adoptive
> brother, had built alongside it. Rimbu told us that he often put up
> European guests in his palatial home. I felt a tightness in my throat
> and a hollowness in the pit of my stomach. We'd been cheapened!
> With so many Europeans around we'd go unremarked, and with the
> glut of luxury goods we would lose our superiority. In a flash our
> relationship with Rimbu and other villagers appeared in stark
> outline: it was based on inequality, and once 'democratisation' took
> place we would lose our structural advantage.

Under the spell of this dream with its dark entailments of repressed
consciousness, I intended at first to write a paper on 'The Anthropologist's
Power'. But once I began to hunt through my fieldnotes for concrete displays
of that power what I found instead were instances of feeling thwarted, of
being treated negligently, of not being notified of important events which
were never delayed for my sake, and of an intense awareness of marginality.
At the same time, the burning desire to count for something in the village
was tempered by a vestigial resistance to incorporation. So the dream had

deceived me, it was another example of my lack of confidence and fear that I was not highly regarded in the village.

In one respect, it brought to mind Marilyn Strathern's paper on the Hagen *hausboi* (1985), where she writes that the perception of inequality in the relationship was the master's model, not the *hausboi*'s (or servant's). My case was slightly more convoluted. It was not part of my conscious ideal to live in unequal relationships in the field, indeed I always thought of them as being symmetrical at some level. In so far as I was treated as being in a superior position, I considered this to be *their* model, not mine. Then, horror of horrors, a dream reveals how I actually had nurtured an unconscious or repressed model of superiority. Of course, my interpretation of my dream probably just illustrates how ill-versed I am in that art. A better reading may be that it revealed to me that I had never believed in my repressed model of superiority, and, moreover, suffered qualms over my deficient commitment – hence the panic.

Background

The dream recounted above is just one of a score of dreams I have had which, however interpreted, exemplify at the very least a preoccupation with the moral aspects of my relations with my fieldwork hosts. It seemed a fitting introduction to this chapter, which seeks to develop an argument along the following lines: Beyond a culturally relative particularity, there is moral behaviour that crosses cultures. Ethnographers experience this when fieldwork creates them as moral persons who recognise and are affected by this morality. My chapter pursues these questions by juxtaposing ethnographic experience with the theories of moral philosophers. It finishes by turning to the academic milieu, and considers the problems encountered when the ethnographer attempts to carry into that milieu the moral virtues which were part of ethnographic practice.

Anthropologists go to the field armed with some core precepts about ethical fieldwork behaviour. These are general rules, usually in the form of proscriptions (avoid causing harm, exploiting informants, etc.) drawn from their own systems of morality and informed by past fieldwork experience. We tend to think of fieldwork ethics in this negative way, almost as rules of avoidance – what not to do. But when we go to live and interact with people in the field, we need to establish a positive relationship. It is not possible to live with people without encountering ethical and moral situations and having somehow to resolve them. Being informed by what is considered right and proper and ethical where we come from is, of course, a beginning – what Geertz (1983) has called 'common sense'. But treating people respectfully and being true according to our own lights is not the same as establishing relations with them. Relations create intricate situations in which we have to act beyond the breviary of general rules. Becoming 'immersed' or 'submerged' in the field, or giving up one's own beliefs and ways of knowing for those of local people are strategies fraught with problems. They are also passive strategies that suggest the dissolution of the subject rather than the active imperilling of the self.[1] The authenticity of the ethnography and its success to evoke a lived reality will depend on that transformative relationship achieved in the field. The philosopher Merleau-Ponty wrote of the *cogito* that it must reveal me in a situation (1962: xiii); so too must fieldwork and ethnographic writing.

The ethics and morality at issue here, then, do not just concern external, quasi-legal rules about treating people appropriately.[2] They are requirements for relationships without which good fieldwork could not be achieved. In this chapter I consider the relationship between anthropologist and subject from two aspects. The 'magic of presence' in my title refers to the empathy or the intersubjective, reflexive understanding achieved in the personal relations developed in that encounter, while the 'metaphysics of morality' refers to a commitment to treat the other as an end, an autonomous moral agent. Although this commitment is made on the basis of an intellectual and philosophical judgement about morality, it also originated in the fieldwork encounter. It was not arrived at by abstract reasoning but by the experience of moral behaviour in the field.

On the way to developing these arguments I have to contend with relativistic theories of morality, with their postulates that moral virtues are inextricable from their context in the social structure. It is well known that anthropology is the discipline *par excellence* – or ex officio – of cultural relativism. But in this discussion I use, quite deliberately, the vocabulary, concepts, and syllogistic style of reasoning of moral philosophers (note that they don't argue – they *reason*). I have good reasons for this, but also strategic ones.

From the discussion of moral behaviour in the field I develop an understanding of empathy as a virtue, not just a pragmatic strategy but a moral component of all our relations with people. My final step is to consider how the moral virtues which were part of ethnographic practice can be carried over into the academic milieu. The transfer is problematic, because the academic milieu is subject to contradictory pulls from both the ethics of academic practices and the compelling needs of institutions, and this tug-of-war has a determining influence on academic culture.

Being there: The magic and the artifice

A good starting point is a consideration of two aspects of fieldwork. On the one hand, the conceptual and historical positioning of fieldwork as the bedrock of anthropology; on the other, the practical positioning and experience of the ethnographer.

For most anthropologists, fieldwork is an artificial positioning from which they observe other people's real lives. As postgraduate students, budding anthropologists are prepared for the field with a grounding in the discipline's history, theory, and classical ethnographies. On the basis of this we construct a hypothesis for PhD fieldwork. Our returns to the field may be less hypothesis-driven, but this initial, prolonged fieldwork is normally the defining bedrock of academic careers. We are taught fieldwork ethics and have impressed on us the importance of 'grasping the native's point of view'. Our own cultural background we must 'bracket' or even deny, though we are aware that it will be active in the development of our analysis. The field is a sacred space, given wholly to the quest for knowledge and understanding. We are to conduct 'participant observation' there while remaining respectful guests, sympathetic and non-judgemental.[3] Yet no matter how immersed we become, those surface, day-to-day activities that reproduce our host community engage us mainly as objects of study, offering at most temporary hardships. For that reason our fieldwork positioning can be seen as artificial. Meanwhile, local people go about the business of everyday life, untroubled about the methodological concerns of fieldwork and the epistemological questions of knowledge and empathy. But for us their lives are rich veins which our febrile imaginations mine to construct edifices that describe and explain the world. Fieldwork experience attempts to make fieldwork into a *thing*, an ethnography, something about which to have a meta-discourse.

Yet at the same time, I suggest that the practical experience of fieldwork with its daily challenges has a by-product: a person whose empathy makes possible the ethnography as an object of knowledge. When field experience fashions the anthropologist as an ethical and emotionally committed figure (what I call a 'moral person'), empathy becomes a value in itself.

But what could the foundation of such morality be? A brief look at western moral philosophy will identify challenges to notions of transcultural ethics and morality. It will lead to a discussion of the social strategies adopted in the field, and the compulsion to extend them to the academic milieu.

Theories of morality: The moral philosophers

In his influential book, *After Virtue*, Alasdair MacIntyre describes the heyday of morality in the western world as a time when moral judgements were absolutely binding, 'at once hypothetical and categorical in form' (1984: 60). They posited an authority which was at the same time non-empirical, transcendent, immanent and permanent, founded on a teleological narrative whose purpose was to reclaim a lost patrimony, the eternal paradise forfeited through sin. Divine law had its earthly equivalent in the king's sovereignty, and these two authorities together provided an inescapable framework for action. This morality emerges through a *longue durée*, stretching from classical times to the Christian Middle Ages and the early modern era, until it is dealt a deathblow by the secularising effects of Enlightenment logic. In so far as ideas of the moral 'ought' retained their hold in a later period (as in Kant's treatment of moral judgements as teleological imperatives), MacIntyre saw them as mere linguistic survivals, incoherent fragments of a system once undergirt with practices. The *telos*, or final purpose for human beings, was lost when the modern self was invented as 'the individual'. The resulting situation presented a paradox: the individual was liberated from the external authority of traditional morality, becoming an autonomous, sovereign moral agent, but in the same move the end purpose or *telos* that provided the 'authoritative content' for 'moral utterances' was also lost (*ibid.*: 68). Hence the solipsistic fears of existentialism. Why should anyone listen to us, asks MacIntyre rhetorically, if we speak 'unconstrained by the externalities of divine law, natural teleology or hierarchical authority' (*ibid.*)?

A new teleology was needed to provide t4232he basis for moral action, and several candidates were proposed: practical reason (Kant),4 the passions (Hume), choice (Kierkegaard). The utilitarian, naturalistic teleology of Bentham and Mill derived morality from psychology and paved the way for G.E. Moore's emotivism, which is at the base of modern-day principles of morality. For MacIntyre emotivism is the death-knell of morality, as his (paraphrased) argument sets out:

> Since my precepts of what is good were derived from my emotions, in pursuing the good I am pursuing my own ends. When I subsequently try to influence another person to adopt my precepts, I am treating that person as a means to my ends. Moreover, the very fact of deriving moral action from psychology '[entails] the obliteration of any genuine distinction between manipulative and non-manipulative social relations'. That distinction can be made only by 'impersonal criteria', which alone can determine what is in the other's interests. Since my emotions are elevated to criteria that determine the general good, they usurp the role of 'impersonal criteria', but without posing as impersonal. My treatment of the other as a means to my own ends is justified by the elevation of my emotions to the status of moral criteria. To treat someone as an end, by contrast, is to be unwilling to influence that person 'except by reasons which that other he or she judges to be good' and on the basis of 'impersonal criteria'.
>
> (MacIntyre 1984: 23–4)

The usurpation of the critical role of 'impersonal criteria' by emotional ones has led to the paradoxical character of contemporary moral experience, characterised by MacIntyre as the impasse of autonomy versus authority. Because we are taught to see ourselves as autonomous moral agents we resist manipulation by others, but we also claim authority for our personal (autonomous) moral convictions. Our strategy for achieving this authority consists in attempts to 'incarnate' our principles in our shared practices. Since these principles are not derived from 'impersonal criteria' our attempts to make them the basis of practices can only create 'manipulative modes of relationship', precisely of the type 'which each of us aspires to resist in our own case' (*ibid.*: 68).

To recap MacIntyre's argument: His original premise is that systems of morality and virtue are inextricable from their context in the social structure. The social structure that embodied the western system was always based on the external authority of religion and social hierarchy. With the advent of the sovereign moral agent in the person of the autonomous individual, authority disappears and so does the basis of morality. No rational vindication for morality can be offered, and emotivism, or personal preference, becomes the only basis for moral judgements.

I now present my own data and arguments through an examination and critique of four of MacIntyre's premises:

- That psychologically derived principles of morality treat the other as a means for one's own ends.
- That only 'impersonal criteria' can consider others as ends.
- That virtues are inextricable from their context in the social structure in which they occur.
- That the project of morality is unintelligible without a teleological framework.

Emotivism and morality

There is currently a fast-growing cottage industry on emotions in anthropological theory. They have been analysed, *inter alia*, as forms of cognition and as 'embodied thoughts' (Rosaldo 1984: 143, emphasis removed), as interpretations (Solomon 1983), as social activity and as forms of symbolic action (Lutz 1988), and as systems of meaning and communication (Lutz and White 1986). Building on the insight that emotions have meaning and are social rather than purely private in nature, Lutz and White (1986) take a leap into the abyss and deny altogether that emotions are internal states or passions. For Abu-Lughod and Lutz, emotions are not expressive vehicles but forms of discourse, 'pragmatic acts and communicative performances' (Abu-Lughod and Lutz 1990: 11). Solomon, a philosopher who has influenced some anthropologists, argues that an emotion is not a feeling but an interpretation, and treats emotions as forms of judgement and logic in the Kantian sense: 'those basic judgements and concepts through which ... we constitute the world of our experience' (Solomon 1983: 251; quoted in Lyon 1995: 258). Other anthropologists prefer to turn to Spinoza and rediscover his radical identification of mind and body, in the space where emotions, no longer in the realm of pure individuality, enter an interactive world of mind and body. They are neither meanings nor feelings, but 'experiences learned and expressed in the body in social interactions through the mediation of systems of signs, verbal and nonverbal' (Leavitt 1996: 526). But even without the intercession of Spinoza, it is possible to declare emotions to be both physical and cultural, to do with meaning and feeling (Desjarlais 1992).

This brief review suggests that there is more to emotion than the 'emotivism' made up of 'personal preferences' on which, MacIntyre fears, morality must founder (see Lyon 1995, Leavitt 1996). In what follows I discuss emotion from one perspective only, namely its role in our understanding of others during fieldwork. This small window will nevertheless allow me to claim an intimate and even causal relationship between emotion and morality.

In so far as the reflexivity of 'being there' entails empathy as an emotional response, it is crucial to the moral person who, I argue, is created in the field. In a recent paper that discussed the role of emotions in everyday life I began with a picture of the sense data assaulting the anthropologist in the field. Slowly they acquired meaning, as I acquired discernment. This is how I summed up the experience:

> Emotions animate all local-scale interactions through which life is lived and culture is produced. They create a vibrant, living community, its moods and tempo. They are felt within a group, not necessarily experienced in a phenomenological, intersubjective way, but palpably, as forces, moods, omens, pacifiers, sources of anxiety and morbid interest, magnetic fields outside the individual. They create a maelstrom of human passions, where resentment blows about with complacency, apprehension and fear brush past and darken a brighter mood, greed collides with jealousy, scorn circles around infuriated frustration, generosity becomes tainted with hubris and runs headlong into suspicion and wariness. And all the while humour hovers above everything, not entirely benignly but maintaining a certain alertness, mediating some sort of understanding. It was in this maelstrom that I gained my understanding of the Kewa.
>
> (Josephides forthcoming a)

The maelstrom is what I call empathy. Though I began with an impressionistic ethnographic picture, gradually my accounts became coherent anecdotes that showed people as acting and strategising agents, their actions and statements constantly eliciting the responses of others. But this was just a first step. Clearly, resentment, apprehension, greed and generosity are not sense data. They are subsequent interpretations of expressed emotions as I perceived them. My own emotions had acted as Kantian forms of judgement, in the way that Solomon (1983) describes above. Specifically, they formed moral judgements about what was human. Empathy, an emotional response, became a moral quality.

During fieldwork what I thought of as 'ethical' became more conscious, concretised and extended. I continually judged myself, scrutinised my every action for its motive and effect on others and double-checked my frankness in attributing a motive to it. Another ethnographic vignette from my fieldnotes makes this point.

> When Kengeai demanded a large payment from Rimbu and his brothers in return for transporting their dead father's body, I fulminated against making the payment, telling myself and others that my anger stemmed from my concern that they were being cheated. But was I really viewing the case from the perspective of their interests, or was I being petulant and resentful because I disapproved of the situation from my own perspective? A complex chain of negotiations eventually revealed that a large payment on such occasions was appropriate, not only socially and politically but also emotionally and in accordance with the local value system. My own emotional responses as empathy had allowed me to understand the Kewa, but as *amour-propre* they could also lead me astray.

What was crucial at this juncture was that I had developed the critical ability of juxtaposing emotions as moral judgements. My moral stance derived from emotion, but it could provide a successful basis for my actions and my evaluation of the actions of others in the field. It did not have to result in the manipulation of the other into an instrument of my purpose, as in my initial, unchecked response. As a consequence of this rigorous self-questioning, ethical behaviour became not only what I wanted for myself, but a necessary precondition for meaningful human relations. I thought of it as a measure of people, and judged others in the field on the basis of whether or not they acted according to the precepts of accountability, responsibility and consideration.

The example also shows that my concept of ethics included a sort of *social knowledge*, the ability to judge situations and what they called for. My own stance became crucial in the legitimacy of my descriptions and interpretations, and to that extent empathy became separated from strategy. It was no longer something I had to do in order to carry out fieldwork; it had become a value in itself, as I began to see the commitment to looking from the other's perspective as the only legitimate basis for relations with others.[5] Ethics came to stand for the attitude and understanding that underlay the sort of communication that crossed cultures. Rather than elucidate any particular moral code, fieldwork brought out most clearly the importance of acting morally in a transcultural way.

So far I have been using 'ethics' and 'morality' almost interchangeably. Distinguishing between them at this stage will also help to identify a route for thinking about a morality that crosses cultures. Terminologically, ethics can be defined as the science (or philosophy) that human beings have constructed to guide the transition from 'man-as-he-happens-to-be and man-as-he-could-be-if-he-realised-his-essential-nature' (MacIntyre 1984: 52). This meaning of ethics (originally Aristotle's) presupposes an account of rational beings with a *telos* and the potentiality to act in order to achieve it (*ibid.*), and opens the way for Ricoeur's (1992) more conceptual distinction between 'moral' and 'ethical'. The ethical aim here (as in Aristotle) is the general teleological aim for the good, which is not tied to any particular moral code but instead pursues those ends that are compatible with human 'flourishing', as Nussbaum (2000: 169) puts it. But the deontological moment of action – when one acts out of duty – finds its actualisation in a moral norm. The passage from a universal ethical aim to a particular moral norm poses different problems for philosophers and for anthropologists. The former must legitimate the elevation of the particular moral norm to the universal, while the latter must legitimate the applicability of the general to the particular (or the subordination of the particular to the metaphysics of universality, usually seen as simply a preferred or privileged particular). Ricoeur's perspective, which is also mine, is to see the equivalent of the universal in the particular moral norm as 'nothing other than the idea of humanity', which eliminates 'all radical otherness' (1992: 224). Translated to anthropology, this does not mean to seek a universal morality in a common denominator for all particular moral codes, but to focus on a shared ontology of the human – how human beings everywhere believe it is proper to treat human beings.

Impersonal criteria

It is necessary to distinguish between what MacIntyre says 'impersonal criteria' *are* and what he says they *do*. What they do sounds virtuous and moral: they force us to consider others as ends and thus discourage manipulative behaviour. MacIntyre tells us less about what these criteria *are*, beyond his strictures against emotivism posing as a legitimate candidate. But he does describe a previous situation when external 'certainties' existed in the form of the authority of religion and social hierarchy, which together provided a 'rational vindication for morality'.

I limit myself to two brief points. First, I presume that MacIntyre is not advocating a return to the dark ages of those external authorities, fraught with philosophical as well as political problems (for instance, can one be moral if one is not a free agent but acts out of ignorance, fear, or obedience?). Second, I observe that these criteria were part of hierarchical regimes which allocated political and religious power to some over others. Such an exercise of power would create manipulative relations, in which some used others for their ends; it follows, by MacIntyre's own definition, that such forms of authority could not constitute 'impersonal criteria'.

As a consequence of these criticisms, MacIntyre's stance concerning 'impersonal criteria' may be seen as cynical. Since he does not believe the claims of these old 'certainties' to be true descriptions of a 'natural' hierarchy, his alternatives are to consider them either as false or else as dishonest, used in a hypocritical manner. How, then, can he present false or hypocritical premises as efficient impersonal criteria for moral action? His search for impersonal criteria must therefore be either a red herring or a wild goose chase.

Embeddedness of morality

Two premises in MacIntyre's argument pose a challenge to my project of outlining a morality that crosses cultures. First, that virtues are inextricable from their context in the social structure, and second, that morality needs the basis of a *telos*, a total coherent system and a rational vindication.

When MacIntyre tells us that virtues are inextricable from their context in the social structure it is because he sees morality, quite rightly, as 'always to some degree tied to the socially local and particular' (1984: 126). But if 'there is no way to possess the virtues except as part of a tradition in which we inherit them' (*ibid.*: 127), how can I be moral in a society whose tradition I do not share and in whose local structures I am only partially and provisionally placed? I may see myself as a moral person, but can I appear so from their point of view? Clearly I often do, when Kewa people approve of my actions and treat me as a serious person. Is this because I have stumbled on a practice that is part of their moral code, or is there something else, beyond the particular form, which they recognise in my actions and general demeanour?

Ethnographic illustrations to clinch such arguments inevitably appear suspect. I offer the following as one of the defining moments of understanding I experienced among the Kewa. At the same time, I cannot deny that I have crafted this account, perhaps not precisely to make this point but with such general questions in mind. The vignette addresses a neglected aspect of the ethnographic encounter, the economic basis of the relationship.

Case 1: The ethnographer and money

Before going to the field I had heard tales of researchers adopting an embarrassed attitude to money and I was determined that my case would be different. I began by making a distinction between monetary relations (which I somewhat disdained) and gift giving (which I valued as part of the culture). Keeping my generosity for the latter, I entered the prestige economy wholeheartedly. While remaining aware of my local value as a potential source of cash, I coupled necessity with principle right from the beginning by making a point of driving hard bargains. During negotiations over my house building, Koai, a prominent man from a neighbouring village, suggested I pay the six workmen a total of 120 kina (PNG currency) instead of the 100 kina previously agreed upon, or, alternatively, that I employ five men instead of six and pay them 20 kina each. In high-sounding phrases I stuck to my guns, and appeared to have carried the day. Yet when the work was completed I found that I had picked up two extra workmen. I forked out without a word. The question was not so much whether they had hoodwinked me into paying more, which they may have done. But in the interim I had realised that their demand was based on principles not made up expressly in order to fleece me. I learned that their calculations were person-centred, not job-centred. Their starting point was not the 'costing' of a job in the manner of builders offering competitive quotations in their bid for a contract. Instead, they started with the person. How much should a person get for contributing to the work? How many persons were involved? Multiply these two amounts and there's your cost. You could employ only five people and pay less, but then the work would take longer. The person-rate was determined by a consideration of such nebulous factors as the going rate, the personal work that would suffer neglect, compensation for effort, subsistence needs, perceptions of what I could afford and how far I could be pushed beyond my initial offer. More trivially but not inconsequentially, 100 kina was awkward to divide between six. Twenty per person was a nice round figure. Perhaps coincidentally, 20 *was* a whole person (man) in the local counting system.

I did not merely record the lesson I had learned as a description of people's culture, but I operated by these principles myself in further interactions. I was not just humouring them, doing as the Kewa did in Kewaland. I could never see morality in culturally relative terms. A second ethnographic vignette, about a dispute, drives the point home. It shows how all of us concerned in the dispute, whatever our different cultural or moral principles, were involved in a contest over being treated as autonomous agents. The outcome was to force each one of us to recognise and acknowledge this autonomy.

Case 2: The anthropologist becomes a social person

On my return to the village after a lengthy absence I distributed various gifts to the villagers. In the past I had always consulted Rimbu about my distributions and handed gifts to people through his mediation. On this occasion I handled my own distribution. The result was resentful mumblings and indirect complaints from Rimbu, a swift and furious, potlatch-style response by villagers, who threatened to return my gifts, and a public arraignment in which Rimbu got his come-uppance. Throughout the unfolding of the dispute I was aware that all our concerns were with strategies for advancing our own claims, rather than with upholding any norms. I wanted to be a strong woman with my own networks; Rimbu wanted to have control over them; the others wanted a more direct relationship with me, and to teach Rimbu a lesson. The most enduring outcome of the incident was that it tied me publicly in a reciprocal relationship with all the villagers. Previously only Rimbu had this ostensible relationship with me, while relations with others appeared as intermittent or contractual ones mediated through him. It is not an exaggeration to see this as the moment when I emerged as a social person.

My arguments in this section were empirical rather than philosophical. Observing the occasions on which my actions and myself were critically well-received, I assumed a certain moral approval, and therefore tacit agreement concerning what was good, virtuous behaviour. Although I acted within a different framework, yet my framework did produce rules, norms and principles which resulted in actions that spoke directly to other actions produced by other rules. It thus seemed possible to recognise worthy action that arose from other particularities. I never claimed or even imagined, throughout the enterprise of fieldwork and subsequent ethnographic writing, that I was a Kewa, or speaking for the Kewa. Mine was a theoretically informed, empathetic account of synthesising skill.[6] Thus I am not suggesting that the 'moral person' who is the product of fieldwork is the creation of the local moral code. It was not only through an understanding of Kewa morality that I tried to act as a moral person or was created as such in dealings with them. I acted on *my* conscience and my principles, which compelled me to be truthful, trustworthy, consistent and fair, and to treat others as agents. I did not ask myself if these were virtues for the Kewa, though I can easily find evidence that they prize them.[7] Rather than adopt a pragmatic or even sanctimonious strategy of giving way to what I imagined were local virtues, to some extent I engaged in the contest as local people did themselves, namely by struggling to attain 'social knowledge' of how things were done while demanding to be treated as moral agents. To the extent that disagreements remained in my interactions with people, they were hardly more threatening than those endemic to local interactions.

Morality and teleology

MacIntyre's comments about the local contextualisation of morality are embedded in a more fundamental argument: that the project of morality is unintelligible without a teleological framework, a total coherent system and a rational vindication. As we saw, his historical account of western culture's 'degeneration' is marked by the 'grave cultural loss' of what was once morality, and its replacement by emotivism (1984: 22). If he is right, the combination of his two criteria (local contextualisation and teleology) could, barring serendipitous cultural similarities, lead to complete cultural relativism in questions of morality. It would certainly put paid to my claim that morality at its most profound and basic level is not tied to a particular culture. Yet such a conclusion would go against the evidence of anthropological experience, of the sort I discussed in the last section. If this experience is discounted as too soft for evidence, can the criterion of teleology be attacked on home ground?

If the concept of teleology is understood as a final purpose founded in the external authority of hierarchy and religion, it is too formal and abstract. It provides a system of rules but fails to examine practices and beliefs. In particular, it ignores the exclusiveness and elitism of codes (whether heroic Greek or pre-Enlightenment Christian) that left so much of ordinary people's everyday lives untouched. When people behaved 'morally' in the ways suggested by these codes, was it because they had a total, coherent system of morality? Did they require a rational vindication for moral action, or the presence of external authority? How many people did in fact behave morally as outlined in the heroic codes? And how much hypocrisy, opportunism, and repression were at play?

Following my own ethnographic investigation I propose a different perspective. If morality is tied to a certain teleology, it is the kind that is embodied in human beings who recognise virtuous behaviour (cf. Taylor 1989). MacIntyre uses the concept of teleology in its etymological and historical sense, which postulates that human beings were designed for a particular cause or end, in expectation of which they must live their lives in a particular way. But this sense of teleology may render it as arbitrary as emotivism. Though it purports to be external to the person, it is effective only if embodied as personal faith, whose product it then becomes.

Others as ends

Let us then abandon the preoccupation with teleology. Morality is not dependent on it. A more fruitful enquiry is one which takes as its point of departure those actual instances when the other is treated as an end. A starting point for this is a refusal to regard others in the field in generic terms, as typical examples of genus (Watson 1992: 139).[8] Another caution is not to put them in a different time-frame, trapped in the frozen present which is really the past, while the mobile ethnographer inhabits historical time and a present which has a future (Fabian 1983).

Time and mobility are relevant to the question of control of access to the relationship in the ethnographic encounter. The mobile ethnographer decides when to visit the field, when to invade people's lives and when to withdraw. But the distance at which the subjects of ethnographies can be kept is constantly shrinking. Their awareness of the outside world grows, and, aided by education and access to communication media, they respond to the descriptions of themselves. This has a profound effect on our own attitude to our enterprise. A heightened awareness of the possibility of alternative depictions forces us to question the methodologies and implications of our inventions. But treating people as ends in the field would not have needed this future shock.

A major reason for challenging our ability to invent others is the implication that our activity disempowers them. At the same time we suspect that our construction of them is fake, since we are committed to ideological and epistemological trends that consider self-construction to be the only legitimate one. Yet our own agency is at least partially determined by the field situation, how we are placed by the people there and how they choose to reveal themselves to us. In my case, Rimbu had made me his sister. Seremetakis describes how it was she rather than her informants, Maniat people with whom she had kinship links, who was 'objectified, classified, and subjected to a political reading' imprisoning her in a dense web of boundaries (Seremetakis 1991: 10).

All ethnographers have to varying degrees experienced the empowerment of 'having been there' as a sort of hubris, a power to refute an argument merely by saying, 'Yes, the Kewa do this'. I have an authority here that I lack in my own culture, where I may be challenged by so many others and my claim will not have so much weight, since it does not result from the insight of fieldwork. The danger always lurks that we may completely take over people's voices, in the mirage of 'experiencing with them' and 'creating their culture with them' as a fieldwork methodology. Even when we do not deliberately pursue such aspirations, these empathetic revelations may inflict themselves on us, catch us unawares in our dreams. The people in the field themselves, by their positive response to our assimilation, may gently manoeuvre us into a belief that we speak for them. However it comes about, it is always dangerous to adopt the authoritative voice that removes the boundary between itself and the thoughts, feelings, experiences, perceptions and intentional cultural creations of the people it describes. Seremetakis' powerfully brooding and fascinating account carries us into a landscape of such intense and compelling meaning that we have no space to fall into an alternative interpretation. If these are Maniat women speaking, looking into the distance and seeing what the author describes so evocatively, who are we to gainsay them? Seremetakis creates her own story which she presents as their story. If she really is one of them there is a sense in which reflexivity becomes authorial voice (see Josephides 1997).

My own presentation of 'portraits' is an ethnographic strategy, developed from the particular manner of my incorporation into village life, that tries to let people's stories tell their story (Josephides 1998). Though I asked people to tell me about their lives I never presented them with a blueprint of what is a 'life story'. In my writing I reproduce the context of the telling, including current concerns and actual happenings in the village, in what (following Carrithers 1995) I refer to as minimal narratives (Josephides forthcoming b). Thus people's accounts of their lives did not isolate them as individuals in the distorted way Abu-Lughod (1993) cautions against. Quite the contrary, the narratives constructed people's personhood within a moral and social universe. My work (with insights from Mead 1964 and Merleau-Ponty 1974) investigates anthropological knowledge *through* accounts by means of which people negotiate social knowledge and make it explicit.

Social strategising in the two milieux: The field and the academy

In the 'background' to this chapter I wrote that anthropologists view fieldwork as an artificial positioning from which to observe people's real lives. Fieldwork also remains the refuge of lofty pursuits, where the ethnographer is given wholly to the quest for knowledge and understanding. The academic milieu, by contrast, is viewed as constructed space. Here, our real but cynical positioning is involved in unending compromises between the revered truth of scholarship and the pragmatic opportunism of academic politics.

In the field I developed an understanding of social effectiveness which I called social knowledge. On the basis of social experience, Kewa people negotiated their positions and what was due to them in actions and strategies designed to elicit desired understandings. Simultaneously, they claimed that these negotiated understandings were the products of their culture. I saw these as strategies for self-creation rather than moral actions springing from either a sense of justice, or attention to basic facts, or concern with the other. I linked lack of success in these endeavours to poor social skills and lack of *savoir faire*.

Elsewhere I have described in detail this eliciting activity of self-making and social strategising (Josephides 1998). In particular, I reviewed the case of a woman who was repudiated by her husband, despite her repeated efforts to elicit his respect and recognition. Though she had real grievances – what she perceived as unfair treatment – I held her responsible for a social delict, an incompetence. She had failed to strategise sufficiently astutely with cultural norms. Yet I did not think the same social competence was required of me in the academic setting. When I experienced a setback that might have been avoided by a cleverer strategist, I viewed my position differently from that of the repudiated Kewa wife. This was because I valued a forthrightness which I associate both with fieldwork and with scholarship. In the case of fieldwork, it was a selective association that applied only to my own relations with people. I did not look for forthrightness in people's strategies as they engaged in negotiating cultural norms among themselves. But I considered my relationship to the academic milieu in quite a different light from the relationship of the people I studied to *their* cultural milieu. Was this position justified? I attempt an explanation that combines an ambiguous moral commitment to the academic cultural milieu with a critical distance from it.

As already discussed, my field experience had fashioned for me an ethical and emotionally committed figure for the anthropologist. On my return to the academy I wanted to extend to relations there the ethical and empathetic mode of interaction learned in the field. But the academic milieu did not present itself as a moral community. I was struck by what seemed to me a central contradiction. As academics we are an organic part of this milieu, which is our workplace and means of livelihood. But in so far as the academy espouses a critical stance, in a meta-discourse which imagines itself part of a game for higher ends, its own cultural traditions and strategising techniques can only be adopted ironically or cynically, like opportunistic devices.

To clarify this convoluted sentence, let us take the example of the UK Research Assessment Exercise (RAE) to which all of us working in the academy have to submit (see Strathern 2000a and 2000b). The RAE is designed to measure research productivity, but it also has practical consequences: departments are ranked and funding is allocated according to its findings. Some of its exercises may seem unexceptionable. Staff must publish books and articles, attract research funding and draw postgraduate students. Nothing nefarious or cynical about that – it is what academics are supposed to be doing. But a lot of anthropological research does not require a large funding base. Anthropology is traditionally a lone trade, yet departments are now encouraged or required to construct programmes of common research interests. Many anthropologists find this an encumbrance and an unprofitable way to develop their research. The burden increases with the extra administrative and bureaucratic work required to operate the mandatory auditing exercises.

With the example of the RAE in mind, my convoluted sentence could be rewritten like this: The RAE is a meta-discourse about academic research. Academics' own discourse on what the RAE is about is a meta-discourse about the RAE. Academics adopt a critical stance towards this discourse. They don't believe they need the RAE to carry out good research or generally do their jobs well. Thus their own meta-discourse about the RAE is imagined by them to be a game for higher ends; they have to play along, but only in order to keep themselves alive and ahead so that they can accomplish the real scholarly works that academics are supposed to accomplish. From this perspective, the cultural traditions and strategising techniques of the academy which are marshalled in the preparation of RAE statements are adopted ironically, and to some extent cynically and opportunistically.

These deliberate academic tactics also feed off a set of psychological and emotional conditions, whose oppositional operation may remain unacknowledged. In the field we 'bracket' or even deny our own culture, stripping it of content while using its critical form; in the academic milieu we take on, rhetorically, the culture of our studied people, and this transubstantiation confers authority on us. Relations in the academic milieu have at their base ethnographic knowledge, or the idea of it; for instance, when Melanesianist anthropologists are addressed as 'Melanesian wallahs', it is the product of our own collective disciplinary imagination that we are such wallahs. Thus, while our influence in the academy derives from the disciplinary expertise conferred by field experience, in the field, by contrast, our status derives from association with a putatively powerful outside. Michael Lambek's comment 'In the field I am a student, but at home I am supposed to be an expert' (1997: 44) stresses only the humility in the first half of the proposition.

To recapitulate my argument so far: the academic milieu is an inherently contradictory one, because the items of value that circulate within it (scholarly knowledge) are framed by a moral code with quite different principles from those shaping academic bureaucracy and the measuring (auditing) rules of academic productivity. My refusal to strategise was a reluctance to scramble contexts. But a sharp academic lesson taught me that strategies are especially necessary in situations where we entertain a cynical view of our position. I move next to a closer consideration of the nature of academic relations, and in particular the changing moral culture of the academy.

The culture and morality of the academy

MacIntyre's definition of virtue and practice provides an apt opening for this discussion. He argues that virtue is an acquired quality which enables us to achieve goods internal to practices. He clarifies his meaning with the example of a child who is taught to play chess by being offered a reward as an incentive. As long as the child's only motive is to win a game of chess in order to receive this reward – which is a good external to the practice of chess playing – it will cheat when it can. Only when the child develops the desire to play the game by its proper rules will it reap the goods internal to the practice. Thus, for any practice, its goods can be achieved only by subordinating ourselves within it, which includes taking risks and criticism and recognising what is due to other practitioners.

MacIntyre makes an important distinction between practices and institutions when he writes that, without the virtues of justice, courage and truthfulness, 'practices could not resist the corrupting power of institutions' (1984: 194). Anthropology is a practice with internal goods, anthropology departments and universities are institutions, and institutions are concerned with external goods. The problem facing academic scholarship is the constant impingement of institutions on practices, what MacIntyre calls 'the corrupting power of institutions'.

My discussion draws on comments by Stephen Hill and Tim Turpin, who write on the contradictory value pulls in the academy. On the one side, there is the weakening grip of the cultures traditionally associated with the constitution of scientific knowledge; on the other, the ever firmer grip of commercial market systems insinuating themselves into those cultures (Hill and Turpin 1995: 141, 135). There is a parallel here between the work of MacIntyre and that of Hill and Turpin. MacIntyre locates the loss of moral authority in the incoherent conceptual scheme inherited from the Enlightenment, when 'the externalities of divine law, natural teleology or hierarchical authority' were replaced by the sovereign individual (1984: 68). Hill and Turpin trace the transformation of academic values to 'a shift from the modernist culture that reified the liberating power of science to ... a post-1960s culture that has shrugged off the emancipatory certainties of science and erected commercial marketplace values and pluralistic images in its stead' (1995: 135).

Their thrusts are different. Hill and Turpin are concerned with science in the academy (the impact of the marketplace on scholarship), MacIntyre with virtue and morality. But at another level both are talking about the cultural and epistemological contexts of practices, and the relationship between practices and institutions. It is possible to see Hill and Turpin's collision of cultures, and the invasion of one culture by another (the academy by the marketplace), in terms of MacIntyre's discussion of the relationship between practices and institutions. When MacIntyre writes that 'without justice, courage and truthfulness, practices could not resist the corrupting power of institutions', he is not only stressing the necessarily different character of practices and institutions; he is also suggesting that the virtues of practices depend for their upkeep on individual practitioners. They are the ones who need to act with justice, courage and truthfulness.

From the Enlightenment's shattering of moral, religious and political certainties, and through positivism, reason, utilitarianism, and emotivism, MacIntyre takes us to an individualist relativism that cannot authenticate any authority. Picking up the trail from postmodernity's shattering of positivism, Hill and Turpin leave us with the pluralistic images of commercial marketplace values, driven by the need to homogenise, quantify and evaluate on the basis of immediate results. They use a different discourse from MacIntyre to a similar purpose. This is especially clear when they talk about 'elements of the activities that people formerly constructed within their lifeworlds' – such as bringing up children, producing food, solving health, emotional and family problems – being 'turned over to "systems", systems of education, industrial systems, health systems, counselling systems, administrative, power, and, most important of all, market systems' (*ibid.*: 141). The term 'activities turned over to systems' is equivalent to 'practices subordinated to institutions'.

For MacIntyre, the justice, courage and truthfulness that belong to practices may fall victim to institutions. For Hill and Turpin, the values of scientific knowledge systems (dedication to knowledge and mastery of discourse, accountability, rigour, openness) fall victim to the values of a commercial system (predicated on money, power, competition, manipulation, quantity of output). This system, moreover, '[engages] in strategic action rather than in communicative action and open discourse'. In such a situation society's values and vision become inextricable from immediate advantage and interest (*ibid.*: 146 and 149). What sort of collegiality and moral as well as intellectual climate for scholarship do these developments presage? Paraphrasing Vered Amit's warning (2000: 233), we should face the reality that neither timidity nor cowardice will save us. But let us not forget Strathern's warning that 'cynicism is a half-way house to self-alienation' (2000b: 298, note 5), and MacIntyre's comments about the goods internal to practices (1984: 191).

Conclusion

This chapter has outlined several contradictory positions and propositions. Though fieldwork is an artificial positioning, it creates a moral person, the quality of whose local relations makes possible the ethnography as a product of knowledge. The ethnographer nevertheless perceives herself as differently placed in her cultural milieu from local people in the field. As a fieldworker the ethnographer is empathetic in cultural understanding and ethnographic writing. As a moral person she is motivated by a double commitment, to the local people and to anthropological knowledge, the combination of which should lead to a rigorous and meticulous ethnographic representation. But as an academic the anthropologist may turn cynical from an excess of morality. A field-derived authority empowers ethnographers in an academic milieu, where nevertheless institutional pulls and incursions of the market threaten collegial relations and encourage a pragmatic opportunism inimical to scholarship.

My underlying aim throughout these transitions was, however, to demonstrate the presence of 'a morality that crosses cultures'. MacIntyre's moral philosophy (as indeed Taylor's), while rejecting the self-indulgence of emotivism and the barren agnosticism of philosophies of language, nevertheless baulks at reclaiming Kantian and Aristotelian ethics in their entirety (as one would expect since times have changed). I have tried to dig a path out of the impasse that traps MacIntyre in a modernist maze, primarily by broadening two troublesome concepts, those of emotivism and teleology, but also by stressing the importance of empathy in our decision to treat others as ends. The latter move dissolves any contradiction, in my own fieldwork, between being considered a moral person by the Kewa and acting morally according to my own lights. The double commitment, to fieldwork subjects and to the discipline, has the effect of heightening rather than compromising our moral stance – until the new Trojan horse unloads its cargo in the academy. But if we have a certain faith in the empathetic potential of human beings to respond to what is human in any cultural context, humanity should prevail, as long as (following Aristotle through to MacIntyre) we continue to act with justice, courage and truthfulness.

Notes

1 Taussig refers to the relationship as one in which 'something crucial about what made [myself] was implicated and imperilled in the object of study' (1993: 253).
2 Pels (1999, 2000) provides a detailed historical and theoretical account of ethical codes in anthropology, which he traces back to Malinowski's 'purified ethnographer' and the 'confessional' styles of Bohannan and Powdermaker.
3 Following these principles I wrote an ethnography that recorded the observed surface of things (Josephides 1985). But in faithfulness to the theoretical interests of my discipline, its aim was to uncover a hidden structure.
4 Kant's moral philosophy is based on two maxims: 'Act only on that maxim through which you can at the same time will that it should become a universal law' (Paton 1948: 29), and 'Act in such a way that you always treat humanity ... never simply as a means, but always at the same time as an end' (ibid.: 32). Moral worth results from the formal maxim itself, not from any results the action may attain, so it follows that the contingent ability of human beings to carry out such actions is not important. The categorical imperative is deontological: it imposes law-abidingness, appearing to us as a law that we ought to obey for its own sake.
5 Pels (see note 2) describes how ethics originated as a set of rules designed to guard the professionalism of the discipline so as to enhance the reliability of the research it produced (2000: 139). While I also 'investigate the notion of ethics as (part of a) technology of the self, (ibid.: 138), I see the construction of the moral person as happening in the field, not at the stages of 'professionalism' before and after fieldwork.
6 In later writing I became increasingly reluctant to construct my ethnography through empathetic substitution and strove instead to let the people's own words speak. But even then I did not give the Kewa the chance to be the judges of what I wrote about them. Thus an ethnography runs the risk, as MacIntyre describes for some novels, of allowing 'the manipulative mode of moral instrumentalism', whether benign or not, to triumph (1984: 24).
7 For instance, Rimbu showed regard for consistency when he told a parliamentary candidate he could not support him as he had already pledged support to another candidate and could not change sides. It is useful to remember that 'ethical' originally meant 'pertaining

to character', so it had to do with one's own makeup in behaving systematically according to that character.

8   Although Watson (1992: 139) stresses individuality and cautions against the tendency to generalise others, at the same time he paradoxically calls for the deconstruction of the myth of the other which stresses difference between 'them' and 'us'. Thus he argues simultaneously for individuality or specificity and for similarity or a merging of the one into the other.

Bibliography

Abu-Lughod, L. (1993) *Writing women's worlds*, Berkeley: University of California Press.

Abu-Lughod, L. and Lutz, C.A. (1990) 'Introduction: emotion, discourse, and the politics of Everyday Life', in C.A. Lutz and L. Abu-Lughod (eds) *Language and the politics of emotion*, Cambridge: Cambridge University Press.

Amit, V. (2000) 'The university as panopticon: moral claims and attacks on academic freedom', in M. Strathern (ed.) *Audit cultures: anthropological studies in accountability, ethics and the academy*, London: Routledge.

Carrithers, M. (1995) 'Stories in the social and mental life of people', in E.N. Goody (ed.) *Social intelligence and interaction*, Cambridge: Cambridge University Press.

Desjarlais, R.R. (1992) *Body and emotion: the aesthetics of illness and healing in the Nepal Himalayas*, Philadelphia: University of Pennsylvania Press.

Fabian, J. (1983) *Time and the other: how anthropology makes its object*, New York: Columbia University Press.

Geertz, C. (1983) *Local knowledge: further essays in interpretive anthropology*, New York: Basic Books.

Hill, S. and Turpin, T. (1995) 'Cultures in collision: the emergence of a new localism in academic research', in M. Strathern (ed.) *Shifting contexts: transformations in anthropological knowledge*, London: Routledge.

Hudson, W.D. (1970) *Modern moral philosophy*, London: Macmillan & Co.

Josephides, L. (1985) *The production of inequality*, London: Tavistock.

—— (1997) 'Representing the anthropologist's predicament', in A. James, J. Hockey and A. Dawson (eds) *After writing culture*, London: Routledge.

—— (1998) 'Biographies of social action: excessive portraits', in V. Keck (ed.) *Common worlds and single lives: constituting knowledge in Pacific societies*, Oxford: Berg.

—— (forthcoming a) 'The hubbub of emotions', in K. Milton and M. Svasek (eds) *Mixed Emotions*.

—— (forthcoming b) *The production of ethnography*, book manuscript in preparation.

Lambek, M. (1997) 'Pinching the crocodile's tongue: affinity and the anxieties of influence in fieldwork', *Anthropology and Humanism*, 22 (1): 31–53.

Leavitt, J. (1996) 'Meaning and feeling in the anthropology of emotions', *American Ethnologist* 23 (3): 514–39.

Lutz, C. A. (1988) *Unnatural emotions: everyday sentiments on a Micronesian atoll and their challenge to Western theory*, Chicago: University of Chicago Press.

Lutz, C.A. and White, G.M. (1986) 'The anthropology of emotion', *Annual Reviews in Anthropology*, 15: 405–36.

Lyon, M.L. (1995) 'Missing emotion: the limitations of cultural constructionism in the study of emotion', *Cultural Anthropology*, 10 (2): 244–63.

MacIntyre, A. (1984) *After virtue*, Second edition. Notre Dame, IN: University of Notre Dame Press.

Mead, G.H. (1964) *On social psychology: selected papers*, A. Strauss (ed.), Chicago and London: Phoenix Books and University of Chicago Press.

Merleau-Ponty, M. (1962) *Phenomenology of perception*, London: Routledge.

—— (1974) *Phenomenology, language and sociology: selected writings*, J. O'Neill (ed.), London: Heinemann.

Nussbaum, M. (2000) 'Non-relative virtues: an Aristotelian approach', in C.W. Gowans (ed.), *Moral disagreements: classic and contemporary readings*, London: Routledge.

Paton, H.J. (1948) *The moral law: Kant's groundwork of the metaphysics of morals*, London: Hutchinson University Library.

Pels, P. (1999) 'Professions of duplexity: a prehistory of ethical codes in anthropology', *Current Anthropology*, 40 (2): 101–36 (with *CA* comments).

—— (2000) 'The trickster's dilemma: ethics and the technologies of the anthropological self', in M. Strathern (ed.) *Audit cultures: anthropological studies in accountability, ethics and the academy*, London: Routledge.

Ricoeur, P. (1992) *Oneself as another*, Chicago: University of Chicago Press.

Rosaldo, M.Z. (1984) 'Toward an anthropology of self and feeling', in R.A. Shweder and R.A. Levine (eds) *Culture theory: essays on mind, self, and emotion*, Cambridge: Cambridge University Press.

Seremetakis, C.N. (1991) *The last word: women, death and divination in Inner Mani*, Chicago: University of Chicago Press.

Shore, C. and Wright. S. (1999) 'Audit culture and anthropology: neo-liberalism in British higher education', *Journal of the Royal Anthropological Institute*, 5 (4): 557–75.

—— (2000) 'Coercive accountability: the rise of audit culture in higher education', in M. Strathern (ed.) *Audit cultures: anthropological studies in accountability, ethics and the academy*, London: Routledge.

Solomon, R.C. (1983 [1976]) *The passions*, Notre Dame, IN: University of Notre Dame Press.

—— (1984) 'Getting angry: the Jamesian theory of emotion in anthropology', in R.A. Shweder and R.A. Levine (eds) *Culture theory: essays on mind, self, and emotion*, Cambridge: Cambridge University Press.

Strathern, M. (1985) 'John Locke's servant and the hausboi from Hagen: thoughts on domestic labour', *Critical Philosophy*, 2: 21–48.

—— (2000a) 'Introduction: new accountabilities', in M. Strathern (ed.) *Audit cultures: anthropological studies in accountability, ethics and the academy*, London: Routledge.

—— (2000b) 'Afterword: accountability ... and ethnography', in M. Strathern (ed.) *Audit cultures: anthropological studies in accountability, ethics and the academy*, London: Routledge.

Taussig, M. (1993) *Mimesis and alterity:: a particular history of the senses*, London: Routledge.

Taylor, C. (1989) *Sources of the self: the making of modern identity*, Cambridge, MA: Harvard University Press.

Watson, C.W. (1992) 'Autobiography, anthropology and the experience of Indonesia', in J. Okely and H. Callaway (eds) *Anthropology and autobiography*, London: Routledge.

4

THE YANOMAMI

Anthropological discourse and ethics

Stephen Nugent

The furore surrounding the publication of Patrick Tierney's *Darkness in El Dorado* (2000) (hereafter *DED*) has been both overtaken and undertaken by events. It has been overtaken by wide journalistic coverage of the book's contents and critiques of those contents, subsequently rendered more modestly scandalous and hence, apparently, un-newsworthy. At the time of writing (December 2001), there is very little press attention to the furore. It has been simultaneously subject to a review of the charges (by a professional body, the American Anthropological Association) that has resulted in an interim report (aaanet.org – a site at which extensive documentation of *DED*-related discussion can be found) which, if it bears any resemblance to the final report, will be judiciously restrictive in terms of adding fuel to the fire. Among the most useful post-mortem discussions is a set of commentaries in the April 2001 issue of *Current Anthropology* (42: 2).[1]

Introduction[2]

The organised defence of the rights of indigenous peoples in the New World has a short and recent history, and professional anthropology – only in existence for the last 100 of the 500 years of what is euphemistically known as 'contact' – while being implicitly an advocate of such rights, has only very erratically raised the political role of the field to the top of the scientific agenda. Nonetheless, the very fact of taking native peoples seriously has granted the field a crucial diplomatic – and occasionally activist – role as expert. The complexity of that mediating role has never been well articulated. It is a source of continuing debate within anthropology itself and proves baffling to most outsiders.

With the publication (or, rather, the threat of publication) of Patrick Tierney's *Darkness in El Dorado: How Scientists and Journalists Devastated the Amazon* (2000), the numerous uncertainties about anthropology's relationships with its subjects are rendered in brutal form. Jungle fever, genocide, duplicity, ideological posturing, vendetta, preposterous accusations, hysteria, the real anthropological heart of darkness, furore, professional misconduct, fascistic eugenics, unparalleled violation of scientific ethics, smear campaigns, even – dipping ever further for the perfect encapsulation – 'the academic equivalent of the Jerry Springer Show' (*New York Times*, 8 October 2000): these are some of the phrases bandied about since the controversy emerged.

While the flagging of the imminent publication of *DED* prompted a variety of responses along a spectrum ranging from 'genocide' to 'hoax', there has been general agreement that *DED* would alter, perhaps irrevocably, public understanding of what anthropology is.

The discussion here concerns three things: the character of the commentaries surrounding publication of the book; the way in which debates about anthropology-as-science are reflected in disputes about focal issues in the book; and attempts to make ethical judgements about the conduct of anthropologists.

Demonisation in anthropology and *Darkness in El Dorado*

It is striking that even with the dismissal of the most serious charge of Tierney's book – genocide through vaccination – this now hollow accusation continues to provide a thematic unity to a set of materials that is hardly new. The relationship between Chagnon and the Yanomami has been the subject of serious attention and critique for decades and Chagnon's version of Yanomami fierceness has been challenged as much on the basis of his science as on the ideological position he is said to represent (see Albert 2001). What is new about the current scrutiny is only the weft provided by the apparently unsustainable charges against Neel (see Lobo *et al.* 2001). That weft allows commentators such as Grandin to open a review of *DED* with the statement that,

> In the shadow of Hitler and Stalin and in the wake of the Vietnam War, theorists from Theodor Adorno to Donna Haraway have been concerned with the ways in which science has colluded with acts of barbarism.
>
> (Grandin 2000: 12)

before conceding later in the review that,

> *DED* unconvincingly attempts to trace this shameful history directly
> to Neel ... unfairly describing him as an extreme eugenicist. This is
> unfortunate, for Tierney could have written a more powerful book by
> demonstrating how the cold war produced acts of barbarism
> regardless of individual motive.
>
> (*ibid.*, p.17)

To paraphrase: the charges against Neel are false, but they could be true in a larger sense, even if in this case they are not.

There is no shortage of bathetic ironies in this affair. Leaving aside for the moment the accuracy of the charges against Chagnon and Neel (along with those against filmmaker Timothy Asch and anthropologist Jacques Lizot), the distressed prospects of indigenous peoples around the world are rarely newsworthy, and the likelihood that the current coverage will enhance the life chances of the Yanomami are not great. Second, in a field in which there is a strongly professed desire for connecting with public culture, this event is unlikely to serve as an example of 'best practice'. Third, the field of anthropology presented to and by public culture – via the *New York Times* or *Forbes*, say – is itself deeply divided, and hardly speaks as one voice on this or other matters. When the dust settles, the concrete matters remaining are likely to be those readily available for scrutiny in about 30 years – the accuracy of Chagnon's data and the propriety of his research methods.[3]

By most reputable estimates, more than 80 per cent of the populations of indigenous New World peoples had disappeared long before they became a matter of serious scholarly interest. As the subjects of a new science – anthropology – contemporary Amerindians over-represent anthropological inquiries into the character of pre-historical and pre-capitalist societies and under-represent the peoples of which they are legatees. Those few peoples who still survive in Amazonia are probably atypical in relation to their antecedents. The former are interfluve or remote forest-dwelling small-scale hunter/gathering societies while the latter were proto-state riverine social formations. Of all the Amazonian societies still extant, the Yanomami are exceptional: they are numerous by Amazonian standards (around 20,000) despite the fact that they occupy a remote locale which is non-riverine (i.e. away from the main course of the Amazon River). They are also, largely due to the work of Napoleon Chagnon and the very wide dissemination of several editions of his book, *The Fierce People* (1968), extremely well-known as products of the anthropological culture industry, icons of 'classic' tribal Amazonian peoples. That the Yanomami were the focus of the scandal announced by an e-mail from Turner and Sponsel which was subsequently forwarded many times to many anthropologists and others meant that this was not a narrowly professional issue, but one that significantly addressed a larger public. In the midst of a storm of character testimonials and denunciations, two events were anticipated: the publication of the volume in question (shortly preceded by serialisation in the *New York Times,* 8 October 2000) and a public discussion at the AAA meetings in San Francisco on 15–19 November 2000.

The bald charge of the Turner/Sponsel reading of the galley-proofs of the Tierney volume is that Napoleon Chagnon's Yanomami research was part of a larger project organised by James Neel, world-class geneticist and physician in the employ of the US Atomic Energy Commission, and that, in pursuit of eugenicist goals, Neel intentionally inoculated Yanomami with a measles vaccine (Edmonston B) which would strip out from the Yanomami population non-Alpha males. In fact, the precise experimental reason for inoculating the Yanomami was not easy to deduce, for it was unclear what it was hoped to gain, but the gross allegations were pretty emphatic: human experimentation, genocide, anthropological collaboration with an agency of the US government, subterfuge, promotion of sociobiological engineering, lying, non-consensual exploitation of primitive peoples.

The book

DED is poorly sub-titled: *How scientists and journalists devastated the Amazon.* Certainly, on the evidence presented, scientists and journalists may not have an exemplary record with regard to Amazonia, but are they the key figures in its devastation?

The claim inflates the roles of both 'scientists and journalists' as pathological agents in the devastation of the Amazon and disregards almost completely the major players: the Brazilian state, the Venezuelan state, multi-lateral agencies, private investors and the usual modernisation suspects. By pinpointing a group that, although hardly irrelevant, does not have an influence on the scale of these major players, it does not accurately reflect the established causes of devastation, nor does it provide appropriate historical contextualisation. It exploits a received view of Amazonia-the-lost-world known to civilisation only through the heroic efforts of contemporary anthropologists, explorers, missionaries, scientists and writers.

DED is almost exclusively concerned with the relationship between the Yanomami and a few anthropologists, by no means representative, for whom the Yanomami have served as major research subjects. The citation of contemporaneous ethnographic studies is selective, with the work of Ramos, Albert, Colchester, Ferguson, Peters and Early – to name a few – only tacitly acknowledged. The strong impression given is that the Yanomami as anthropological subjects are pretty well covered by the work of Chagnon – just as he himself would appear to believe – and such a brazen figure as Jacques Lizot is dwelt upon – it seems – less for his contribution in confirming or refuting Chagnon's work than for the high profile of his sexual peccadilloes.

Thus, in short, the front-cover packaging of the book does not appear casual, but neither is it authoritative. The devastation of the Amazon river basin is not seriously dealt with, and the scientists and journalists actually implicated in the narrative are not representative of encounters between and among anthropology, journalism and Amazonia.

Turning the book over, the dust-jacket reveals another problem: the authors of the blurb are none other than Terry Turner and Leslie Sponsel, who also wrote the flame-fanning e-mail which set off the 'scandal'. This e-mail gives the strong impression – or minimally leaves open the possibility of strong inference – that Turner and Sponsel had only recently become aware of the imminent publication of a book which would scandalise anthropology and that they are performing a public service by warning the anthropological community in advance. Yet, far from being mere messengers, Turner and Sponsel appear to be insiders. Both are thanked in the Acknowledgements section, have been consulted by Tierney over a number of years, and could hardly be regarded as disinterested actors.

There is a larger issue here for which the book in question holds no direct responsibility, but which is indicative of why such a book should have – or appear to have – such broad appeal (it is, after all, a National Book Award nominee and the subject of much public hair-tearing and chest-beating). This is that the Amazonian backdrop is that of Conan Doyle's *Lost World*, resolutely pre-modern and cliché-ridden, the nineteenth-century naturalists' playground in which limiting case primitive society is contained by green hell doctrinal nastiness. Such a representation is a matter of some consequence in view of the privileged role that anthropologists have claimed as authoritative mediators between public culture and esoteric peoples. The Amazonia presented in *DED* is not a fictional Amazonia, but it is a very particular one: frontier Amazonia of stone-age Amerindians, virulent disease, poor transport, isolation, adventurers and heroic explorers, hallucinogens and visions, larger than life characters, depraved anthropologists, tropical licentiousness. All in all, a standard Hollywood account.

Shortly following the Turner/Sponsel e-mail and a flurry of electronic responses, a portion of *DED* was serialised in *The New Yorker*, a magazine well known for the scrupulousness of its fact-checking brigade. This was for most commentators the first opportunity to see Tierney's text, and the reputation of *The New Yorker* – as well as that of Tierney's publisher, W.W. Norton – together with a body of circumstantial evidence lent considerable plausibility to the accusations. As John Tooby noted in *Slate*, 24 October 2000:

> Pre-publication galleys of the book show why it inspired such trust. Tierney's argument is massively documented, based on hundreds of interviews, academic articles, and items uncovered under the Freedom of Information Act, not to mention his own visits among the Yanomamo. Through 10 years of dogged sleuthing, it would

seem, Tierney dragged a conspiracy of military, medical, and anthropological wrongdoing into the light. Last week [*c.* 17 October], when finalists for this year's National Book Awards were announced, *DED* was listed in the nonfiction category.

'There is', Tooby observes, 'only one problem: The book should have been in the fiction category. When examined against its own cited sources, the book is demonstrably, sometimes hilariously, false on scores of points that are central to its most sensational accusation.'

I have quoted Tooby at some length because his article is one of the clearest examinations of the key charges against Neel and Chagnon, and because, as President of the Human Behaviour and Evolution Society (of which Chagnon was also a member), as a former colleague of Chagnon at the University of California at Santa Barbara, and as a key figure in the scientific anthropological camp, his discussion touches on the wide range of issues invoked by the *DED* scandal: ethnographic controversy, ethical controversy and controversies associated with the polarisation of anthropology into so-called scientific and anti-scientific camps.

That the debate over *DED* is highly polarised should not blind us to the fact that a definitive appraisal of all the claims and counterclaims is unlikely to be resolved unambiguously. The events reported have taken place over a period of more than 30 years, and many depend on unverifiable observations and interviews. Additionally, the volume of commentary is so great as to be impossible to summarise. Furthermore, significantly, the tension over political correctness – or, preferably, the more ironic ideological soundness, as we used to say – is considerable, and leads to occasionally bizarre and hard-to-judge positions. Susan Lindee, for example, an early commentator on the scandal, posted a defence of Neel based on her pre-*DED* familiarity with Neel's work. Lindee is the author of *Suffering Made Real: American Science and the Survivors of Hiroshima* (1994), a study of Atomic Energy Commission studies in Japan in which Neel was a key figure. She has had access to Neel's papers, yet saw fit to note that, despite the fact that Neel did not appear to be guilty of human experimentation, he was still a 'classic cold war warrior', much in keeping with Tierney's claim that the 'conservative' Neel's politics were 'too extreme for Reagan's council on aging'. Neel's own publications (such as *Physician to the Gene Pool: Genetic Lessons and Other Stories*, 1994), however, show him to be a supporter of Al Gore, in favour of nuclear disarmament, a Reagan–Bush basher, pro-choice and anti-eugenicist. The fact that he was a geneticist appears to demonstrate automatically for some critics the championing of 'extreme eugenic theories' and fascistic eugenics (T/S e-mail, p. 3–4). Turner and Sponsel (p. 2) also go to some lengths to characterise Neel's position in an unfavourable light, while conceding that his complicity is not established. Thus, he was involved in studying the effects on Marshall Islands peoples of the radioactivity from experimental atomic and hydrogen bombs to which they were subjected, and Turner and Sponsel note that

> our colleague May Jo Marshall has a lot to say about these studies in the Marshalls and Neel's role in them. The same group also secretly carried out experiments on human subjects in the USA. These included injecting people with radioactive plutonium without their knowledge or permission, in some cases leading to their death and disfigurement.

However, they concede that 'Neel himself appears not have given any of these experimental injections' (p. 2). So, no evidence, but demonisation by association.

The two key charges levelled by Tierney are that Neel and Chagnon experimented on the Yanomami and that Chagnon has 'cooked' his data in order to provide confirmation of his view that Yanomami men who are successful killers are demonstrating selective fitness, acquiring greater than normal numbers of women/reproductive partners in the course of their Alpha-male work-outs and hence increasing the distribution of their superior genes.

The first charge does not appear to stand up to the facts. The measles vaccine that Neel and Chagnon administered to the Yanomami (Edmonston B) is neither lethal nor ineffective, as alleged by Tierney, and therefore does not seem capable of playing the experimental role with which it is credited. Samuel Katz – co-developer of Edmonston B – says that of almost 19 million people immunised, the only fatalities have occurred among a handful of individuals suffering from immuno-depressive disease or leukaemia. There has not been a single case of an Edmonston B vaccinee transmitting the disease. Turner has publicly retracted his support for the claim that Neel was experimenting on the Yanomami, but, in a letter to the *New York Review of Books* (16 April 2001), he states that examination of Neel's archives shows that 'vaccinations against measles and several other diseases were originally planned' (see Grandin *ibid*.). If the measles outbreak associated with the 1968 visit of Neel and Chagnon to the Yanomami was not prompted by their vaccination efforts, then it appears that they used the vaccine precisely for the reasons they offered: they were attempting to forestall a wild measles epidemic.[4]

The second charge – that Chagnon has shaped the data to fit his theoretical tendencies – is more complicated but hardly novel, and certainly does not provide Tierney with any justification for claiming that he has taken the lid off a long-brewing anthropological scandal.

There are two strands here. The first concerns the way in which Chagnon has mobilised his ethnography in the name of making a theoretical point that has divided professional opinion. The second concerns the standards of evidence widely employed in anthropology in making claims for adequate sociological generalisations. Chagnon is an unabashed neo-Darwinian, a fact frequently invoked by critics to discredit his characterisation of the Yanomami. For many, such an approach is anathema, and polarisation over the issue of the relevance of biology to the study of culture is extreme (see Tooby and Cosmides 1982; Ehrenreich and McIntosh 1997 for commentaries). It is the deep-seatedness of this issue that has in large part provoked such a spirited response to *DED*. With this division into mutually exclusive theoretical camps it is not surprising that the ethical dilemmas posed by ethnographic research are difficult to approach and define.

The Yanomami as ethnographic subjects: Science, scholarship and anti-science

Brian Ferguson's *Yanomami Warfare* (1995) provides a widely cited and respected overview, one conclusion of which is that the Yanomami portrayed by Chagnon are exceptional rather than typical. The significance of warfare and feuding recorded in most other ethnographic accounts of the Yanomami is hardly lacking, but as a cardinal feature of Yanomami sociality, it holds a much lower position. Let me look at just two available explanations for this discrepancy.

The explanation offered by Tierney (and by Turner, who cited this in his AAA appearance), which is supported by much anecdotal if not necessarily systematic evidence, is that it was Chagnon's particular form of intervention in Yanomami affairs which led to the increase in aggressive behaviour. His generous distribution of steel tools such as machetes is said to have exacerbated inter- and intra-village conflicts.[5] Second, it is suggested that in seeking to compile genealogies – in order to establish arguments concerning selective fitness based on success as killers – he transgressed local prohibitions on speaking the names of the dead; indeed, that he is proud of his skills as an ethnographer in overcoming proscriptions regarding disclosure of names. He is alleged to have sought genealogical information through bribing and playing informants off against each other, thereby creating a climate of mistrust and accusation.

It is this aspect of Chagnon's research that is the still-standing thematic pillar of *DED*, but the depiction by Tierney of the shortcomings of anthropologists goes far beyond Chagnon himself, enhanced most particularly by the portrayal of Jacques Lizot and character references offered by Chagnon's co-workers, students and other associates. Lizot comes in for particularly unflattering portrayal, afflicted by green hell satyriasis. He is employed by Tierney as an example of anthropologist basking in licentious, savage sexuality, a man whose vocation and avocation converge under the canopy of tropical amorality. In anthropological circles, this is scarcely news.

However, as an example of what anthropologists typically get up to in the field – purveyed to a general audience – it has a different impact.

The filmmaker Timothy Asch and the anthropologist Kenneth Goode are used to flesh out the characterisation of Chagnon as demagogue manipulator, and they are shown as collaborators whose unwillingness to stick with the programme results in expulsion from the inner circle. Those portions of the text dealing with the complex relations among these key figures are highly revealing of academic politics.

The second explanation is quite different. It evades the claustrophobia of controversies focused on Chagnon's career (and readings of it) and examines, with some clinical distance, not the Yanomami tied to particular, individualistic accounts (i.e. the serial ethnographic representations attributed to particular authors), but Yanomami groups converging and diverging over time, from 1930 to 1996. In *The Xilixana Yanomami of the Amazon*, Early and Peters (2000) present a demographic analysis of eight Yanomami villages. The cycles of life and death of Yanomami villages are extremely varied over the four periods considered: pre-contact – 1930–57; contact – 1957–60; linkage – 1960–81; Brazilian – 1981–1996; they are thus hardly generaliseable. The analysis precludes definitive refutation of any particular account of 'the Yanomami', but instead redefines what is at issue: the implausibility of taking a case study (whether Chagnon's or anyone else's) and deriving a general account from it. The account by Early and Peters neither fully supports nor fully refutes Chagnon's analysis. It does, however, implicitly castigate a mode of ethnographic research in which an isolated case study is used as the basis for unwarranted generalisation.

That the scandal promoted in Tierney's book could become 'a scandal' at all speaks ill of anthropology. Weight of argument would seem to count for less than plausibility of hyperbole. This is not a new feature of anthropology. In 1994, Eric Wolf wrote that:

> Anthropologists need to arm themselves professionally and ethically against such dubious practices of anonymous character assassination, directed in this case against an anthropologist (Chagnon) who has built up an exemplary body of data through long-term and often difficult fieldwork. Even those among Chagnon's colleagues who might disagree with his neo-Darwinian premises (and these include the present writer) acknowledge his extraordinary devotion to anthropology as science, which has provided us also with the information that allows us to debate his interpretations and suggest possible alternatives. This was recognised most recently in a meeting at the New York Academy of Sciences on September 27, 1993 … The search for relevant questions and good answers should not be inhibited by demonisation.
>
> (AAA Newsletter, March 1994)

The demonisation addressed by Wolf is a persistent feature of modern anthropological discourse. Scholarship is judged, often intemperately, as much on the basis of theoretical affiliation – real or imagined – as it is on the arguments and data presented. So-and-so is a narrow transactionalist, ahistorical functionalist, bloody positivist, mechanical reductionist, febrile leftist, swirling sophist and on and on. This provides, at times, an interesting idiom for the conduct of anthropological debate, but it has certain defects – perhaps fatal ones. In the first place it places a premium on performance and presentational skills the successful deployment of which may have absolutely no bearing on the scholarly matters at issue. In the second place it deprives the field of historical dynamic. Theoretical development tends not to be measured in terms of the production of increasingly explanatory models, but in terms of affiliation. Not only do we end up walking around with bumper stickers – postmodern zealot, vulgar materialist, idealist airhead – but we collect all the bumper stickers and inflict on students the demand to learn not just about the principles of anthropology, but about all the models of all the cars that once bore those bumper stickers – whether they have had lasting roadworthiness or not. Third, we become increasingly unintelligible outside a fairly narrow, academic anthropology eco-niche.

Given the subject matter of anthropology, it is not surprising that cross-cultural awareness/cultural relativism produces an institutionalised scepticism towards unambiguous conclusions. Who knows? Maybe twins are birds. And certainly a rich corpus of ethnography is available. But available to whom and for what purpose?

Work on the Yanomami, for example, has in some cases been more beneficial to Yanomamologists than to the Yanomami themselves. Certainly some of the actions of anthropologists have – obliquely perhaps – been positively destructive. If, as alleged, Chagnon's research methods have resulted in the exacerbation of feuding and warfare, then that is a moral as well as a scientific issue, but at present the scientific versus anti-scientific polarisation appears so pronounced as to preclude much useful discussion – and *DED* hardly improves the situation.[6] At another level, the promotion of the 'fierce people' characterisation of the Yanomami gives licence to the Brazilian government to militarise the area in order to protect Brazilian nationals from the nasty savages, and it leads invading goldminers to adopt a very aggressive, shoot-first stance towards native peoples. At yet another level, it sends to the public a message which feeds reactionary denunciation. A writer in *Forbes*, for example, notes that:

> the credulous reaction of so many anthropologists bespeaks a mind-set aching for activist causes … sprawling all over the AAA website today are the organisation's position statements on issues that have only the most tenuous connection to anthropology – statements

about gay rights, violence against women, hate crimes – but just come naturally to political activists. Rational underpinning to all this: If anthropologists run out of Stone Age tribes to investigate, they will at least have some political hot buttons with which to attract undergrads to their courses.

(Seligman 2000)

Or this from the *National Review*: 'If conservatives hailed the Mead debunking as a case study in the dangers of cultural relativism, it's the Left that now wants Chagnon's head' (Miller 2000).

While the *DED* furore has clear anthropological referents, it bespeaks a more general dispute that suggests only the dim prospect of a temperate outcome. The soundbite 'science wars' is, as noted by Sokal and Bricmont, unfortunate (1998: 174), for neither is war (other than the sandbox variety) being waged, nor are such 'wars' about science. The expression is a catchphrase whose distribution is largely, but not exclusively, limited to classes of mental labourers mainly confined to universities. According to Ross:

the Science Wars [are] a second front opened up by conservatives cheered by the successes of their legions in the holy Culture Wars. Seeking explanations for their loss of standing in the public eye and the decline in funding from the public purse, conservatives in science have joined the backlash against the (new) usual suspects – pinkos, feminists and multiculturalists.

(1995: 356, cited in Sokal and Bricmont 1998: 174)

That is one gloss, and one that Sokal and Bricmont take apart with precision, but with no discernible lasting effect. The article by Sokal in *Social Text* (1996) that prompted the writing of their book *Intellectual Impostures*, is classed not as a contribution to resolving the 'two cultures' debate, but as a 'hoax', a prankish attempt to distract attention from the shaky footing of the temple of postmodernism. For the *Social Text* editors, epistemological pluralism is less inclusive than might be imagined.

Many years ago, the problem was outlined in the following way by Chomsky in response to a query about the difference between theoretical linguistics and sociolinguistics: what sociolinguists do is interesting, but it is not linguistics. Rather, it is sociology, the study of the way language usage is implicated in broad sets of social acts. Linguistics asks a different question: what must be true of language structure (universal) in order to make possible the kind of cultural diversity that sociolinguistics examines? In other words, there are different projects asking different questions; they are linked in ways that are not well understood (and may never be), but they don't cancel each other out, nor is there any reason for thinking that the posing of one is anathema to the other.[7] Yet a precept of the 'science wars' (or at least the local, anthropological version) is that they cannot co-exist, not – I think – because the argument can be shown to be manifestly absurd, but for a number of other reasons:

- many negative cultural associations of science (as revealed/indicated in the Ross quote above);
- reasonable scepticism *vis-à-vis* the fetishisation of science by a political apparatus;
- commercial exploitation of the idiom of science by way of socialising the costs of science;
- poor popular scientific journalism;
- an overvaluation of humans as cultural beings disconnected from biological structure and constraint (postmodernism being a particularly exaggerated version, relegating even social structure to the dustbin: lots and lots of agency). That the field of anthropology could be scientifically oriented while critical of scientism does not seem that much of a problem or challenge, but the trends are clearly the other way, and to anthropology's loss.

There is a third protagonist/antagonist in the anthropological science wars that has not yet been mentioned (although Wolf has been cited). This is the faction that, if dismayed by the field's polarisation into extreme relativism and extreme biological reductionism, locates the serious debates as much outside the academy as within it. What anthropologists say to (and about) each other has professional salience, but perhaps only that. What anthropologists say in the context of public culture is a different matter, but the terms according to which anthropologists are able to engage with public culture (and its scientific enclaves) are restricted by a squaring off between the intransigent relativist and the rationalist.

Ethics

Anticipating that the publication of Tierney's book would bring to public awareness a compromised relationship between anthropology and some of its subjects, the American Anthropological Association and the Royal Anthropological Institute/Association of Social Anthropologists issued position statements. The RAI/ASA Joint Statement was released in September 2000. An AAA 'pending' statement was issued at about the same time, followed up by a resolution of the Executive Board released on 15 November 2000 (Interim reports may be found at aaanet.org).

Both statements convey the message that the professional associations do not have criteria according to which they would be willing to pass ethical judgement on the activities of their members. Such statements are not manifestly unreasonable, but they do seem rather vapid in a discipline in which the normal criterion for membership is fieldwork carried out in what are almost by definition ethically ambiguous or dubious situations. The access that anthropologists have to field subjects is premised on a political asymmetry for which anthropology is not itself directly responsible, but without which it would not have the configuration it does. Not only would a Yanomamo probably not be welcome to reside in an Oxford quad for two years of fieldwork, s/he would not be likely to be in any way motivated to do so. These circumstances in no way obviate the possibility that anthropological research is, in the best circumstances, and even maybe in most, relatively benign in terms of reproducing the most deleterious effects of the historically grounded asymmetry of the conditions of existence of those who study and those who are studied. However, even the mitigations implied in 'studying up', namely reflexivity, polyvocality and stakeholder approaches, do not substantially alter the basic relationship.

These points are not new, but neither – it appears – are the positions of the professional bodies. The hysterical response (in some circles) to Gough's 'handmaiden of imperialism' article (see Gough 1968) and to the collection edited by Asad (1973) indicated the dimensions of the problem: the probity of professional practice could not be articulated in terms of scholarly practice, in part, I would argue, because scholarly practice was – and is – so ill-defined. To take the example of research involving human subjects: most research applications by academics must be scrutinised by an ethics board in order to ensure that there is informed consent, that no harm will befall the subjects, that the stated goals are the real goals, and so on. One hazards the guess that most anthropology applications, unless they involve some kind of bio-medical study or heavily flagged intervention are passed without much discussion, while a psychological study of US undergraduates' capacity to tolerate sleep deprivation would undergo more detailed scrutiny. In effect, the ease with which anthropological study is ethically vouchsafed has less to do with the nature of the study than it has to do with its being an *anthropological* study (i.e. folk with credentials studying folk without credentials).

Lest it be thought that I am arguing for the introduction of increased surveillance of anthropological activities, let me declare that I am not. What is at issue is the invocation of ethics (the official statements of the professional associations) less for the defence of those for whom unethical behaviour has real consequences than for the defence of the associations themselves. When doctors, lawyers, schoolteachers, police, social workers or university lecturers are challenged by professional or civil bodies there is typically an unambiguous legal outcome. When events such as *DED* (and those detailed in *DED*) occur there is an uneasy compromise between universalistic and relativised criteria. And it is hard to see how this compromise could be evaded.[8] Given the wide variety of societies and circumstances in which anthropologists function, how can one be sure of protecting research participants and honouring trust, anticipating harms, avoiding undue intrusion or negotiating informed consent? (These are the first four of eight guidelines listed in the 'Relations With and Responsibilities Towards Research Participants' section of the current ASA *Ethical Guidelines for Good Research Practice*.)

So, we have informal guidelines that indicate the professional associations' interest in demonstrating a concern for the parameters of ethical behaviour without prescribing those parameters with precision. Signing off dubious environmental impact statements? Collecting myths? Taking genealogies? All of these misdemeanours (or worse?) may be seen to be addressed by one or other of the guidelines, but what about the consequences? A code of ethics not rooted in the historical reality of relations between the studiers and the studied is doomed to triviality. It seems unlikely that an anthropological participant-observer among killers would be censured as an accessory to murder (Chagnon, for example, has not been held culpable), yet there is clearly some possibility of transgressing boundaries.

In an article in *The Nation* (20 November 2000) David Price has reviewed the AAA history of dealing with misdemeanours (and dissidence) by its members, and the account is salutary. When Boas, in 1919, proposed the censure of four then un-named anthropologists who, he said, had 'prostituted science by using it as a cover for their activities as spies', the AAA's governing council voted instead to censure Boas. Three of the four accused voted in favour of Boas's censure. As Price states,

> The AAA's governing council was concerned less about the accuracy of his charges than about the possibility that publicising them might endanger the ability of others to undertake fieldwork. It accused him of 'abuse' of his professional position for political ends.

He goes on to note that 'The AAA's current code of ethics contains no specific prohibitions concerning espionage or secretive research.' (Nor, as far as I can tell, does that of the ASA.) According to Price, the AAA collaborated with the CIA in the early 1950s by way of providing a cross-listed directory of AAA members showing their geographical and linguistic areas of expertise along with summaries of research interests. Furthermore, Price contends, 'When the CIA overthrew Arbenz in Guatemala in 1954, an anthropologist reported, under a pseudonym, to the State Department's intelligence and research division on the political affiliations of the prisoners taken by the military in the coup.' He also notes that, wnen, in 1971, it was reported that anthropologists had secretly used their ethnographic knowledge to assist the war effort in Indochina, a fact-finding committee headed by Margaret Mead 'manoeuvred to create a report finding no wrongdoing on the part of the accused anthropologists'.

It might seem bizarre that this was the professional body to which Turner and Sponsel turned in order to reveal the (now apparently spurious) charges mounted in the Tierney volume, but where else might they have turned? To scholarly journals? The Chagnon material has been extensively examined and discussed and has excited little public comment until linked with the discredited charges against Neel.

The official response from the professional bodies is somewhat muted, and that is not surprising in light of the response by the AAA to the 1989 letter to the association from the Brazilian Anthropological Association (Carneiro da Cunha 1989) that tried to alert the AAA to 'the harmful effects of careless renderings of Yanomami life'.[9] The AAA Executive Board has resolved to take a number of actions on allegations made in *DED* (15 November 2000), namely, to 'consider, report, suggest, recommend, examine, consult'. The key phrase appears in Part II, in which the Committee on Ethics is charged to consider developing additional draft guidelines to the Code of Ethics: 'Consideration should be given to common dilemmas faced by anthropologists conducting research in field situations.' The joint statement by the RAI and the ASA in September 2000 makes a similar point: 'The ASA statement of ideals, in its own words, "does not impose a rigid set of rules backed by institutional sanctions" … Instead, they are aimed at educating anthropologists, sensitising them to the potential sources of ethical conflict and dilemmas that may arise.'

The character of the *dilemmas* identified in both documents is diffuse, in fact so non-specific as to be anodyne. There *is* a basic dilemma, however, that is not included in the guidelines. It is not the one involving ethical decisions that may or may not have to be dealt with in the field. Rather it is that anthropological fieldwork is transgressive, bespeaks political asymmetry between the studier and the studied and is significantly rationalised on the grounds of making some kind of contribution to 'scientific research' (loosely or rigidly defined). Anthropology is not the often derided tourism/travel-writing/exploring, but an activity with explicit ethnographic, cross-cultural, comparative and non-trivial aims. Now the fact that research may not actually result in a great deal of useful knowledge is neither here nor there. The underlying rationale – however wonderful or sad the ultimate results – is that the anthropologist is systematically engaged, not as a casual observer, but as a motivated researcher.

So, looking at the dilemma from this vantage point, perhaps the problem of ethics merges with the one of science versus scepticism of science. Logically, it is hard to see how anthropology can evade some kind of association with science (by which is meant here little more than systematic and formulated knowledge). However, for many people, any overt association with scientific purpose is taken to be an endorsement of the whole cultural package, from nuclear weapons, to workers in lab coats, to vivisection and two-headed sheep experiments. That there is a critique of the culture of science is obviously highly desirable – it is after all a vital, not to say overwhelming, feature of being modern – but the highly charged 'science wars' debate often appears an infantile turf-war of little discernible benefit.

It is hard to see in the particular case of *DED* who the beneficiaries are and how the evident talent mobilised in various quarters of the debate is being usefully engaged. I suspect that the public scandal aspects will recede. Chagnon's position will be strengthened. The 'science wars' lines will become hardened. Anthropology's public reputation will remain as inscrutable as ever. Anthropologists will continue to retreat to specialist sub-fields of sufficient critical mass to sustain them, and ethical guidelines will perforce reflect the relativised nature of the enterprise.

As Albert has argued in another context (1997), however, contemporary analysis of the ethical obligations facing anthropologists is also strongly shaped by a conception of 'the ethnographic situation' that often bears little relationship to current circumstances in which the mediating role of researchers has at times been radically transformed by the expectations of modern anthropological subjects. The Malinowskian Yanomami may have expected machetes in exchange for collaboration, but the post-Malinowskian Yanomami want machetes and training in microscopy.

Conclusion

Despite early media interest, debates about *DED* have largely been confined to anthropological communities, and it seems unlikely that circumstances will change. Geertz's review in the *New York Review of Books* and Sahlins' in the *Washington Post* are likely to serve as representative commentaries. The epistemological disputes that actually drive the debate are likely to continue to evade general discussion (although see Ehrenreich and McIntosh 1997).[10]

When Sokal and Bricmont published *Intellectual Impostures*, their critique was similarly domesticated. In that book they did not engage in a rhetorical denunciation of Lacan, Kristeva, Irigary, Latour *et al*. They acknowledged that these people were taken seriously in their respective fields, and declined, on the basis of non-expertise, to measure the accuracy of local, professional and discipline-specific judgements, limiting themselves to documenting the shortcomings of these authors in their outlandish appropriation of quasi-scientific formulations to bolster the arguments. The exposure of such impostures appears to have done little to diminish the credibility or stature of these highly public intellectuals, but this is not because the arguments of Sokal and Bricmont were refuted: they were simply ignored.

Anthropology is a field very different from any of those represented by the subjects of Sokal and Bricmont's book. If anything, overt scientism is heavily policed by anthropology and hardly provides an unproblematic, authenticating entry-ism. But the response to the refutation of the core claims of *DED* appears to be just as flat as was the response to Sokal and Bricmont.

The transformative effects of anthropological practice on its subject peoples constitute an important issue, and one that when focused on – as in the cases of Asad's *Anthropology and the Colonial Encounter* (1973) and Hymes' *Reinventing Anthropology* (1972) for example – has provoked widespread critical reassessment and increased sensitivity to the complexity of the anthropological project. *DED*, however, is only passingly galvanising because the 'scandal' it attends to is not the socio-historical relationship between anthropology, its subjects and public culture, but a putative face-off between good guys and bad guys. That the Yanomami, whose precarious position has to a significant degree been mitigated by anthropological work, should now bear the added weight of destructive celebrity is to add injury to injury.

Acknowledgements

This is a version of a longer piece presented at a seminar at Goldsmiths. I am grateful for the comments of participants in that seminar, to a number of anonymous reviewers, and to Joel Kahn, Scott Atran, Stephan Feuchtwang, John Gledhill, Mike Rowlands, Mark Harris and Ian Jack.

Notes

1 For extensive documentation and discussion see: www.anth.uconn.edu/gradstudents/ dhume/darkness_in_el_dorado/index.htm and www.tamu.edu/anthropology/Neel.html and www.publicanthropology.org.

2 The account below began as a research seminar paper on ethics in anthropology, a version of which was subsequently edited for publication in *Anthropology Today* (Nugent 2001) with much of the background material excised and with an expanded section on the demonisation of science in anthropology.

3 As Albert (2001) has pointed out, a discussion largely absent from analysis of the research goals of Chagnon and Neel is the institutional system, particularly with respect to Atomic Energy Commission funding and the use of Yanomami blood samples by the Human Genome Diversity Project.

4 In one of the more bizarre performances at the AAA meetings, 17 November 2000, responsibility for this particular measles outbreak was actually claimed by a member of the Summer Institute of Linguistics. In a letter read out by Thomas Headland – an SIL officer – a missionary by the name of Wardlaw claimed that it was his daughter, Lorraine, who came down with measles following a trip to Manaus some months before the appearance of Neel and Chagnon. This naming of names was met not with incredulity and a call for immediate expulsion of bible-bashers, but with applause.

5 Albert (2001) deals with this in some detail.

6 The measured tone of the Public Anthropology Roundtable on *DED* is in marked contrast (www.publicanthropology.org).

7 Stitch and Mallon (2000) have recently offered a very similar formulation of the problem, one harking back to Chomsky: what separates the Standard Social Science Model and that

of rationalists (represented in this case by evolutionary psychologists) is a mis-understanding about terms.

8 See Albert (2001: 75–8) for a discussion of the difficulties in affirming both cultural particularism and universalist ideals.

9 The 'fierce people' characterisation, for example, emboldened both the military and goldminers in Brazil to justify violence towards the Yanomami.

10 For a splenetic counter-example see *Current Anthropology* commentary on Gil-White (2001).

Bibliography

Albert, B. (1997) '"Ethnographic situation" and ethnographic movements. Notes on post-Malinowskian fieldwork', *Critique of Anthropology*, 17 (1): 53–65.

—— (2001) 'Reflections on *Darkness in El Dorado*, Pts. I–III', *Documentos Yanomami*, 2: 43–114.

Asad, T. (ed.) (1973) *Anthropology and the Colonial Encounter*, Ithaca, NY: Humanities Press.

Cantor, N. (2000) Statement from University of Michigan, www.umich.edu.~urel/darkness.html

Carneiro da Cunha, M. (1989) Letter to the Committee on Ethics of the American Anthropological Association from the President of the Brazilian Anthropological Association, *Anthropology Newsletter*, January.

Chagnon, N. (1968) *Yanomamo: the Fierce People*, New York: Holt, Rinehart and Winston.

Early, J. and Peters, J. (2000) *The Xilixana Yanomami of the Amazon*, Gainesville, FL: University Press of Florida.

Ehrenreich, B. and McIntosh, J. (1997) 'The new creationism: biology under attack', *The Nation*, 9 June.

Ferguson, B. (1995) *Yanomami Warfare*, Santa Fe: School of American Research Press.

Forbes.com (2000) 'The science of self-preservation', www.forbes.com/forbes/2000/1127/6614086a

Gil-White, F.J. (2001) 'Are ethnic groups biological "species" to the human brain?', *Current Anthropology*, 42: 515–54.

Gough, K. (1968) 'New proposals for anthropologists', *Current Anthropology*, 9: 403–7.

Grandin, G. (2000) Review of *Darkness in El Dorado*, *The Nation*, 11 December: 12–17.

Hymes, D. (ed.) (1972) *Reinventing Anthropology*, New York: Pantheon.

Lindee, S. (1994) *Suffering Made Real: American Science and the Survivors of Hiroshima*, Chicago: University of Chicago Press.

—— (2000a) posting (www.ameranthassn.org) http://www.psych.ucsb.edu/research/cep/eldorado/lindee.htm

—— (2000b) Neel's field trip in 1968 (www.ameranthassn.org) ccat.sas.upenn.edu/hss/faculty/neel.htm

Lobo, M.S. de C. *et al.* (2001) 'Report of the medical team of the Federal University of Rio de Janeiro on accusations contained in Patrick Tierney's *Darkness in El Dorado*', *Documentos Yanomami*, 2: 15–42.

Miller, J. (2000) 'The fierce people: the wages of anthropological incorrectness', *National Review*, 20 November.

Neel, J. (1994) *Physician to the Gene Pool: Genetic Lessons and Other Stories*, New York: John Wiley.

Nugent, S. (2001) 'Anthropological public debate: the Yanomami, science and ethics, *Anthropology Today*, 17, 3: 10–14.

Price, D. (2000) 'Anthropologists as spies', *The Nation*, 20 November.

Ross, A. (1995) 'Science backlash on technoskeptics', *The Nation*, 2 October.

Seligman, D. (2000) 'The science of self-preservation, *Forbes*, 11.27.00.

Sokal, A. (1996) 'Transgressing the boundaries: toward a transformative hermeneutics of quantum gravity', *Social Text*, 46/7: 217–52.

Sokal, A. and Bricmont, J. (1998) *Intellectual Impostures*, London: Profile Books.

Stitch, S. and Mallon, R. (2000) 'The odd couple: the compatibility of social construction and evolutionary psychology', *Philosophy of Science*, 67: 1: 133–54.

Tierney, P. (2000) *Darkness in El Dorado: How Scientists and Journalists Devastated the Amazon*, New York: W.W. Norton.

Tooby, J. (2000) 'Jungle Fever: did two U.S. scientists start a genocidal experiment in the Amazon, or was *The New Yorker* duped?', Slate.msn.com/code/story/action.24.10.

Tooby, J. and Cosmides, L. (1982) 'The psychological foundations of culture', in J. Barkow, L. Cosmides and J. Tooby (eds) *The Adapted Mind*, New York and Oxford: Oxford University Press.

Turner, T. and Sponsel, L. (2000) – email (www.ameranthassn.org).

Turner, T. (2001) 'Life among the anthros', Letter to *The New York Review of Books*, 26 April, p. 69.

Wolf, E. (1994) 'Demonization of anthropologists in the Amazon', *Anthropology Newsletter*.

Zalewski, D. (2000) 'Anthropology enters the age of cannibalism', *New York Times*, 8 October.

5

'THE BLIND MEN AND THE ELEPHANT'

The challenge of representing the Rwandan genocide

Nigel Eltringham

Introduction[1]

Whenever faced with a very complex and complicated case the human mind looks for ways of simplification. For instance, whenever people look at the Rwandan tragedy, they always ask you to narrow down the problem into a simple equation, easy to grasp in one hearing, and failure to do so is often taken either as hiding something or simply complicating a matter that in itself should be easy to understand. The truth, however, is always like the elephant in the blind men's story. Asked to identify what an elephant is, the blind men come up with different answers depending on what part of the elephant they had touched. The one who touched the side thought the elephant was a big wall, the one who touched the leg took it for a big tree, the one who touched the tusk thought an elephant was just a dry branch, while the one who touched the large trunk said it was a long, soft hose. But the truth was just there in the middle – as big as an elephant!

Many have looked and still look at the Rwandan tragedy as the result of ethnic hatred, others as the consequence of bad politics and power struggle, some take it for the direct outcome of colonial and neo-imperialist manipulations, while others take it to be the outlet of socio-economic frustrations, and so on. Blind men with a big elephant in the middle to identify! And the truth again is there in the middle – as big as all those elements put together.

(Rwandan Protestant church worker,
personal communication, Kigali, March 1998)

Few non-Rwandese commentators would take such a pragmatic position regarding Rwanda. Too few would admit that any attempt to describe or explain the Rwandan genocide of 1994 will encounter multiple perspectives, many of which defy synthesis. As a consequence, it may seem more expedient to essentialise and stabilise the conflict as 'ethnic/primordial', 'political', 'economic', 'post-colonial' – in short, to impose a simple equation. Consequently, much of the literature takes one of two forms, either realist, transparent descriptions of the events as a whole, stripped of contingency, or those that focus on a particular aspect, such as the role of the United Nations (Melvern 2000), development aid (Uvin 1998) and so on.[2] Analytically, such a division of labour is desirable. But such works are in danger of trying to isolate a golden key that will unlock the mystery of this horrific cataclysm. Even if this is not the intention of the authors, the artificial slice may take on a life of its own. Having been plucked from the whole, this may be the facet that is privileged while the whole is discarded. This raises the question of whether, when people have finished taking the pieces apart, they are willing to concede that, once reassembled, the genocide remains 'a tangled skein of order and disorder' (Taylor 1999: 29).

Reductionism and essentialism are to be expected, but the apparent order they generate does not correspond to the fragmented, partial experience of those who witnessed the genocide or the multi-causal morass from which it emerged. We are faced with a bewildering enigma, the answer to which can never be in the singular, but must be multiple, stretching across disciplines and our conceptual categories, and, above all, stretching our patience for complexity. Despite this, as my informant observes, the world appears to want 'a simple equation, easy to grasp in one hearing'.

This poses a challenge to anthropologists. If we wish to take part in the essential endeavour to understand and raise the profile of events such as the Rwandan genocide, does our gaze, our professional pedantry, help or hinder the sending of a clear message? If the world's attention is conditional on providing a golden key – a simple equation or a realist transparency – to what extent does our stress on contingency and cognitive partiality dilute that message? Yet it is clear that multiple interpretations and representations of violence are inevitable and that violent conflict is experienced as a chaotic, fragmented and often irrational experience. Each witness brings her or his own interpretation and perspective. Furthermore, in the context of Rwanda the two interpretative filters that inform post-1994 reflection – the ubiquitous reference to 'history' and the category of 'genocide' – aggravate the generation of multiple representations. This article draws on three sets of research material: my experience working in Rwanda for a 'conflict resolution' NGO (1996–9); interviews conducted among members of the Rwandan government (1998); and further interviews among the Rwandan diaspora in Europe (1999).[3]

Legitimacy and historical narratives

Rwandese themselves legitimately invoke historical narratives to 'explain' the cause of the 1994 genocide, but their narratives are not identical. In contrast, among many non-Rwandan commentators there appears to be an assumption that a single, neutral history is attainable and that divergence is a sign of intentional distortion and myth-making (the latter term used pejoratively). Of course, one cannot rule out intentional distortion, but even without this, divergent narratives are inevitable. It has become axiomatic to consider that the past is used selectively to understand the present: that it is a resource and not a progression of neutral facts. At the same time, however, we are aware that history is not just a figment of the historian's mind (see Peel 1989). There thus remains a substantive difference between the 'past' made up of recorded time-and-place specific events and entities – what we may call a chronicle of facts – and the genre of history-writing. There is a difference between the chronicle of facts and the 'real time', selective narratives of history (see Lang 1992: 307). 'History' is not only concerned with whether (the past) but with how and why. The answers to how and why questions do not inhere in the chronicle itself. Rather, the historian (professional, lay, journalist) is required to integrate disparate entries into the chronicle, to impose an order, to demonstrate where they fit on a line of causality, temporality and logic (see Errington 1979: 239). A narrative is required if a selection of atomised entries extracted from the chronicle is to be integrated and fulfil the canons of cause-and-effect and progressive interconnectedness that are imperative in history-writing as genre. It is by this means that history produces an illusory, but necessary, reality effect. To progress from the chronicle of facts to a meaningful narrative requires interpretation. But in the wake of interpretation comes indeterminacy.

First, given that there is simply too much of the past to simply recreate as it happened, a historian must choose to focus on a particular aspect: to ask a particular question of the chronicle. The production of history is, therefore, necessarily selective. Furthermore, because a question is asked of the chronicle, the narrative contains an answer – an argument. Between the chronicle and history there exists an interpretative space. Given this freedom of manoeuvre, other possible, concurrent narratives, still true to the chronicle, may be envisaged. Two different narratives on the same event or event sequence are, therefore, not necessarily incommensurable; rather, they are the outcome of asking different questions of the past, which in turn generate different interpretations. Yet these multiple narratives, as long as they remain within the exterior limits set by the chronicle and do not intentionally distort it, may be considered as history.

The key issue, therefore, is what question the historian asks of the chronicle. Maurice Halbwachs (see Coser 1992) and Peter Berger (1984: 68ff.) argue that the present determines the questions asked of the past. In such contexts we should not ask 'how-did-the-past-create-the-present?' but 'how-did-the-present-create-the-past?' (Chapman *et al.* 1989: 5). Furthermore, the transient present (from which such questions emerge) is both differentiated synchronically (among actors) and evolves diachronically. The questions posed in the present are both heterogeneous and evolving. Consequently, the question(s) asked by historian(s) of the past are multiple, a factor which leads, if any answer is to be forthcoming, to divergence in selection, interpretation and argument.

This rapid run through of the nature of history demonstrates two things. First, we should not be troubled by multiple historical narratives (as long as they remain within the exterior limits set by the chronicle). Second, such an approach elevates history from being merely a prologue to both description and explanation and transforms it into a window on how actors understand what is currently at stake. Consequently, in my own research I treat the substance of historical narratives as secondary to exploring how they reveal contemporary cognitive maps of Rwanda. With such an approach, multiple representations are not a hindrance, but a means by which the 'conflict about the conflict' may be explored.

Such an interpretative approach to history is not controversial in the context of a 'history for pleasure' (as in the work of Schama, Starkey, *et al.*), but there are obvious ethical questions regarding my critique in contexts where what passes as history can act as an instrument of polarisation and ultimately of annihilation. In other words, does my approach detract from the palliative function played by history as Rwandese seek to explain such a catastrophic event? In order to explore this question, I need to be aware of two issues: first, the 'pioneering' role played by colonial anthropologists in introducing the appeal to history as a central component of Rwandan politics (especially the 'Hamitic hypothesis'); second, that my approach sets me in direct opposition to the actor's own reliance on the explanatory power of history.

Genocide and ethnicity

Similar issues arise when one considers the category of 'genocide' in relation to Rwanda. All the Rwandese I interviewed assert, as I do, that between April and July 1994 as many as 507,000 Tutsi (about 77 per cent of the population registered as 'Tutsi'; see Human Rights Watch 1999: 15) were killed in a genocide. This seems unassailable, yet ambiguity remains. For example, where to place the so-called 'Hutu moderates' – those Hutu who, as opponents of the Habyarimana regime, were killed by other Hutu?[4] These Hutu were not killed because of their 'ethnic' affiliation, but as political opponents and do not, therefore, fall within the enumeration contained in the United Nations Convention on the Prevention and Punishment of Genocide (UNGC).[5] Of course, those responsible for murdering 'Hutu moderates' can be charged with 'crimes against humanity'.[6] But in contemporary Rwanda it is through the lens of the UNGC that the categories of victim and perpetrator are constructed. As a consequence the 'Hutu moderates' remain anomalies and the challenge they pose to simple, Manichean views of the genocide and Rwandan society remains unanswered.[7]

Furthermore, why 'political groups' are omitted from the UNGC is a matter of intense debate. In a number of UN documents[8] the enumeration included 'political groups'. But, in the final Convention (adopted on 9 December 1948) they were removed.[9] In the literature, two inter-related reasons are given. There was a fear among a number of national delegates that the inclusion of political groups would obstruct internal suppression of 'subversive movements' and that this would deter 'sovereign nations' from ratifying the Convention. Second, it was argued that 'political groups' (and socio-economic groups) were too mutable to be accorded protection, unlike 'permanent and stable' ethnic groups.[10]

From an anthropological perspective, the assertions regarding mutability are clearly problematic – if only because they ignore the empirical observation that political movements are often constructed around so-called 'ethnic communities' regardless of where these come on the real/imagined continuum. Furthermore, a perpetrator can present his/her actions as directed against a 'political' group, when the target group is considered by the former to be just as 'permanent and stable' – as 'objectively identifiable' – as any pre-existing category based on religion or ethnicity.[11] Indeed, given the segmented nature of identities, individuals are always members of both protected and unprotected groups (see Drost 1959: 122–3). Our sociological knowledge of the constructed, situational nature of identity – whether ethnic, religious or political – and the porosity of such categories indicate that such archetypal characterisations are inadequate. They miss the point that it is perpetrators who define their targets, not victims.

Consequently, there need be no correspondence between the identity of a group and the identity that marks them out as targets of genocide. In some cases the perpetrators' definition will be based on a group's own, self-ascribed identity; in other cases group identity is merely a figment of each perpetrator's imagination (see Fein 1993: 13). In this sense, should defining mass killing as genocide depend on an exogenous, universal lexicon of archetypal groups (religious, ethnic and so on) or on the fact that a perpetrator delimits a target group by whatever criteria he or she chooses? In other words, would it not be better to determine genocide according to the endogenous, situational definitions of target groups as used by perpetrators, rather than by using some universal, abstract set of archetypes?[12] For it is inevitable that decontextualised, exogenous, abstract categories will throw up anomalies and inconsistencies. These will, in turn, generate efforts to (re)contextualise, and different representations will emerge. Again, the single 'simple equation' or the 'realist transparency' will escape our grasp.

This situation poses difficult ethical questions. It is anthropology that provided the terminology and 'scientific method' upon which the drafters of the UNGC relied. While our disciplinary thinking may have progressed, we still bear responsibility for the claims made by our forebears. Although we may now view the social world as indeterminate, we often carelessly still use the same reified, analytical concepts found in the UNGC. Furthermore, is our view of group identity really relevant? Whatever we may have to say about 'imagined communities', the real consequences of those imaginings are all too apparent in the piles of mutilated corpses in Rwanda. More than ever, we are reproached by W. I. and D.S. Thomas' dictum 'If men [sic] define situations as real, they are real in their consequences' (1928: 571–2).

Consequently, although an extensive literature has argued for the inclusion of both political and socio-economic groups in the Convention,[13] I still feel unease in questioning the UNGC *once applied*. In more than one seminar, anthropologists have asked me why I felt I had to make explicit my reasons for believing that the events of 1994 must be defined as genocide. Because, unlike other areas of study (and in parallel with writings on the Holocaust), any movement away from the received representation of events may be treated with suspicion and denounced as revisionism. Any critique of the accepted framework, even if it wishes to strengthen that framework, can be portrayed as 'denial-by-stealth'. It pays to be explicit. But in being explicit I am not just protecting my reputation. I want to see perpetrators brought to justice. To do this, I must recognise that, however much legal discourse and practice may subvert anthropological thinking ('whatever it is the law is after, it is not the whole story' Geertz 1983: 173), I would readily jettison my anthropological proclivities if more people were brought to justice. Yet there remains the overwhelming feeling that our anthropological knowledge of group identity could contribute to both the detection and the prevention of genocide by preventing perpetrators from exploiting the malleability of group identity to their obfuscatory advantage.

So, the critiques of the writing of 'history' and the usage of the term 'genocide' have their ethical pitfalls. What is the alternative?

'Let the facts speak for themselves'

Much of the literature on the Rwandan genocide has been written by journalists who follow a 'let-the-facts-speak-for-themselves', reportage style where the emphasis is on a progression of observed, 'objective facts'. In this context, the most significant has been Philip Gourevitch's *We Wish to Inform You That Tomorrow We Will be Killed With Our Families* (1998), winner of the Guardian First Book Award in 1999. By using interviews and personal testimony, Gourevitch provides an absorbing insight into the genocide. His book is, undoubtedly, a powerful contribution to the corpus of work on Rwanda and should be valued as such.

Gourevitch's work could be considered as 'popular', a term I use with caution since in academic circles it is often understood pejoratively. The term is also used as a reproach because it implies accessibility. The persuasive feature of Gourevitch's book is that it is presented as a series of factual narratives, allowing witnesses to 'tell-the-story-in-their-own-words'. As such, the narratives are powerful testimony to lived experience. As Elie Wiesel said of survivors of the Holocaust, '[A]ny survivor has more to say than all the historians combined about what happened' (quoted in Cargas 1986). Gourevitch certainly appears to be a 'neutral conduit' revealing the genocide (and its aftermath) 'as it actually happened'. Thus, 'everything is of one piece, a seamless fabric of tightly interwoven strands' (Kress 1985: 72). But, while Gourevitch may give the impression of unmediated 'truth', he fails to demonstrate that all representations of a given conflict are actually structured, first by his informants and then by himself – there is thus no 'pure', unmediated stream of experiential 'data'.

My argument is not that Gourevitch's book is intrinsically wrong or misleading. No one can deny that informing the 'general public' about genocide is a worthy endeavour. Rather, I pose the question (both to other anthropologists and to myself) as to why a work that lacks contingency and reflexivity, in which facts are presented as objective – when they are clearly selective and partial – should remain so appealing? If the 'just-give-us-the-facts' approach is so pervasive (and persuasive) what added value can anthropology offer?

There are a number of problems with this reportage style. First, those to whom Gourevitch 'gives a voice' did not experience the genocide as an integrated, single narrative, but as a fragmented, chaotic, incoherent set of different experiences to which actors have legitimately assigned some semblance of coherence. Gourevitch therefore confronts a 'chaos' already constituted. Gourevitch has then imposed further order, editing and integrating isolated fragments in order to demonstrate how they interconnect. This has required interpretation, for the isolated fragments (the 'stories') themselves do not tell us how they are interconnected. Clearly, such a process is inevitable for any form of inquiry (including ethnography) but it should not be confused with 'letting-people-speak-for-themselves'.[14]

Gourevitch, like the ethnographer, is in an artificial, privileged position which precludes being a 'neutral conduit'. Both synchronically and diachronically Gourevitch has access to a wider field of vision than any single witness or informant to whom he seeks to 'give a voice'. Consequently, he knows where his book is going whereas the reader does not. Yet Gourevitch's wider field of vision is obscured as the reader's eye/ear is drawn to the witnesses/informants who 'speak' – so that the stories 'appear to tell themselves' (see Wilson 1997: 143). In reality, it is the metanarrative (of which only Gourevitch is aware) which tells the 'whole' story, not the vignettes. It is the metanarrative that provides linkages and thus coherence to the progression of otherwise discrete stories. The metanarrative does not inhere in the isolated stories themselves, but is a product of interpretation and selectivity. Thus, although Gourevitch still appears as a neutral conduit, the very framework within which the personal stories are situated is reliant on an artificial, omniscient perspective, one that benefits from his foresight about where the book is going. Such a vantage point places Gourevitch far beyond the perspective of those who appear to 'do the talking'. An obvious question is whether this framework *pre*cedes or *pro*ceeds from the stories? Ultimately, the dialectic between the stories and the metanarrative is too intertwined to answer this question. In other words, without the stories there is no metanarrative, and without the metanarrative, the stories could not be told in this form. Does Gourevitch himself know which was the determinant?

We are aware, therefore, that, in the process of excluding or including certain facts and testimony, an 'analytical' position has already been taken (even if Gourevitch may not be able to tell us exactly what it is). Gourevitch appears to be a disinterested conduit of impartial information, rather than being an adjudicator of knowledge; the illusion of a realist transparency is maintained; actors appear to speak for themselves. Yet motivated by a desire to describe a single, factual reality, Gourevitch fails to demonstrate that conflict is, in essence, a contest over how to interpret reality.

Despite this, Gourevitch is writing what he assumes (probably correctly) his imagined audience wants to hear. He is not expected to leave the world unresolved and say, 'well maybe it's like this, or maybe it's like that. One person told me one thing, but another person told me something else, so I don't know – you choose.' He is not expected to provide his readers with a menu of alternative realities, but to 'give-them-the-facts'. Whether we like it or not, anthropologists must accept that certain readerships require indisputable facticity to attribute meaning to particular events or entities. For them, 'meaning' is not obscure (and does not have multiple incarnations) but is evident in transparent 'facts' themselves. Arguments of representation and partiality carry little weight. Thus anthropologists may be left asking what is the added value of a deconstructionist approach. Ethically, are we not duty-bound to give voice to the reality of events such as genocide in all their horrifying detail? By deconstructing discourse, do we not simply obscure reality while claiming to demystify it?

The anthropologist representing

Having worked for a conflict prevention/resolution NGO in Rwanda I am all too aware of the extent to which 'facts' are rarely incontestable. First, what we are exposed to is often a result of happenstance. Second, we should not forget that others use apparently self-evident 'facts' to incite people to kill, and to dissuade others from intervening. Anyone can present 'facts' as indisputable. Conflict, however, is intrinsically processual. For all concerned, any conflict is chaotic and protean, constantly resisting a single, standardised, static and unitary portrayal. Even 'facts' have chameleon-like qualities (see Davies 1994: 2) since at any given moment they are being cited, (re)constructed, dismissed and reworked – some brought to the foreground and others conveniently forgotten. Today's fact can become tomorrow's fiction. To stop the clock at any moment is an arbitrary, albeit necessary, decision for any writer, academic, or journalist. We should remain aware, however, that facts are discursive resources, synchronically multiple and diachronically fluid. To make them concrete in our writing is to freeze-frame this process. The plasticity of 'facts' themselves, and the negotiation of what is and is not accepted as being 'factual', is not subsidiary to conflict but is central to it. If we treat 'facts' as anything other than contingent, we may be left in a position not only of failing to understand conflict but of asking why, if everything was so clear, conflict was possible. 'Facts' rely on hindsight; they are literally 'post facto'.

Yet the very accusations I level at Gourevitch could be levelled at me. My 'imagined audience' (anthropologists) wants me to deconstruct, to problematise, to be reflexive and so on, yet such a 'mandate' still requires a framework, that of my own metanarrative. Ultimately, if we (journalist or anthropologist) want to demonstrate our perception of the how and the why – the interconnectedness of events – then exclusion, editing, synthesis and interpretation are inevitable. Is this not the cost of all representation? If so, then selectivity and metanarratives are not suspect, but inevitable. Therefore, it is not a question of whether or not my research is superior to that of Gourevitch. There are no real criteria to make such a judgement, and no judges who could make that decision. On the level playing field of partiality there are no winners (although we hope for complementarity). And yet, the question remains, if the story has already been told as an eloquent, integrated set of narratives, what is left for me to contribute?

I could argue that Gourevitch's metanarrative elucidates only one perspective on Rwanda. Of course, I must concede, paradoxically, that my own view, which is that there are many perceptions/representations, is also a perspective. Furthermore, at least Gourevitch remains true to the project of his informants who are intent on stabilising events with a single, coherent representation. In contrast, my own desire to demonstrate the multiplicity of representations is not how actors themselves operate, i.e. they do not recognise the partial veracity of all, or most, representations. Similarly, my claim that an actor holds one of a multiplicity of possible perspectives implies that for each implicated actor, I can isolate a static, dogmatic perspective that remains unaltered by context. In actuality, such perspectives are dynamic, strategic, evolving and situational. Thus in my drive to demonstrate the polyvocal nature of conflict representation I may artificially stabilise discrete multiple perspectives in the same way as Gourevitch constructs a single perspective.

If I had been in a different position (a journalist like Gourevitch, for example), how might I have gone about writing on Rwanda? Is it merely my presence in an academic institution that requires that I find new and 'innovative' (pedantic?) ways to discuss Rwanda? In other words, would I have been better off writing a straightforward, 'factual' narrative of Rwanda? Such an approach would have enabled me to side-step the dangers of unbridled postmodernism, and avoid the deferential nods to Foucault *et al.* Above all, such an approach would have allowed me to stay well clear of the ever-present charge of revisionism, the charge that by going beyond conventional narrative and 'transparent facts' I have some hidden agenda that questions the deaths of more than half a million Rwandese.

It would be disingenuous of me not to state explicitly the pragmatic agenda that underpins the nature of my research. The issues it considers grew directly from working for a conflict resolution/prevention NGO in Rwanda. As one would expect, I initially believed that a single 'reality' of the conflict existed. As my knowledge of the situation grew, new information was conveniently incorporated into my personal understanding of Rwanda. As time passed, however, I became aware that I was forced to privilege certain representations, that no single perspective could integrate all possible positions, and that such a positivist goal was unattainable. With this realisation there also came an awareness that I was not, as I had at first thought, dealing with diametrically opposed positions. It was not only the case that divergence was far more nuanced than I had anticipated, but that these positions were dependent on shared practice and a persistent dialogue between counter positions as protagonists conducted a long-distance argument. Such a realisation could have put me in a position of acute vulnerability. It became apparent, however, that rather than being an obstacle to my work, the imperative to find reconciliatory spaces could be served by embracing this divergence and sacrificing the unattainable certainty of a single representation.

By taking a consciously artificial position in which all representations must be considered as contingent, I hope to demonstrate[15] that, while conflict may have indisputable, physical manifestations in violence and coercion, these are peaks in a process that is most of the time enacted in discourse and competing verbal representations. Only by giving all such partial representations due attention, and abandoning the fruitless search for a single grand narrative, can true reconciliatory spaces be found.

At the same time I am acutely aware that in my own work two kinds of 'facts' are often missing. First, in the drive to unpack and compare representations, I may omit what others consider to be important details (dates, names, places) from the body of the text. Second, I may fail to state explicitly my own position on what is 'true'. For example, one eminent academic, who has written extensively on Rwanda, suggested that while my history chapter includes the historical narratives of those I interviewed, should I not have introduced the chapter with a sketch of Rwandan history? He, of course, immediately saw the problem. I cannot write a 'history' of Rwanda without pre-empting and/or dismissing aspects of my informants' narratives. I cannot write a 'true' history of Rwanda. The debate would be prematurely foreclosed. Another colleague questioned my dismantling of discourse not only on anthropological grounds, but on logical ones too, suggesting that I was in danger of losing touch with reality in the process. Hemmed in by the desire to be impartial, to avoid accusations of revisionism, am I elevating discourse above any concrete reality or facticity? I hope not. Any utterance is potentially both factual and fictional, or more correctly, 'fabricated' and partial. It is in the act of interpretation, of trying out a particular utterance against our own biography, experiences and life circumstances (and the partial 'additional facts' we possess), that we decide whether that utterance is true or not.

But my own hidden discourse remains that of conflict resolution and it influences what I choose to include, exclude and emphasise. Such a discourse forces me consciously to take an artificial position in which I try to uncover not only why, but how representations compete. As such, my own hidden discourse can be viewed as much as an attempt to impose order on chaos as can those discourses which I seek to analyse. I should stress that I am conscious of this underlying motivation and hope that my analysis is sufficiently comprehensive not to be accused of glossing the reality of the conflict in the drive towards reconciliation.

Ethics and representation

For those who write on Rwanda, any representation runs the risk of being considered partial or misleading. In the context of Rwandan history, it is assumed that one can identify a writer's position from the stance that she or he adopts on key issues (often presented as pro-Hutu or pro-Tutsi). For example, the debate about whether ethnicity was the creation of colonialism ('pro-Tutsi'), or whether it existed prior to colonisation ('pro-Hutu'). Likewise, it is not just these alternative positions that are of importance, but the degree of context a writer considers appropriate. As context is potentially infinite, there can be no definitive contextual boundary. In such a minefield, desired impartiality is almost impossible to achieve. However creative (and careful) a writer attempts to be there will always be room for accusations of bias towards one side or the other. This has important implications for the question of ethics.

As anthropologists we are rightly concerned with the ethical dimension of our work, particularly as it relates to the intellectual property rights of those with whom we carry out research. Much is made of taking findings back to the field. In the context of my research, however, those I interviewed were not giving me privileged access to a private and encoded world, my representations of which should rightfully be made available for their assessment and comment. Very few of the Rwandese I interviewed had experienced the genocide at first hand. Their discourse was concerned less with personal than with 'objective' analysis of the causes of the genocide.

I do not claim that my research is an exhaustive treatment of *all* Rwandan discourses on the 1994 genocide. First, there are the discourses of ordinary Rwandese – rather than the political élite among whom I conducted my research. There are also discourses of those who were not willing to be interviewed (many of whom are implicated in the genocide). In addition, there are the hidden discourses (the *'non dit'*) of those who *were* interviewed. Out of necessity, therefore, my concern is with public discourses, conducted in an international setting, among and between people who are actively engaging with one another. In other words this discourse(s) exists independently of my research and not because of it. Rather than giving victim testimony, the Rwandese I interviewed articulated a public, analytical discourse, one that they had already expressed in numerous encounters with journalists, diplomats and other academics. More importantly, they were aware that I would talk to the 'other side'.

As the objective of the research was to investigate both the nature and the substance of this discourse, neither side could be privileged. To put it bluntly, in a conflict situation (one marked by persistent discursive forms), the incorporation of these different discourses would automatically make my work suspect to either side. Neither side wants to share the stage. I have consequently found myself in a position where the results of my research could not be usefully assessed and critiqued by those involved. The fundamental characteristic of these various discourses is that, while they may employ the same mechanics, they cannot exist in the same space. Their incorporation in my work is, in itself, contrary to their intended purpose. Given that from the outset the placing of these discourses side-by-side would be contrary to the expectations of those involved, how can I hope to satisfy informants that I have correctly presented their points of view? The very act of giving voice to other discourses questions the veracity of their own point of view. In a situation in which dialogue between informant and researcher is made problematic from the outset, how does one apply an ethical framework to the question of representation?

I should still, of course, provide my informants with the opportunity to read and assess my findings, but I am aware that I will not receive feedback that would respond to what I have written in a particularly constructive manner. The very act of placing these discourses side-by-side will always make my research problematic, however much I try to highlight the generic nature and power of discourse.

Perhaps all this angst is a reflection of my own position sitting at a computer trying to represent an event as horrific as genocide in a country thousands of miles away, and an atomised, amorphous discourse. In the process of writing one creates a 'virtual' imagined landscape of one's place or region of interest, a landscape around which we navigate as we try to form our arguments and arrange our material. Our representations of conflict are amalgams of multiple message fragments (the conversation, the interview, the newspaper report, the academic article), pieced together in a never-to-be-complete mosaic. Some fragments are observed or empirical, some intuitive, some specific to the conflict itself and some universal and abstract. Message fragments are potentially infinite, so the mosaic is constantly augmented and modified.

Occasionally, we try to anchor this virtual landscape in a vaguely remembered conversation, or a single personality. By this, I do not mean the sanitised interview transcript or the name on the page, but the emotional reality of an encounter. And yet, writing insists that we create our own universe. The inadequacy of all of this is thrown into sharp relief on returning to the field and finding it is not, and never will be, tamed by our writing. Is it not the case, however, that the actors implicated in our research are also navigating around a virtual and imagined landscape of their own?

Conclusion

To return to the questions raised above. What is the integral value of a deconstructionist approach of the kind used by anthropologists? If multiple perspectives are unacceptable to the actors involved, why should one expect a general readership to accept such a position? Ultimately, of course, there would be no conflict if there were only one shared understanding of diachronic cause and effect. Conflict, by nature, is about competing perspectives. Yet while, as individuals, we make moral judgements about those involved in conflict, anthropologists cannot shy away from listening to and interrogating multiple perspectives. Of course, anthropologists must always avoid unnecessarily rationalising and relativising violence and conflict (see Nordstrum and Martin 1992: 3). Nonetheless, our contribution to understanding conflict places us in a difficult position. It puts us at odds with our informants, and it puts us at odds with a general readership who want to know why a conflict has occurred, rather than being asked to choose from a menu of myriad causes.

So, will my research make a contribution to 'reconciliation' in Rwanda? Throughout my engagement with Rwanda, Rwandese have expressed dismay at the ubiquitous use of the term reconciliation by non-Rwandese. The term is often used as if it can be achieved by fiat. Following Priscilla Hayner (2001: 155) I would like to draw a distinction between individual reconciliation and national or political reconciliation. The concern of my research is the discursive basis on which national or political reconciliation (a re-imagining of society) may be achieved. As stated above, the discourse I consider is a public, predominantly depersonalised, analytical discourse. That is not to suggest that political/national reconciliation and individual reconciliation are discrete, for they clearly inform one another. However, while individual reconciliation remains a personal and intractable issue, I would hope that my research can contribute to challenging the discourse of both those who currently exercise political power in Rwanda and those who aspire to hold (or share) that power in the future.

I am not claiming that the analysis contained in my research offers some kind of panacea for the situation in Rwanda. While the sentiments expressed above may automatically bring to mind Noam Chomsky's comment that 'it is the responsibility of intellectuals to speak the truth and expose lies' (1969: 325), I would resist using the words 'truth' and 'lies'. Rather, I would prefer to use another quote by Chomsky, regarding the contribution that intellectuals can make to the struggle for peace and justice, 'to serve as a "resource", to provide information and analysis' (1988: 372). I would hope, therefore, that my research can not only make a contribution to the corpus of work on Rwanda but that it can also provide a resource both for those who seek to understand the horror of the events of 1994 and for those who continue to play a part in efforts towards conflict resolution in Rwanda and elsewhere.

In conclusion, books such as that by Gourevitch are important because they respond to, and are written for, a readership that demands the 'just-give-us-the-facts' approach. In a world in which drawing attention to deeply shocking events such as genocide is difficult at the best of times, we should welcome books that find a responsive readership. Anthropology, however, has the unenviable task of providing alternative approaches to the understanding of conflict. We must hope that such approaches will be recognised as being complementary to these other works, rather than being dismissed as obscurantist. Conflict is ultimately about disagreement. To properly understand conflict we must give voice to these disagreements and demonstrate how they are articulated. The real challenge is not to choose between the relative value of representations, but to create the conditions in which separate realities can inform one another. It is to be hoped that such an approach helps to highlight the processual nature of conflict itself. From such a perspective, disagreements about the nature and 'truth' of conflict have less to do with the sanitised, objective and inevitable progression of 'facts', than they do with an informed engagement with the confused and confusing world of discursive strategies, partial 'truths' and conflicting subjectivities.

Notes

1 An earlier version of this article appeared in the web-journal *Anthropology Matters* (www.anthropologymatters.com). I am indebted to Damian Walter for his comments on an earlier draft.

2 One notable exception is Taylor (1999).

3 I am grateful to the Central Research Fund of the University of London and the Harold Hyam Wingate Foundation for their contribution to the fieldwork.

4 According to René Lemarchand (2000) between 30,000 and 50,000 were killed.

5 Article II: '[A]cts committed with intent to destroy in whole or in part a national, ethnic, racial, or religious group.'

6 According to the most recent definition 'crimes against humanity' include persecution against any identifiable group or collectivity on political, racial, national, ethnic, cultural, religious, gender or other grounds that are universally recognised as impermissible under international law' (*Rome Statute of the International Criminal Court*, 1998, article 7.

7 Likewise, although as many as 10,000 ethnic Twa were killed in 1994 (see IRIN 2001) they are absent from most discussions of the genocide.

8 General Assembly's Resolution on Genocide (Resolution 96(I), 11 December 1946), in the Secretariat Draft (1947) and in the Ad Hoc Committee's Draft Convention (1948).

9 And yet, six years later, in 1954, the UN Convention Relating to the Status of Refugees defined a refugee as someone who, because of a 'well founded fear of being persecuted for reasons of race, religion, nationality *membership of a particular social group or political opinion*, is outside the country of his or her nationality' (Article I(2); emphasis added).

10 They argued that 'because of their mutability and lack of distinguishing characteristics [political groups] did not lend themselves to definition, [which] would weaken and blur the whole Convention' (Kuper 1981: 26, quoting the Polish delegate).

11 Examples given by Chalk (1989: 151) include the killing of some 500,000 Indonesian communists in 1965–6; the murder of members of the Awami League in 1970–1 during the breakaway of Bangladesh; and the planned annihilation by the Khmer Rouge from 1975 to 1978 of 'enemies of the people' – thus defining the victims as 'effectively as any pre-existing division of religion or race' (Fein 1993: 77).

12 For example, although the Tutsi victims of the 1994 genocide were undoubtedly targeted as members of an 'ethnic' group, for the International Criminal Tribunal for Rwanda (ICTR), the categorisation of Rwanda's Tutsi was not straightforward. As William Schabas notes, 'the categorisation of Rwanda's Tutsi population clearly vexed the Tribunal. For the Tribunal, the word "ethnic" came closest, yet it was troublesome because the Tutsi could not be meaningfully distinguished, in terms of language and culture, from the majority Hutu population' (2000: 131). Despite this, the Tribunal employed the 'ethnic' classification in applying the concept of 'crimes against humanity', finding *Akeyesu* guilty of a 'widespread or systematic attack on the civilian population on ethnic grounds': *Prosecutor v. Akayesu*, (Case no. ICTR-96-4-T), judgement, 2 September 1998, paragraph 652.

13 Even the United Nations' own Special Rapporteur for the Commission on Human Rights, Benjamin Whitaker, recommended in 1985 that the UNGC be expanded to protect political, economic and social groups (see Whitaker 1985).

14 Note that the subtitle of Gourevitch's book is *Stories from Rwanda*.

15 In my forthcoming book *Accounting for Horror: Post-Genocide Debates in Rwanda*. London: Pluto Press.

Bibliography

Berger, P. L. 1984 [1963]. *Invitation to Sociology: A Humanistic Perspective*. Harmondsworth: Penguin.

Cargas, H. 1986. 'An Interview with Elie Wiesel'. *Holocaust and Genocide Studies* 5.

Chalk, F. 1989. 'Genocide in the 20th Century: Definitions of Genocide and their Implications for Predication and Prevention'. *Holocaust and Genocide Studies* 4(2): 149–60.

Chapman, M., Tonkin, E. and McDonald, M. 1989. 'Introduction: History and Social Anthropology'. In *History and Ethnicity* (eds) E. Tonkin, M. McDonald and M. Chapman. London: Routledge.

Chomsky, N. 1969. *American Power and the New Mandarins*. New York: Pantheon Books.

—— 1988. Excerpts from Noam Chomsky's Written Responses to Questions from Celia Jakubowicz. In *Language and Politics* (ed.) C. Otero. Montreal: Black Rose.

Coser, L. (ed.) 1992. *Maurice Halbwachs on Collective Memory*. Chicago: University of Chicago Press.

Davies, S. (ed.) 1994. 'Knowledge is Power? The Use and Abuse of Information in Development'. *IDS Bulletin* 25(2): 1–13.

Drost, P. N. 1959. *The Crime of State,* Vol. 2. *Genocide*. Leyden: A. W. Sythoff.

Eltringham, N. P. (forthcoming) *Accounting for Horror: Post-Genocide Debates in Rwanda*. London: Pluto Press.

Errington, S. 1979. 'Some Comments on Style in the Meaning of the Past'. *Journal of Asian Studies* 38(2): 231–44.

Fein, H. 1993. *Genocide: a Sociological Perspective*. London: Sage.

Geertz, C. 1983. 'Local Knowledge: Fact and Law in Comparative Perspective'. In *Local Knowledge* C. Geertz. New York: Basic Books.

Gourevitch, P. 2000 [1998]. *We Wish to Inform You That Tomorrow We Will be Killed With Our Families: Stories from Rwanda*. London: Picador.

Hayner, P. 2001. *Unspeakable Truths: Confronting State Terror and Atrocity*. New York and London: Routledge.

Human Rights Watch, 1999. *'Leave None to Tell the Story': Genocide in Rwanda*. New York: Human Rights Watch: International Federation of Human Rights.

IRIN, 2001. 'RWANDA: Twa Community Concerned over Gacaca System'. United Nations: Office for the Co-ordination of Humanitarian Affairs Integrated Regional Information Network for Central and Eastern Africa. Tuesday 6 June.

Kress, G. 1985. 'Discourses, Texts, Readers and the Pro-nuclear Arguments'. In *Language and The Nuclear Arms Debate: Nukespeak Today* (ed.) P. Chilton. London and Dover, NH: Frances Pinter.

Kuper, L. 1981. *Genocide: Its Political Uses in the Twentieth Century*. New Haven/London: Yale University Press.

Lang, B. 1992. 'The Representation of Limits'. In *Probing the Limits of Representation: Nazism and the 'Final Solution'* (ed.) S. Friedlander. Cambridge, MA: Harvard University Press.

Lemarchand, R. 2000. 'Coming to Terms with the Past: The Politics of Memory in Post-Genocide Rwanda'. *L'Observatoire de l'Afrique Centrale* 3(27). http://www.obsac.com.

Melvern, L. 2000. *A People Betrayed: The Role of the West in Rwanda's Genocide*. London: Zed.

Nordstrom, C. and Martin, J-A. 1992. 'The Culture of Conflict: Field Reality and Theory'. In *The Paths to Domination and Resistance, and Terror* (eds.) C. Nordstrom and J-A. Martin. Berkeley and Oxford: University of California Press.

Peel, J. D. Y. 1989. 'The Cultural Work of Yoruba Ethnogenesis'. In *History and Ethnicity* (eds) E. Tonkin, M. McDonald and M. Chapman. London: Routledge.

Schabas, W. S. 2000. *Genocide in International Law*. Cambridge: Cambridge University Press.

Taylor, C. 1999. *Sacrifice as Terror: The Rwandan Genocide of 1994*. Oxford and New York: Berg.

Thomas, W. I. and Thomas, D. S. 1928. *The Child in America: Behaviour Problems and Programs*. New York: Knopf.

Uvin, P. 1998. *Aiding Violence: The Development Enterprise in Rwanda*. West Hartford, CN: Kumarian Press.

Whitaker, B. 1985. *Revised and Updated Report on the Question of the Prevention and Punishment of the Crime of Genocide*. New York: United Nations Economic and Social Council, Commission on Human Rights (E.CN.4.Sub.2.1985.6: 2 July 1985).

Wilson, R. 1997. 'Representing Human Rights Violations: Social Contexts and Subjectivities'. In *Human Rights, Culture and Context, Anthropological Perspectives* (ed.) R. Wilson. London: Pluto Press.

Part II

DILEMMAS

6

EVERYDAY ETHICS

A personal journey in rural Ireland, 1980–2001

Marilyn Silverman

Introduction

There is today, among many parties and interest groups, a deep concern with the ethics and practice of research which involves human or animal subjects. To some extent, the issues being raised are similar to what anthropologists have long talked about, at least since my own graduate student days during the mid-1960s. However, the present concern has a different context. It is largely driven by an obsession with accountability and auditing which permeates contemporary institutional life in the public sector. Interestingly, this dovetails with, and is also now driven by, postmodern and post-colonial critiques of anthropology which emerged in the mid-1980s. The various practices which have been developed to address these concerns mean that, in theory, all parties can now be satisfied: the institutions through which we practice anthropology (government bureaucracies, universities, funding agencies), our more reflexive-style anthropological colleagues and the people among whom we do research and about whom we write.

In this chapter, however, I question what this recent ethical turn has accomplished for socio-cultural anthropologists. I do this by comparing monitoring procedures and reflexive moments with the materiality of daily life in the field and in writing ethnography. I do so by exploring my own experiences as a Canadian academic doing anthropological research in Ireland over the past 21 years.

Defining and auditing ethics in the academy

At York University in Toronto, anxiety about ethical behaviour in research has given rise to a permanent 'Human Participants Review Sub-committee' consisting of a multi-disciplinary cross-section of academics. The sub-committee must formally approve any research project that involves human subjects before it can begin.[1] Its aim is to ensure ethical research, through

115

'informed consent', that is, to ensure that no harm will come to subjects/participants and that all participants have been thoroughly informed about the research and have made an explicit decision to take part.

These aims are pursued by requiring university researchers to fill out a questionnaire which is vetted by the sub-committee. The questions include what informants will do (e.g. 'stimuli, ... tasks, ... tests, questionnaires, interviews, number of sessions and time required') and whether there are 'any foreseeable risks and benefits' for participants. It also asks how the researcher will inform people about the research so as to obtain their consent. There are three choices. The researcher can ask participants to sign a form which contains a description of the research. The researcher can send potential participants a letter outlining the research and their roles in it. Or the researcher can tell potential participants about the research and obtain their consent verbally. If verbal consent is to be used, the researcher must provide the sub-committee with 'a rationale on why the informed consent form is not being used' and 'provide a draft of the verbal statement'.

The York University questionnaire assumes a formalism in research design which posits highly structured interactions between researcher(s) and participant(s). No gesture is made to the main activity of anthropological research, namely, participant observation and its location in such everyday, on-going interaction as attending public meetings, buying meat from the butcher or chatting with people at the petrol pump. This omission is not accidental. That the questionnaire not only requires anthropologists to justify *not* using a formal consent form but also requires them to produce a formulaic speech, suggests that there is grave suspicion in the academy about how anthropologists produce their data, about those who do not conform to positivist stereotypes and about getting everything in writing. What does such practice have to do with ethics in anthropology?

Permission granted!

Since 1980, my partner and colleague, Philip H. Gulliver, and I have carried out long-term, intensive research on a small town (population 1,450 in 1991) and rural hinterland (population 600) in south-eastern Ireland. Over the years, we have spent numerous long summers, an autumn and two sabbatical years in this locale (Thomastown, County Kilkenny). We have accumulated extensive archival materials, semi-formal interview data and field notes from participant observation. It was in 1995, as I was filling out the ethics questionnaire in order to gain access to a new research grant, that I realised I was under suspicion. I therefore made an especial effort to explain to the non-anthropologists on the York sub-committee what it is that we do most of the time. I was pleased with my efforts (Case 1); so was the sub-committee. I was not only given research permission but I was commended for my clear and thoughtful statement. Thus did I allay the fears of vigilant outsiders and

116

define, through their idea of informed consent, the essence of ethical behaviour for anthropologists.

Case 1: 'Informed consent' in anthropology – a 1995 application

Anthropological fieldwork is premised on a mutual rapport which must develop between those who are doing the research and those whose society and culture are being studied. Usually, all the participants – anthropologists and locals – are adults. The relationship between them is mediated by mutual trust: a breach of such trust, by either side, destroys the rapport which sustains the research and may destroy the entire project. Anthropologists therefore must tread carefully, and always with respect for local and interpersonal mores. For the behaviour of the anthropologist is subject always, and continuously, to community approval.

In such a research context, formalising consent to a piece of paper or a formulaic recitation destroys what it is intended to protect. It does this, first, by breaching interpersonal etiquette because it questions the trust that must underlie the interpersonal relations on which the research is based. In other words, it removes the right of local people to consent to the research in the way in which they believe their consent ought to be given: by their intimacy and their participation with the anthropologist's work. Second, given that anthropological fieldwork is long-term and on-going, over months and even years, formal consent – whether written or verbal – at one point in time removes people's right to withdraw consent at a later time, and to deny their past involvement, if they later wish to do so. In effect, it disempowers people and leaves the way open for the abuse which the form was designed to prevent.

Thus, it is unwritten and non-formalised verbal consent which best typifies participant observation in anthropology. It means that people's consent must be renewed each day – through their continuing interaction with the researcher and the project, through their help, co-operation and assent. This is the accepted style and nature of ethical anthropological research. Phrased another way, anthropological research can only take place in the light of informed consent – given continuously, openly and graciously because we are behaving, and have behaved, properly.

Informed verbal consent: Crafting identities and rapport (unconsciously)

The sub-committee had agreed with me that 'continuity' and 'mutuality' underlay ethical anthropological research in terms of rapport, trust, respect, etiquette and rights. The lengthy questionnaire however, and the sub-committee's happy acquiescence, started me thinking about the implications of what I had written. Could I really behave so well? Had I? Was everyday life so transparent?[2]

Clearly not. My response, like the sub-committee's questionnaire, had been concerned with establishing parameters and practical rules. Despite being time-consuming, this exercise had been fairly easy. Life in the field, however, has been far more complicated: it has never been simply about codes and canons but about better or worse choices. What standards, criteria and norms did I in fact use when in the field? Why?

Identity formation as ethics and field technique

The recent anthropological concern with authority and representation has tended to ignore what one of my graduate students said (and what I have long felt) about fieldwork: 'When you're dependent on people for information which you desperately need to write a thesis, it's hard to believe that you're the one with the power. I have never felt so powerless in my life.' In Thomastown, County Kilkenny, even after two decades of 'being there', my sense of being dependent has never left me. In fact, it has become more complicated through time.

Initially, when Philip Gulliver and I first settled into Thomastown in mid-1980, local people[3] were concerned to discover 'who we were' — especially, as we were later told, after the tourist season had ended and we were still around. We explained to anyone who was interested or curious, or anyone we wanted to speak to, that we were Canadian university professors writing a history and description of the parish. This was understood and acceptable.[4] However, it only answered the question of *what* we were doing. It did not address the more fundamental and important question of *who* we were.

Thomastown people had long had experiences with 'outsiders': in-marrying spouses, in-coming migrants and notables, tourists, visitors, and so on. The result was that this category had little import in the locality. Instead, so-called outsiders were always assigned more nuanced identities. In Philip's case, he spoke with an English accent which several people, as a result of sojourns in England, had been able to trace to the Midlands. He clearly and explicitly wasn't a Catholic. Was Philip then a Protestant? Not really, as it gradually became obvious that he never attended services, that he did not enter the local Protestant network and that he professed, openly, to be an agnostic. Nor did he have any Irish 'connections' (kin). Philip, therefore, could be labelled a 'blow-in' — one of the many English who, over the years, had wandered into the area, stayed a while and then left, and whose political attitudes were suspect. Philip's 'outsideness' was known and knowable.

In contrast, I was Jewish. In 1980, I was the first Jew that the vast majority of people there had ever encountered. As one woman noted: 'I thought you were different. You're dark.' Seldom, if ever, did anyone take this further and express an interest in Jewish belief, practice or history or in my own ancestors' migratory past.[5] I was, simply put, exotic and strange – an 'other'. This was bolstered by my anomalous gender: I was in my mid-thirties and childless; I was a professional (confirmed by the post office delivering letters to Dr Silverman, not Mrs Gulliver); and not only did I lack crucial homemaking skills but I was never at home anyway. Even my one familiar feature, that I spoke with an 'American accent', was vociferously belied by my repetitious claim that Canadians were different.

In such ways, our outsider status became fixed as 'blow-in' and 'other'. Interestingly, these definitions gradually became part of our own sensibility as to who we ourselves were in Thomastown – as individuals and a couple and as anthropologists. On the one hand, it affected how we comported ourselves. Tales of the marital squabbles of other blow-ins from the past led us never to exchange a cross word with each other in public. Consciousness of Ireland's colonial past vis-à-vis England made us ultra-Canadian. So, when we brought forward in conversation our own experiences as analogies (e.g. about buying cars, weather, farming, road traffic and so on), we never used English examples, only Canadian ones. We colluded in being the butt of mild humour: 'Here come the Canadians, better turn on the heat.' I listened, always silently and sometimes painfully, to tales of privation and poverty, but was never asked about the pogroms and violence in my own mother's past. Awareness, too, of my incomplete role as a woman led me into several homes to learn how to bake amid unspoken amazement at my faulty education.

On the other hand, and at the same time, Philip and I slowly began, albeit only in part consciously, to use our identities as blow-in and other as a means for cutting through the formalities and privacies of much of local life and for establishing rapport, eliciting information and building the social life which would ease participant observation.[6] For example, we began inviting people to dinner in the evening – a very unusual way of socialising at the time. And we invited couples, in a world where the social activities of men and women were largely separate. We took long walks over farmers' fields in a rural space devoid of walking paths, hikers and country strollers. We met several (surprised) farmers that way and were rewarded with lengthy conversations. Most important, perhaps, in our visiting, talking on the street or in shops, and in simply being visible, we cut across the status–class and class barriers that comprised the socio-cultural map of the locality: we were seen by farmers as we spoke with farm labourers, by workers as we spoke with capitalists, by shopkeepers as we spoke with the elderly poor, by professionals as we talked with the unskilled. Our identities, as blow-in and other, gave us the freedom to bend conventions and to craft novel situations and relationships. We used this more and more consciously and unashamedly as time went on.

Reciprocity and confidentiality

Essential features which underlie social and cultural life in Thomastown are reciprocity and equivalence. These permeate all extra-household life, from the most accidental encounter to the most structured. From casual greetings on the street and comments about the weather, through to casual and thence intimate gossip, from pub behaviour to extending favours, gift-giving and proffering invitations, it is imperative for people to maintain a semblance of balanced exchange and both moral and material symmetry in all relationships and interactions. All local residents – natives, blow-ins and others alike – are invariably implicated in this behavioural code.

One of the most important exchange items which moved along local networks was gossip, shared in varying degrees with others according to a person's knowledge.[7] Most important was the fact that gossip was communicated according to an expectation of reciprocity. As anthropologists, we were seen entering and leaving homes, driving in a particular direction, talking to people, attending public functions, joining local clubs and associations. Who we became acquainted with, as well as what we were learning about the locality and its people, invariably became part of the gossip which circulated. Conversely, people approached us to learn what we might know. We had no professional or personal problem with being the objects of gossip. However, how far could we actively trade in this currency? How far could we afford not to?

To elicit information required that we provide information. How could this be done without breaching the promise of confidentiality which we continually emphasised? How could we even put information about ourselves into circulation by chatting with some people since this suggested a favouritism which might limit our access to others? After several months in the field, we found ourselves unable even to articulate to local people who else we had met. We had become closed-mouthed, unsociable and inaccessible.

We gradually came to realise, however, that in so doing, we had put another item into circulation which could be used in exchange for information. This was our promise of absolute confidentiality combined with our growing knowledge of the past. Through our archival work, we were collecting information which, we decided, could and should be shared with the people whose ancestors it concerned. We thus began to exchange genealogical knowledge and gossip about the past for information about the present as well as about the past. We became known as experts in local history and tracing 'connections' (genealogy) and, for most people, as unwilling to share any information except with those whose pasts and ancestors it concerned. This solution to the ethical dilemma had the unintended effect of adding to the pressures which were pushing us more and more into an exploration of Thomastown's past – as we mined for information to exchange, as we happily saw a way out of an ethical conundrum and, more importantly as time passed, as we ourselves became increasingly fascinated with that past.

During our early years of fieldwork, this exchange worked well. This does not mean that everyone spoke with us, that those who did shared more than the most superficial information, or that everyone came to trust our promise of privacy. It did mean, however, that we spent more and more time in archives and that our lives in the locality came to conform more and more closely to the segmentary model which an informant had once described for her own social world: 'There are those people I know to see', she said. 'Then there are those I chat with about the weather. There are then those I gossip with and, finally, there are a few who will tell me almost anything.' Invariably, and perhaps predictably, as we kept coming back to Thomastown over two decades, the most intimate zones began to yield up new moral contradictions. What happened, in other words, when informants became friends?

Escalating ethical choices

In mining for historical information about the Thomastown locality, we began to move from seeing data in terms of their exchange value to seeing the material as objects for detailed examinations of the processes of socio-cultural change, the political economy of domination and exploitation, the patterns of continuity and discontinuity over the *longue durée*. We quickly found that other local people, long attuned to the emphasis on history through various educative institutions, were also interested in Thomastown's past, usually as a matter of excavating facts or as antiquarian preservation. Over time, as we ourselves became more immersed in the past, many of the people whom we came to know best were those who also had a concern with history. Enter another ethical problem: how far should we share archival information with local historians? These historians had themselves often collected materials about the distant past (the nineteenth century or earlier) and sometimes had had access to sources no longer available. We thus began to share archival data, such as records of deeds and property conveyances, through multiple photocopies and carbon paper notes. This quickly became the norm. More recent materials – such as parochial records and civil registers of births and marriages in the latter half of the twentieth century, or probated wills – proved difficult.

However, anthropologists know that friendship ties can bear a good deal of imbalance. As Sahlins famously said: 'gifts make friends but friends make gifts'. Friendship, in other words, does not always depend on balanced exchange but can move towards a relation based on more generalised reciprocity. Thus, the longer we have remained in the field, and the more often we have come back to Thomastown, the more has the emphasis on balance slowly given way to more generalised exchanges with numerous people. We have become increasingly able to withhold what we deemed were sensitive archival data without ever having to explain explicitly that we were doing so. Local historians, our friends, came to know that we freely shared most materials but, when not sharing, we were not only respecting the privacy of others but also demonstrating that, equally, we would protect the privacy of our friends. Friendship and trust, alongside reciprocity, had thus allowed for boundaries to be drawn and expectations to be defined and respected in relation to archival materials.

In relation to gossip about contemporary people and events, our solution became easier as time went on. This was because, as we became more connected with local networks, we were more privy to common, public information. It was public because it always began with: 'Did you hear about ... ?' Thus, we happily exchanged this information, giving out what most people already knew. Conversely, we never spoke about those whom we had interviewed; we never passed on personal/private information; and we never even mentioned the names of people whom we knew or had interviewed or to whom we had spoken.

Most recently, however, such moral certainty has been undermined. The canons of long-term, intimate friendship (mutual visits across the ocean; wedding invitations; financial help) increasingly and invariably demand informality and the ever-more-loose exchange of information. This conflicts, many times a day when in Thomastown, with the need to retain the confidentiality of far less intimate others. Where does my professional self end/begin and my personal self begin/end? Can anthropologists really maintain intimate friends in the field site?

Informed verbal consent in everyday life in the field

Within the general context of the decisions which we made about the presentation of our public selves, inserting ourselves into local networks, and reciprocity and confidentiality, moral choices embedded in the minutiae of everyday life became relevant. First were the daily decisions which had to be confronted on the spur of the moment, and quickly, when we bumped into people casually. The second took place in more formal meetings which we arranged to visit people in their homes to talk to them about their family histories and enterprises (farm, shop, business) or to discuss their particular areas of expertise (e.g. the community council, workfare, trade unionism). Moral dilemmas in this setting could often be anticipated and choices made beforehand. This did not mean, however, that we always got it right.

Cases 2–5: Moral choices in everyday fieldwork

(2) Thomastown had a business enterprise which had evolved from an artisanal shop in the later nineteenth century into a factory and multiple

retail outlets after the Second World War. The current owner was a sociable man but, like all of Thomastown's shopkeepers, he 'kept himself to himself' and maintained firm control over the information which circulated about his business. We wanted to talk to him – about the history of his family's enterprise, his entrepreneurial strategies and whether and how he saw himself as a town notable. We already 'knew him' well enough to talk about the weather and casually gossip. Now, we wanted more. Our first few suggestions for a semi-formal meeting were deflected. How far should we pester him?

(3) While interviewing a farmer and his wife one evening, we were going through our usual array of topics – family-farm history, kinship relations and contemporary farming systems – when, arriving at a point in his family tree which required him to explain what had happened to his father's sister, he suddenly said: 'Don't write this down!' We ostentatiously put down our pens and he proceeded to explain how she had married a labourer 50 years before and had emigrated, never to be heard from since. Should we write down this information after we left him?

(4) While talking to another farmer and his family, our genealogical records indicated that his father's sister had had an illegitimate child 30 years before. Given the stigma which surrounded such births at the time, we decided that we would leave her out of the list of kin about whom we asked. As soon as we had finished our list, the farmer looked at us and said: 'You left out my aunt Mary. She lives in Waterford and has a shop.' We apologised for the oversight under the unblinking gaze of the entire family.

(5) One of the archives in which we worked was the Deeds Registry in Dublin. Minutes of all registered property conveyances, from 1830 on, are to be found there. Our use of this source became known after we published our first book (Silverman and Gulliver 1986). On a subsequent visit, we were approached by a middle-aged Thomastown woman who asked if we had found a record of her cottage being registered. We asked why. The answer was quickly forthcoming. She had lived with and taken care of her widowed mother for many years; her brother had emigrated 30 years before, leaving the two women to cope as best they could. Her mother had died recently without leaving a will. Her brother had now returned and claimed half the cottage. She could not afford a lawyer to check in the Deeds Registry but she needed to know if her mother had ever transferred the cottage to her, as she had once promised to do. Should we give her access to our records?

In effacing aunt Mary from the records according to one moral code (stigma), we had offended another value (family privacy). In continuing to pursue the businessman and finally catching him, we obtained some superb insights into Thomastown's commercial sector and into the transformation of an artisanal enterprise. In later writing down what we had been requested not to record (but red-circling it to remember for ever how we came by the information), we were able to fill in our own understanding of status–class endogamy in the locality. And by providing a woman with information which lay clearly in the public domain but which required an outlay of cash, we made the apparatus of the state less inaccessible.

All this, however, should not be seen as a recipe for contemporary research in Ireland or even in Thomastown today. Moralities, values and codes change continually; and they certainly have done so during the two decades during which we have been doing research in and about the locality. For example, the town's businessmen have become increasingly unapproachable, inaccessible and uninterested as, more and more, they have come from well beyond the locality and region. Status–class endogamy has been reproduced but, in so doing, the categories have been transformed as have the boundaries, beliefs and interactions which are maintained through them. Illegitimacy and a history of tuberculosis no longer deface a family's reputation. The Deeds Registry is now open to anyone who wants information about his/her own property.

These changing materialities and moralities mean that anthropologists who have been there for over two decades are still having to negotiate their ethics, every day.

Informed verbal consent: The ethics of (re)presentation

Researching among a highly literate, English-speaking population seemingly resolves one ethical issue by removing the boundary between writer (anthropologist) and reader (local people). Yet, this erasure – and the fact that Thomastown people can read anything that we write – brings to the fore, more than ever, the moral problems which surround presentation and representation, accessibility and inscription.

During our first and most intensive periods of fieldwork (sabbatical 1980–1; summer 1983), we had commonly told people that we were writing a book about Thomastown. Since the time-consuming work of writing is largely invisible and unknown to most non-writers, we were always being asked: 'When is the book coming out?'. In 1983, we had to decide whether to analyse our materials and write them up for an academic audience or to give precedence to the local one. Which audience had the stronger claim?

Our premise at the time was that we had two distinct audiences. We knew that what most local people hoped to read about was of little interest to anthropologists, and vice versa. Thomastown residents wanted to see the names of their parents and grandparents inscribed in a book, along with any (neutral) details (e.g. occupations, offices, accolades) that we had uncovered. They also wanted commonly known stories about local people wrought in ways that would capture their public personalities and quirks. What they did not want was academic jargon and anthropological theory. Nor did they want unbecoming details publicly inscribed. That Joe Reddy was 'a man of his times' – humorous and a story teller – should be recorded, but not the fact that, as everyone knew, it was his heavy drinking that underwrote his leisure time, humour and persona. That the 'shopkeeper Doyles were so mean that they'd chase a crow for a crust of bread' was equally well-known but not for publication. Seen analytically, what Thomastown people wanted were primary data – facts – about respectable people and respectable facts about all people. Thus, even before it was written, our book had been appropriated by many locals as part of their own public representation of their selves.

We eventually decided to write our first book primarily for a Thomastown audience, largely to fulfil our promise as quickly as possible and to return what had been given to us. It also seemed a good way of easing ourselves into our data.[8] In making this choice, we also had to make two compromises. First, the book (1986) had little that was theoretically explicit and, therefore, little that would interest anthropologists outside Ireland.[9] Second, to avoid offending anyone, we wrote largely about the more distant past, barely venturing beyond the Second World War. What did we gain? A lot of goodwill and legitimacy. But we were also academics, concerned with anthropological theory and debate. We thus published other pieces (Gulliver 1989, 1992; Silverman 1989b, 1993, 1995, 2000; Silverman and Gulliver 1996, 1997) in locations not easily knowable or available to Thomastown people, except for a few close friends to whom we gave copies of some of our work. So far, so good: two audiences (local vs. anthropological), two genres (detailed empiricism vs. analytical ethnography), and two locations (local vs. limited availability).

However, a local history and articles are, relatively speaking, small pieces of work. What were we to do when we wrote lengthy, labour-intensive, analytical anthropological books? Could or should Thomastown people be excluded from accessing such a major endeavour about themselves because of its academic language, limited availability or content? Clearly not. What did this mean? First, we thought about the common tactic of changing all names; but we knew that local people would quickly de-code this. In any case, they wanted to know about people, both past and present. Second, we thought that perhaps we could be cautious in what we included and avoid certain topics. But could we really? How does one write about inheritance patterns without mentioning disputes? The code of respectability without stigma (illegitimacy, alcoholism, disease)? Capitalist enterprises without exploitation? Class relations without antagonism? Gender without violence? Social relations without ostracism? Religious belief without hegemony? Third, how could we theorise about, for example, the petty bourgeoisie, class and world systems (Gulliver and Silverman 1995), and about hegemony and power (Silverman 2001a), without alienating local readers? Finally, perhaps if we stuck to the more distant past, potentially unpalatable names and events could be avoided? Yet, the whole point of writing in the genre of historical anthropology was to explain how the past led into the present (Silverman and Gulliver 1992a and 1992b). Thus, as we contemplated writing academic books, the dilemmas inherent in presentation and representation emerged dramatically, especially as we also tried to factor out paternalistic, over-protective sentiments from a genuine fear of doing harm or of breaching the tenets of confidentiality which, we believed, covered data obtained from historical sources as well as from participant observation and interviews.[10]

Our solutions were as follows. We decided that all topics and theories which had anthropological relevance should be included. However, we also began to develop a 'textual strategy', initially in *Merchants and Shopkeepers* (1995) and then in *An Irish Working Class* (2001a). This strategy allowed parallel readings of the text. Taking the 2001 volume as an example, I put all primary data (extracts of documents, anecdotes, and so on), unanalysed, inside demarcated 'cases'.[11] Enough to constitute a local history on their own, the 167 cases in the 2001 volume can be, and are being, read as such by Thomastown people.[12] We also decided to use real names unless the data or the tales were compromising. What, though, was compromising? Some decisions were clear: the general lack of charitable impulse among shopkeepers or the stigma of alcoholism could not be illustrated using the name of Doyle or Reddy. However, most cases were not as clear; and we found no simple rules. We came, frankly, to depend on our instincts which, in turn, were informed by many years of 'being there'. Even so, as the examples in the next set of case studies illustrate, we can never hope to get it right all the time.

Cases 6–8: Ethical questions of (re)presentation

(6) In *An Irish Working Class* (2001a), I traced the history of radical politics among workers during the 1930s and 1940s. Among the activists were several who were communists. At the time, the stigmatisation was intense. The adults were ostracised and threatened, their children were taunted, the families were denounced from the pulpit. In the book, I changed the names of the families. I knew that elderly local people would know who they were but I thought that young people and, especially, outsiders should be kept in ignorance. The response: members of the present generation of the families were divided. Those who saw the past as heroic wanted their parents named; those who saw the past as compromising current respectability did not. Who should decide?

(7) In *Merchants and Shopkeepers* (1995), we presented, in Chapter 12, detailed descriptions of three shop premises in the town in order to explore the dynamics of retailing through the nineteenth and twentieth centuries. Our data came both from archival sources and from interviews. Together, the cases touched on marriages of convenience, elopements, disappearing dowries,

familial disputes, bankruptcies, alcoholism, improvidence, religious conversion (Catholic to Protestant), marital squabbles, stepfather–stepson altercations. Such features could not be censored, for they, among others, were crucial to patterns of enterprise continuity (inheritance)–discontinuity (sale). The names of families could not be changed; everyone knew who they were. Was there any room for ethical choice here?[13]

(8) Since publishing *In the Valley of the Nore* (1986), we have felt morally obliged to continue writing articles for local and regional historical journals (Gulliver and Silverman 1993; Silverman 1989a, 1990, 1991, 1992a and 1992b, 1994, 1998, 2001b). Thomastown people, such as students writing papers, shopkeepers preparing a brochure, local journalists seeking background information, have mined these works for facts about the locality. So, too, have local historians who have then published our material, often verbatim, in their articles. Our publications are never cited as the sources in these cases. In other words, our work has been appropriated. Should we say something?

Conclusions

When teaching students, whether graduate or undergraduate, over the past 30 years, I have always been struck by the fact that they find the subject of ethics so fascinating. Nothing will get seminar discussion moving more quickly, and encourage more participation, than putting forward a so-called ethical dilemma, such as the ones in Cases 1 to 8 above. I have long pondered this. Is it because anthropology students are particularly sensitised? Is it because moral choices are intellectually or emotionally jarring? What is clear to me, however, is that the kind of auditing which is being done by institutions such as York University has little to do with anthropological practice.

In this article, I have tried to illustrate the profound differences between institutional audits and discourse, phrased at York as 'informed consent', and the experiences of being in the field and of writing up. The former is about rules, standards and formalities which will neatly fit all research projects and keep liability at bay. Yet even when approached through anthropological discourse, such as mutuality, rapport, trust, respect, etiquette and rights, the audit fails to come near my own experiences of everyday moral choices which underlie my anthropological practice. Nor are ethics in anthropology about the stark choices which must be made at dramatic moments and which are beloved of students: do you tell the police if you know that murder will be committed that night?

Instead, everyday ethics is about crafting a persona and identity that will mutually engage both the researcher and the people, without doing damage to either. Then, it is about the continual need for choices, each day. It is about ambiguity, conflicting interests, fine lines, judgement calls and, therefore, about awkward decisions. This means that every research site is different, as is the personal style which every anthropologist brings to the field.

I do not believe that the new culture of accountability or the recent reflexive and post-colonial turns have altered ethical anthropological practice in any real way; at least they haven't done so for me. I cannot recall behaving differently in my earlier field projects in rural Guyana (1969–73) or coastal Ecuador (1978–9). I also do not recall that we, as graduate students in the late 1960s, spoke about ethics in ways that were very different from those spoken of today. What has happened is that the language has changed and some important issues have been lost, such as questions about 'clean' funding for research and how our research helps the material conditions of people among whom we work. Thus, within the strictures carved in stone – 'do no harm and do not cheat' – our discourse spoke of honesty and openness in our explanations of who we were, what we were doing and from where our research funds were coming. We were to 'respect differences' and 'withhold judgements'. This older discourse also included the need to make our 'findings' available to all and, ideally but importantly, to make these findings 'relevant' to informants' lives. We were to be givers as well as takers. Now that we 'produce data' rather than 'collect' them, 'represent' rather than 'present our findings', and 'appropriate' rather than 'give', have our everyday moral lives in the field really changed? Have our choices become simpler?[14]

Like my graduate student who mentioned her abject sense of powerlessness in the field, I too think that the dependence of anthropologists on the people among whom we work needs highlighting here, for this too has moral implications. It is therefore useful, when exploring everyday ethics, also to reflect on how dependence has framed the 20-year trajectory of our work. Succinctly put, our concern not to offend, to do no harm in a field site in which English was the working language, has pushed us towards exploring more of the past and away from documenting the present. Equally, our concern to make our work accessible to a local audience has had a similar impact, given the very clear interests of Thomastown people in reading about their pasts as distinct from their present. However, as I now write up materials for which the above-described research permission was granted in 1995 – to explore socio-economic change in Thomastown since Ireland joined the the European Economic Community in 1973 – I have also decided that I will do this in a way which is relevant for anthropologists rather than for a local audience. To write about the present, I will hide informants and agents, be sparing with the empirical examples, build theory. Having done so much to make our work accessible so much of the time, am I ethically correct in not doing so this time?

For me, anthropology is, every day and with every decision, a 'moral discipline'.

Notes

1 Originating in the 1980s, the present manifestation of this sub-committee is now more formal and extensive in its coverage and more coercive in its demands.

2 It also got me thinking about the behaviour of others who had worked in Ireland. For example, I recall being horrified at the disingenuousness of Mart Bax's comments about how he had sometimes used a hidden tape-recorder during interviews and how this impacted on later rapport (Bax 1976: 5). The present chapter is premised, perhaps naively, on the assumption that all anthropologists follow fundamental ethical guidelines which, certainly in my own experience, have been part of graduate education since the late 1960s. These were simple edicts: do no harm and do not cheat. That even these stark rules could raise ethical dilemmas in some volatile or extreme contexts is further proof of the complexity of moral behaviour in the field.

3 I use the term 'Thomastown people' or 'local people' in a colloquial and indeterminate way. Residents of Thomastown – an unbounded area (of town and rural hinterland) – are neither homogeneous nor all acquainted with each other. These qualities of local life are discussed in Gulliver and Silverman 1990.

4 Note that we refrained from defining ourselves as 'anthropologists'. First, we already knew from our readings about the public and political importance of the Irish historiographic tradition and how it had long been disseminated through the educative organs of society (e.g. schools, voluntary associations, church). To be 'historians', to do history, was valued. Second, in addition to the fact that few people actually knew what anthropology was, to be anthropologists at this time in Ireland was a problem. We were there during an altercation in the national press between Scheper-Hughes, as an 'anthropologist', and Michael Viney, a regular *Irish Times* columnist, over whether Scheper-Hughes' (1979) book had 'betrayed' the people in her village because of its focus on schizophrenia and economic decline and because she failed to protect sufficiently the identities and feelings of her informants (Kane 1979; Viney 1980; Scheper-Hughes 1981; Komito 1982). The debate entered the anthropological record through RAIN (Kane 1982; Scheper-Hughes 1982; Nixon 1983). Because we were doing political economy – that is, how the past informs the present – we felt justified in speaking of ourselves as 'doing history and contemporary description'. The debate around anthropology in Ireland continued for some time and came to incorporate Messenger's ethnography (1969) as well as that of Viney (1983). This altercation and debate became another strand of experience propelling us to privilege the past in our research. However, we had decided, long before arriving in Ireland, that we did not want to study 'the West'. For a discussion of this see Silverman and Gulliver 1992b.

5 A lack of interest in, or a denial of, a past and a history is, of course, a key feature in defining an 'other'.

6 I think that it was the combined identities of 'blow-in' and 'other' which worked so well for us. To some extent, Philip could overcome the blemish of his Englishness in an Irish context by his association with me; I, in turn, could be rendered more familiar through my marriage to Philip.

7 As we described in Gulliver and Silverman (1990), items of gossip are neither universally nor equally distributed in all segments of local networks. Instead, knowledge depends on physical proximity, class, occupation, gender, age and so on. This is why gossip – defined here as the transmission of information, whether known or putative – is so important. It is a scarce, and unevenly distributed, commodity.

8 By 1983, we had accumulated huge amounts of data of various kinds. The problems of sorting and accessing them are discussed in Gulliver 1989.

9 In Silverman and Gulliver 1992b, we described our theoretical journey in relation to our Thomastown research. We showed how, in our 1986 local history book, we had altered the dominant Irish historiographic agenda by exploring topics, events and categories of people which had been ignored. We did so without explicitly noting this. Thus, the reviews of

the book by academics tended to laud its value as 'people's history at its most refreshing and humane' (Kennedy 1987) but, quite rightly, criticised its 'lack of theoretical overview or general interpretation' (Donnan 1987). Within the politics of the academy, and its modes of assessing scholarship, such reviews are construed negatively. This raises questions about the ethical choices which we make as academics when we evaluate the outcome of our ethical choices.

10 We had, very early on, dispensed with the idea of using a pseudonym for Thomastown itself. Some anthropologists in Ireland had done this. The result was that, years later, we were unable to bring their data up to date, or even to use their data, for comparative purposes (see Gulliver 1992: 193–6). In an anthropological world where paradigms and theories change rapidly, old ethnographies become more useful for their data than for their theoretical ruminations. To obscure those data by hiding the regional and national location of a locale seems foolish. In any case, Thomastown people were proud to have a book about themselves; they wanted 'to put the town on the map'.

11 Cases 2, 3 and 4 in this chapter illustrate this textual method.

12 This is different from the use of 'apt illustration' and the 'case method' which was common in the 1960s. Although the outcome may seem similar, the motives are very different. This textual strategy does result in long books, however: *An Irish Working Class* (2001a) is 566 pages in length. For many, then, this ethical solution is obviated by the economics of publishing.

13 As a final comment here: no one in Thomastown that we know of has objected to any of this material.

14 I am not discussing here the new and often exciting topical or analytical ideas which have emerged from postmodern and post-colonial studies. I am querying how we behave, ethically, in everyday life in relation to the people among whom we work.

Bibliography

Bax, Mart (1976) *Harpstrings and Confessions: Machine-Style Politics in the Irish Republic*, Amsterdam: Van Gorcum.

Donnan, Hastings (1987) 'Review of *In the Valley of the Nore*', *Man* 22 (2): 381.

Gulliver, P.H. (1989) 'Doing Anthropological Research in Rural Ireland: Methods and Sources for Linking the Past and the Present', in C. Curtin and T. Wilson (eds) *Ireland from Below: Social Change and Local Communities*, Galway: Galway University Press.

— (1992) 'Shopkeepers and Farmers in South Kilkenny, 1840–1981', in Marilyn Silverman and P.H. Gulliver (eds) *Approaching the Past: Historical Anthropology through Irish Case Studies*, New York: Columbia University Press.

Gulliver, P.H. and Silverman, M. (1990) 'Social Life and Local Meaning: "Thomastown", County Kilkenny', in W. Nolan and K. Whelan (eds) *County Kilkenny: History and Society*, Dublin: Geography Publications.

— (1993) 'Hucksters and Petty Retailers in Thomastown, 1880–1945', *Old Kilkenny Review*, 4: 5.

— (1995) *Merchants and Shopkeepers: An Historical Anthropology of an Irish Market Town*, 1200–1986, Toronto: University of Toronto Press.

Kane, Eileen (1979) 'Is Rural Ireland Blighted?' *Irish Press* (Dublin), 13 November.

— (1982) '*Cui Bono? Do Aon Duine*', RAIN 50 (June).

Kennedy, Liam (1987) 'Review of *In the Valley of the Nore*', *Economic and Social History*, p.123.

Komito, Lee (1982) 'Reply to Ballybran,' Letter to the Editor, *The Irish Times* (Dublin), 16 March.

Messenger, John C. (1969) *Inis Beag: Isle of Ireland*, New York: Holt, Rinehart and Winston.

Nixon, Paul (1983) 'Social Anthropology in Ireland', RAIN 54 (February) 12–13.

Scheper-Hughes, Nancy (1979) *Saints, Scholars and Schizophrenics: Mental Illness in Rural Ireland*, Berkeley: University of California Press.

— (1981) 'Reply to "Ballybran"', *The Irish Times* (Dublin), 21 February.

— (1982) 'Ballybran', RAIN 51 (August) 12–13.

Silverman, Marilyn (1989a) 'Doing Local History in County Kilkenny: An Index to the Probate Court Papers, 1858–1883', *Old Kilkenny Review*, 4: 1, 625–49.

— (1989b) '"A Labouring Man's Daughter": Constructing "Respectability" in South Kilkenny', in C. Curtin and T. Wilson (eds) *Ireland from Below: Social Change and Local Communities*, Galway: Galway University Press.

— (1990) 'The Non-agricultural Working Class in Nineteenth Century Thomastown', in William Murphy (ed.) *In the Shadow of the Steeple* II, Duchas-Tullaherin Parish Heritage Society.

— (1991) 'The Probate Court Papers for County Kilkenny: 1858–1883, Part II', *Old Kilkenny Review*, 4: 3, 900–15.

— (1992a) 'From Kilkenny to the Sea – By River, Canal, Tram or Rail? The Politics of Transport in the Early Nineteenth Century', *Old Kilkenny Review*, 4: 4, 988–1011.

— (1992b) 'The Voices of Conflict: The Inland Salmon Fishery of the River Nore, 1911', in William Murphy (ed.) *In the Shadow of the Steeple* III, Duchas-Tullaherin Parish Heritage Society.

— (1993) 'An Urban Place in Rural Ireland, 1841–1989: An Historical Ethnography of Domination', in Chris Curtin, Hastings Donnan and Thomas Wilson (eds), *Irish Urban Cultures*, Belfast: Institute of Irish Studies Press.

— (1994) 'A Tragedy from 1871: A Study of Stigma, Poverty and Alienation', in William Murphy (ed.) *In the Shadow of the Steeple* IV, Duchas-Tullaherin Parish Heritage Society.

— (1995) 'The "Inhabitants" vs. the Sovereign: An Historical Ethnography of the Making of the "Middle Class" in an Irish Corporate Borough, 1840–1', in Pat Caplan (ed.) *Understanding Disputes: The Politics of Argument*, London: Berg.

— (1998) 'Thomas Fitzanthony's Borough: Medieval Thomastown in Irish History, 1171–1555', in William Murphy (ed.) *In the Shadow of the Steeple* V, Duchas-Tullaherin Parish Heritage Society.

— (2000) 'Custom, Courts and Class Formation: Constructing the Hegemonic Process through the Petty Sessions of a Southeastern Irish Parish, 1828–1884', *American Ethnologist*, 27 (2): 1–31.

— (2001a) *An Irish Working Class: Explorations in Political Economy and Hegemony, 1800–1950*, Toronto: University of Toronto Press.

— (2001b) 'The Borough of Thomastown in Irish History, 1520–1652', in William Murphy (ed.) *In the Shadow of the Steeple* VI, Duchas-Tullaherin Parish Heritage Society.

Silverman, Marilyn and P.H. Gulliver (1986) *In the Valley of the Nore: A Social History of Thomastown, County Kilkenny, 1840–1983*, Dublin: Geography Publications.

— (1992a) *Approaching the Past: Historical Anthropology through Irish Case Studies*, New York: Columbia University Press.

— (1992b) 'Historical Anthropology and the Ethnographic Tradition: A Personal, Historical and Intellectual Account', in Marilyn Silverman and P.H. Gulliver (eds) *Approaching the Past: Historical Anthropology through Irish Case Studies*, New York: Columbia University Press.

— (1996) 'Inside Historical Anthropology: Scale Reduction and Context', *FOCAAL – Journal for Anthropology*, 26/27, Special Issue on *Historical Anthropology: The Unwaged Debate*, 149–58.

— (1997) 'Historical Verities and Verifiable History: Locality-based Ethnography and the Great Famine in Southeastern Ireland', *Europaea*, III (2): 141–70.

Viney, Michael (1980) 'Geared for a Gale: Viney's Irish Journey', *The Irish Times* (Dublin), 24 September.

— (1983) 'The Yank in the Corner: Why the Ethics of Anthropology are a Worry for Rural Ireland', *The Irish Times* (Dublin), 6 August.

7

'TO TELL OR NOT TO TELL?'

Ethics and secrecy in anthropology and childbearing in rural Malawi

Gill Barber

Introduction

The chapter is about ethics and secrecy, confidentiality and disclosure, the issues that arose in my fieldwork in rural Malawi, and how they were handled. I experienced the issues discussed here as dilemmas and they provide the opportunity for an exploration of the ethics of anthropological research, specifically concentrating on secret and concealed knowledge. There appears to be limited evidence in the literature indicating anthropologists' approaches to these tensions, and little specific guidance even in codes of practice. Furthermore, in this fieldwork two very different professions came together and I take the opportunity to reflect on my position as both midwife and anthropologist, the potential disparity between the two and whether their differing ethical stances can be reconciled.

Before discussing the wider issues of disclosure and anthropology, I describe my pre-fieldwork concerns and fears and how I set about addressing them, and look at the background that constructed fieldwork as potentially problematic for me. As Corey *et al.* (1988) suggest, consideration of personal values and why they are held is vital for ethical decision-making. I next consider the dichotomies between the two systems of medicine encountered and the two codes of practice. The traditional village midwives are then introduced, with analysis of what happened and my response.

The concept of secrecy, and more specifically confidentiality, anonymity and the question about whether to tell or not to tell links three areas of exploration for this chapter. One is a reflexive personal account of experience, the second considers my evidence and what it revealed, and the third describes how the anthropologist's dilemma is lived and resolved. Ultimately it is about the politics of whistle-blowing.

The community in which fieldwork was conducted is very poor, with most people undertaking subsistence agriculture on land that is becoming increasingly deforested and overused. The threat of hunger is never far away. The people are of Lomwe, Yao or Ngoni origin and are predominantly Roman Catholic, Seventh-Day Adventist or Muslim. The community is strongly matrilineal with inheritance through the female line and matrilocal residence. Many households are female-headed. The area is located some 20 kilometres from a southern urban area of Malawi and served by a well-respected mission hospital and several schools.

My main fieldwork was carried out with three traditional midwives known as 'traditional birth attendants' (TBAs) in international terminology, *azamba* in the chiChewa translation. Often dismissed in scientific literature as illiterate and unlikely to practise safely and hygienically, many women continue to use the services of these midwives in the context of inadequate access to acceptable 'skilled' biomedical care. Unlike 'professional' midwives who have studied on statutory national training programmes to enable them to take legal responsibility for the full care of healthy mothers and babies, traditional midwives generally have been prepared by an apprenticeship (often to their mothers) and some, in recent times, have received a programme of short government training. Their effectiveness in caring safely for women is partly ensured by regular professional supervision and updating. Women themselves almost always select such midwives and an additional aspect of their legitimacy is that they have themselves given birth.

A final introductory note concerns the current maternal health context: women die in vastly greater numbers in poorer countries, a 'natural' disaster commonly equated to the loss every four hours of a loaded jumbo jet. In Malawi as many as one woman in 20 currently dies through childbearing despite extensive efforts, and the situation, both there and globally, shows no improvement, almost certainly because of increasing deprivation and HIV and AIDS. The global focus is now on skilled care and emergency support, including transport and the quality of service provision, but this policy pays minimal attention to the context in which women live and in which choices are made. The fieldwork that is the subject of this chapter was therefore designed to explore the concepts, knowledge and notions of risk that influence decision-making around childbearing.

Anticipation and reality: The fieldwork – reconciling differences

Before leaving for the field I experienced many qualms about how I would act if a childbirth situation arose that disturbed me. I also anticipated conflicts in people's expectations of me.

What was I to do if I did not like what I saw happening to birthing women? This question is, of course, loaded with assumptions but relates to my attempt to integrate two potentially dissonant personae, the midwife and the anthropologist. How far would I take my awareness that western concepts of medicine did not have all the answers for birthing women and were inadequate as explanatory paradigms for human experience? I expected local birthing practices to be different from those in the UK yet knew that evidence for making judgements was limited. I must 'think on my feet'.

I planned to spend much of my time with *azamba* and in more anxious pre-fieldwork moments thought about how I might act. Would I ever need to intervene in a birth? Worst-case scenarios were witnessing internal manipulations and pulling on the unborn baby, or the application of substances such as cow-dung and pummelling on the woman's abdomen to speed up the birth, all known practices that I had encountered elsewhere. Less anticipated was being privy to secret knowledge but I anticipated needing to be circumspect towards the local authorities. I needed their cooperation and views but was wary of causing doors to close on me if informants suspected I was reporting back.

This perhaps indicates more concern over the consequences of a loss of trust than with the ethics of confidentiality. In fact I found local people to have rather optimistic expectations of my relationships with health service staff – advocacy was expected of me even to government level. Nevertheless confidences and privileged information could be problematic and it was eventually this that caused me more worry than any need to intervene. I had also to take responsibility for the ethical conduct of my interpreters. News travels fast in a small community and I knew attempts at manipulation were possible.

Plummer (1983) believes exploitation and betrayal of subjects to be a crucial ethical issue. I was aware of the potential for harm to my informants and took account of Homans' warning that social researchers could be held accountable for harm 'only at their peril – proceeding without reckoning the likely consequences and implications of their work' (1991: 176).

The issue of secrecy

The theme of secrecy emerged unexpectedly. Many people in Malawi live in fear of being bewitched, often by a jealous neighbour or relative, and may therefore go to great lengths to conceal their property. Improving one's house or harvesting a high-yield crop may lead either to being bewitched or to an accusation of having profited by witchcraft. I was acutely aware of my own potential for precipitating jealousy and learned to be discreet, particularly when providing material assistance. Furthermore, fear of witchcraft makes some women reluctant to divulge their labours or to seek help if problems arise. Another important area of secrecy that emerged in this context concerned the influence of marital infidelity during pregnancy on the progress of labour. The concept that infidelity by the woman or her husband can lead to obstructed labour – a highly dangerous situation when the infant cannot be born – is well known in southern and central Africa. The secrecy element lies in the use of 'telling' the names of sexual partners in order to free up the birth. Waiting for such confession may lead to serious delays in seeking help, compounded in some mainly patrilineal areas by the desire of older kin to monitor the length of labour at home as an indicator of faithfulness. Problems in childbearing may also be seen as the result of bewitching, as happened to Gladys whom I introduce later.

Secrecy has several elements; significant among these is the secret knowledge of women. I gleaned some information by asking how women learned about childbirth now, and saw many tantalising glimpses of the past in people's narratives of 'going to the river' and the 'old ways' of preparing pre-pubertal girls for womanhood and young women for marriage, especially when women danced. (See Plate 7.1.) The overall view was that such ways have now gone for most people, or are practised only in an attenuated form. Wavering on the edge of the ethical issues around anthropological curiosity and the need to know, I finally did not take up an offer to be told the secrets of the old-style initiation of girls which appeared to be largely a discourse on sexuality.

People do not talk publicly about initiation, and their reticence is indicated by the use of the 'going to the river' euphemism. If I had pressed for more information, or taken up the offer made on one occasion, I would then have had to decide what to do with the knowledge. Those who offered to tell me were a group of older women who hugely enjoyed our interview sessions. Would others be as happy for me to know? Would they themselves like to see it written down and perhaps published? What end other than

Plate 7.1 Village *azamba* dancing with other women

curiosity, amounting almost to intellectual voyeurism and ambition to publish, would justify making secret knowledge public?

The secret information that concerned me most had regard to the activities of the *azamba* which I explore in detail later. Should I divulge these or not? The issue was 'to tell or not to tell' both the local supervisor and a wider audience, the latter through the written word. I eventually understood that their activities were not only universally recognised in the neighbourhood, but were instrumental in attracting some of their clients. Matters of confidentiality and anonymity nevertheless still arose about who should know and what should be known. In the end my decision-making was heavily influenced by my initial motivation, which was to explore lesser-known areas of women's lives that influenced what happened to them in childbirth. As a midwife this aim could not be formulated only for curiosity or to add to the global knowledge bank, but indeed for some fairly vague notion of sensitising policy-makers in the hope that women's lives could be ameliorated and the risks they face lessened. The matter of the *azamba*'s herbal armoury was intrinsic to my exploration of the knowledge that governs action in the community, hence I decided that guarding the anonymity of the *azamba* was adequate and that I could publish what I had discovered about their activities.

Before considering what really happened, I need to locate myself in the encounter between two worlds, my familiar world of midwifery and 'the other' as an anthropologist in the field.

Two systems of medicine: Western and local

I trained when home birth was still a common option but hospital birth and medical control was on the ascendant though still comparatively 'low-tech'. I much preferred the relative freedom and rewarding relationships of community practice. Working subsequently in Senegal I failed dismally to get to know local people. My knowledge of local healers and midwives was minimal and my attitudes probably as dismissive as those of my Senegalese colleagues.

I returned eventually to the UK to fit back in with difficulty. Becoming pregnant myself concentrated my mind and I realised I did not want the increasingly medicalised birth that many of my clients were experiencing. I covertly attended natural childbirth classes and picked my own midwife carefully. Mentored by a colleague and influenced by the then leading thinkers on the subject such as Leboyer, Odent and Kitzinger, I soon became a 'radical' midwife, a natural childbirth teacher and eventually a lecturer in midwifery.

So I was already poised uncomfortably between two ways of knowing, raised in the confident atmosphere of the western biomedical paradigm, but aware that alternatives were possible, perhaps even preferable. British midwifery was moving towards peaceful births, in the presence of trusted companions, the avoidance of interference and learning from other cultures. But where should the line be drawn about learning from other ways? Few would doubt the danger of rolling a pounding stick on a labouring woman's abdomen to speed the birth. But the effectiveness of herbal remedies and everyday substances such as Coca-Cola (a Malawian remedy for anaemia) is rarely evaluated. The need for fast action if a woman bleeds heavily is probably undisputed anywhere, but what if a local herb is more effective in stopping heavy bleeding than a long journey to hospital on bad roads, maybe on the back of a bike? It was possible that intervention on my part could itself jeopardise women's safety in some circumstances. How would I determine the wisest action when conducting anthropological research in this unfamiliar environment?

Biomedical accounts of birth are woefully inadequate on their own as explanation for what women experience. Who knows what influence it may have if a woman stands at a crossroads or in a doorway, braids her hair tightly, is 'tied' by a witch or knows her husband has been 'going around with girls' (a not uncommon scenario in Malawi with the celibacy expected of a couple in later pregnancy). Such ideas and their remedies of unbinding and confession are linked in Malawi and further afield with prolonged labour. Influences on the well-being of mother, baby and husband are constant themes in Malawian discourse. Particular emphasis is laid on danger and vulnerability, resulting from imbalances of ritual hot and cold status with their links to moral behaviour and social control. It is plausible that such beliefs, with the attendant fear and its resolution, could influence hormone levels and be self-fulfilling. Yet such a supposition inevitably demonstrates the strength of my biomedical roots as I seek physiological explanations for phenomena, something I found myself doing constantly in the field.

On arrival in Malawi I found a well-developed western-model health service with the informal integration of local forms of therapy. Malawians of all educational levels may turn to traditional healers (sing'anga) alongside formal health care. According to Morris (1998) healers' emphasis lies in using animal and plant material although diviners and sorcerers may also be consulted. Forster's work on religion, magic, witchcraft and AIDS demonstrates the attribution of many diseases to spirits, and shows that the relationship between spirits, witchcraft, sorcery and biological disease is a complex one.

The multi-layered and intermingled nature of local therapeutic systems goes deeper than the mere choice of western-trained medical or 'African' doctors in that sing'anga and azamba, both of whom may act as healers and midwives, themselves use old and new systems simultaneously. Indeed the heavy use of plant remedies which have pharmacological properties suggests a strong biomedical element to the herbalist's knowledge as well as the intrinsic powers described by Morris and the close link between animal substances and the spirit world (1998).

If Malawians could reconcile such differences and move freely between aetiologies and therapies, would I be able to reconcile the forms of care I might observe and, more pertinently, the different professional ethical demands?

Both anthropology and midwifery have codes of practice and guidelines. Would they help me to decide how to act?

Two codes of practice: Anthropology and midwifery

As a UK-registered midwife I am accountable for my practice in whatever environment I find myself. 'In all circumstances, the safety and welfare of the mother and baby are of primary importance' states the Midwives Rules and Code of Practice (UKCC 1998). I would not be entitled to practice in Malawi and in any case I was not there for that purpose, but people might not see it that way and thus I could still be held accountable. The UK code was familiar to midwives in Malawi (Msowoya, personal communication) and the International Code of Ethics for Midwives expects the same of midwives anywhere (International Confederation of Midwives 2000). This encourages respect for cultural diversity while 'working to eliminate harmful practices'. There is no doubt that the interests of mothers and babies, or even the dignity and privacy of individuals such as traditional midwives could never be subordinated to research interests. But what would be in the best interests of mothers and babies and what were harmful practices? This was not as easy to answer.

Still concerned about these issues, I talked them through with the supervisor designated for me by the University of Malawi on behalf of the Ministry of Health. He advised me that the Ministry Ethics Committee approval safeguarded me for either acting in an emergency or choosing to hold back; such dilemmas were well understood.

Yet I considered that even these midwifery codes and the promise of support for my decisions could not determine the appropriate action for me. Could the anthropology codes help?

The latest *Ethical Guidelines* of the Association of Social Anthropologists (1999) articulates the primacy of the interests of research subjects and the need to reconsider the project if this could not be ensured. Confidentiality and anonymity were addressed, the honouring of trust and protection of research subjects. Like the codes for midwives, these guidelines were inevitably general; they were not intended as sets of rules to determine behaviour, but rather as support for decision-making that respects the individuals concerned. They recognise that the researcher's own judgement is necessary, and that this should include regard to the potential outcome, which is situational ethics. As Lewis (2000), an anthropologist with a medical background, found, the point of intervention cannot be determined before the watershed is reached. I knew I would be sensitive to potential for harm and disturbance, and for me the problem was more about identifying that watershed.

I was able to identify differences and similarities in the codes. Common themes are not surprising when codes are based on the same theories of utilitarianism and duty, and the principles of beneficence, autonomy, and avoidance of harm and exploitation. Themes of exploitation are perhaps most evident in the anthropology guidance, perhaps with good reason when the potential is so great for using people with no reciprocal benefit accruing. Research will often serve the interests of the researcher or sponsors more than that of the researched. This applies too within health care but there the client or patient relationship should provide a degree of protection for the latter, notwithstanding the potential power differential between health professionals and their patients. In addition, the health care researcher is perhaps less likely to be isolated from the gaze of peers than is the anthropologist. In the midwifery and nursing codes, there is such a strong emphasis on the duty of care that exploitation hardly features except regarding avoidance of the abuse of privileged relationships with clients and exploitation for commercial gain (UKCC 1992). Inevitably, the strongest emphasis is on doing good. The potential for exploitation in research is addressed more specifically by the Royal College of Nursing (RCN) guidelines, which discuss implications for patients (1993), although these do not have the weight of statutory authority behind them as do the codes of the United Kingdom Central Council (for Nurses, Midwives and Health Visitors) (UKCC).

In both professions autonomy is a common thread. In the anthropological literature (ASA 1999 and AAA 1998) autonomy mainly concerns informed consent to taking part in research and disclosure of information and identity. The midwifery codes address the autonomy of women in making informed choices about care, a prevailing theme in Britain for some years. The RCN code acknowledges the ambiguities and dissonance between research and caring roles while emphasising the importance of knowledge generation. It recommends that intervention by researchers be confined to protection or rescue unless the researcher is employed as carer. Nothing is said about reporting malpractice, the problem that was to emerge for me, but the emphasis on anonymity and the confidentiality of privileged information is strong. The UKCC (1998) ambiguously advises disclosure as sometimes justifiable 'in the wider public interest' and supports the reporting of circumstances that 'jeopardise standards of practice'. The RCN (1993) recognises the potential of research for revealing 'deviations' from normal practice, recommending remedial rather than punitive action and condemning management efforts to uncover concealed identities.

Autonomy of decision-making should mitigate against exploitation when foreseeable and potential risks of taking part in research are articulated and full information is provided. Rational agents can then make appropriate choices although special protection is needed for those who are more vulnerable such as children, the handicapped or mentally ill (Singleton and McLaren 1995). However, no code of practice or ethical guideline can go so far as to determine what to do when individuals are competent but may have limited insight into their potential for harm. Such a concern arose in my relationships with the *azamba* whose experience was largely confined to subsistence farming.

So the codes of practice provided guidance, as did the ethical principles upon which they were based. As Strathern (2000) indicates, they relate individual conduct to a view of good practice. Internalised through years as a midwife, the principles applied as pertinently to my anthropology practice and the codes addressed the same themes. The disparity between them lay largely in the power of sanctions, since, at least in the UK, the midwifery code could be used to support disciplinary action of statutory significance. The world of anthropology could only offer professional disgrace and dismissal from employment. The safety net surely would be 'openness, honesty and integrity' which 'breed trust and respect', and remembering that 'the privilege of research is earned through scrupulous behaviour and carries with it both ethical and moral obligations' (Hicks 1996: 256).

Fieldwork in practice

First I will introduce the traditional and professional midwives who feature in my work, Sissie, Queenie, Gladys, and their supervisor (all pseudonyms). Sissie was my hostess, a literate woman of my own age with many responsibilities within the community. She was my 'fixer' with all the mixed benefits of support, access and loss of autonomy that this entails. Perhaps the most significant difference between us was the opportunity gap – she had eight children, I had two, which inevitably affected our paths in life. Queenie was in her late seventies, and had long been a traditional midwife – in recent years accredited since she had attended the government course. Gladys was her daughter and assistant and it was she who took centre stage in most of my dilemmas. Each highly respected in the locality, they were answerable to a supervisor, again a woman of my age and a registered midwife.

I became acquainted with several *azamba* through visiting their villages with the clinic team, and then approached the chiefs about eventual residence near Queenie, Sissie and Gladys from whom I received an especially warm welcome. For practical and security reasons I eventually lived in Sissie's household. My interpreters and I spent many hours with these *azamba*. I was amazed at their willingness to talk and help; indeed the success of our research was totally dependent on them.

I quickly began to learn from these *azamba* and give here an example of their openness. Walking along a narrow track together, Sissie spotted a particular tree and gleefully tied a few seeds in the corner of her *chitenge* or skirt cloth. I longed to ask what she used them for but it was early days and she was laughingly secretive. Could this be the medicine that was used to speed up women's labours and was apparently responsible for many maternal deaths? Would Sissie fear I might report her? This was my first test. I decided to contain my curiosity and wait, and no more was said.

Much later I did indeed discover what these seeds were. Queenie was talking in her hut about her knowledge and her grandmother's teachings and described the way in which young women used the same seeds to make their bodies more sexually attractive. Returning home, my interpreter Jane amused the women of the household by telling the story (completely forgetting confidentiality, of course) and, amidst great hilarity, Sissie asked me if I wanted some. I knew then that I was gaining access to the privileged knowledge of women and later Queenie showed us how to prepare these seeds.

Despite my concerns I witnessed no dangerous practice. Indeed Sissie's midwifery style was very conventional, not surprising since a retired professional midwife had taught her. Sissie often spoke critically of unnamed others she considered 'dirty'. Discussing ways of helping she thanked God for her success and said: 'The labour pains come differently and there are some elderly women in the village who cause the way [the birth passage] to be damaged … [through] lack of patience – they ask the person to start pushing even when the baby can damage the way.'

Early on Sissie asked me to look at a woman whom she believed to be seriously anaemic and near to her birth. I did not want to be seen as an adviser but Sissie was not going to let me refuse, so we went to see her. I agreed with Sissie and asked her what she thought should happen to her. 'I think she should go to hospital', she replied, and suggested my car could take her. Relieved that we agreed about the risk of bleeding for anaemic women and that no ethical problems arose here for me, I agreed to this.

I found that the combination of cooperation with requests for help, along with judicious questions about what the *azamba* wanted to happen, was a useful strategy. I never interfered, but neither did I refuse help. Their judgements were sound in all cases – a woman in slow labour, another with an open breast abscess, one with a breech baby for whom transport was requested. I agreed to take the last of these to hospital, asking one of the traditional midwives to accompany me as the woman was labouring strongly. We arrived in time with the woman across the back seat, female relative squeezed in beside her and Gladys in front. Gladys escorted her into the maternity unit and returned triumphantly saying the doctor had congratulated her on doing well to bring her in. I will never know whether she requested my assistance because I arrived just then, or whether the long walk would have been unwise in the circumstances.

The midwives may have been selective in choosing those I was permitted to see, or those for whom they wanted transport, but I would have heard of serious problems eventually. Later in my stay they would just call me saying transport was needed. It was in this regard that I had perhaps my greatest disappointment. Near the end of my fieldwork I began to note how rarely there appeared to be women arriving at night. I realised that Sissie had not been rousing me, considering it to be 'disrespectful' to call me at night. This came to light when Gladys arrived at dawn one day to ask for transport. The woman had been in trouble for some hours but they expected me to refuse to drive at night. Few went out then because of the threat of bandits and of evil spirits, and Sissie certainly did not want me out even in my car. Even the local missionary fathers now refused to carry women to hospital at night because of armed hijacking. Neither did Sissie want me to sleep in Queenie and Gladys' village. Not relishing sleeping on a mat on the mud floor anyway, and somewhat scared by recent local events (six rare ritual murders of women and an armed robbery in the birth hut while I was back in the UK), I obeyed. Inevitably then I diminished my opportunities of observing practice as I visited only during the day when births were fewer and anyway could alter only with difficulty our tight schedule of arranged interviews. So issues of intervention hardly arose – until Gladys had 'her accident'.

Gladys was about 45 and taught by Queenie just as the latter had been by her grandmother. They were both very busy; they lived on the route to the hospital from distant villages and women often got no further than their birth house. Undoubtedly they had a reputation for safe and kindly care. Later I recognised that their willingness to help women considered unsuitable by Sissie (such as first-time mothers) was a factor. Gladys was supposed to work under her mother's supervision although conflict was common and Queenie complained she could no longer teach her. Gladys lived life on the run, was active in the church and political party and helped at the baby clinic. Proud and enthusiastic about her work, she was very keen to help me. She had an ambition to have her own 'hospital'. Unsure what this meant, I soon became aware that she and Queenie were healers as well as midwives. I frequently witnessed Gladys advising women with sick children or dressing wounds, then saw Queenie with two young men who came shamefacedly to see her, a teenage girl giggling in the distance. Laughing and wagging her finger at them she disappeared into her hut and emerged with a package: Queenie was the appointed supplier of free condoms. She also told me of the herbs she used to help women who had miscarried but could not afford hospital treatment. Illegal abortion was, they told me, rare as children were so desired. At 75 Queenie was a woman of many parts.

Gladys had a magnificent thatched birth house with decorated walls, two rooms, store, latrine, washhouse and ornate brick-walled placenta disposal pit designed to resemble a Zulu headdress. (See Plate 7.2.) They were Ngoni, a Zulu group who had fled the Mozambican Portuguese a century ago. Given land by the local Yao and Lomwe community, to me they were now indistinguishable from the Chewa but for language, some still speaking

Plate 7.2 Practical and symbolic art: a Zulu head-dress influenced the design of a village azamba's placenta disposal pit

Ngoni. They had even abandoned their customary patriliny and adopted local inheritance through women and matrilocal marriage patterns.

I gradually realised that Gladys' enthusiasm was mixed with unpredictability and a tendency to complicate our work. Queenie would apologise for her as we could wait for hours only to find she was cooking for us or had gone to buy drinks at great expense. Her welcome was always disarming so we often felt beholden and this made it more difficult later. Gladys could nevertheless show great sense and dignity such as when her mother greeted us happily drunk on *chikasu*, her sought-after maize brew, and had to be gently restrained so we could get away.

Gladys had married three times but had no living children. She explained:

> I was bewitched. I had my first boyfriend and we agreed to marry but we were discouraged by the parents – I was already pregnant. When labour started my mother sent my husband's mother to fetch *mankwala* (traditional medicine). It was believed that the problem was due to this medicine – so that the baby must die – the other babies died as well – I was told it was due to witchcraft.

The term *mankwala* was used for many substances, as treatment for problems of health and well-being, and as protection of property. Queenie marched off one day, barefoot, hoe over her shoulder, Jane and I trying to keep up behind. We climbed up through high grass in search of the medicine to 'strengthen the blood' with me watching every step for snakes. I wrote:

> Three types of medicine are mixed to produce 'iron' (one of them produces a red liquid when boiled, think she said one produced black liquid – is there an element of colour symbolism there?) for women who have bled in childbirth.

We then searched her deceased mother's garden – completely overgrown around a tumbledown house – in order to find the other roots she needed which she dug from the ground. (See Plate 7.3.) I was amazed at being given this information when she hardly knew me. I was highly curious about this medicine, wondering if it was knowledge of plant materials which strengthen the blood of anaemic women similar to the one that Bullough (1980) had

Plate 7.3 Digging with a hoe in the long grass, Queenie demonstrates her knowledge of plant materials which strengthen the blood of anaemic women

found to be a very powerful oxytocic, a drug to make the uterus contract. This natural remedy is notorious because it works powerfully, but in a highly unpredictable manner unlike the synthetic one used by doctors throughout the world (although this is also dangerous if used inappropriately). The danger in such drugs lies in forcing the uterus to work very hard when the baby is badly positioned, or too large to pass through the mother's pelvis, which may be small or deformed. In such circumstances the uterus eventually tears and both woman and baby die unless they receive blood transfusion and antibiotics. Such obstructed labour is the commonest cause of maternal death in Malawi, being responsible for about 20 per cent (Malawi National Safe Motherhood Programme 1995). In Zambia 85 per cent of women who died had taken such medicine (Nkata 1996).

I soon realised that this labour-stimulating medicine was also part of the skills for which Gladys was known but the supervisor also clearly knew of her activities and said, 'It is a very strong belief that labour has got to have such medicine.' She told me that relatives would even conceal the medicine in porridge for women in hospital causing them to suddenly commence violent labour. However, she preferred supervision to censure, saying that education and understanding were the key to change. This supervisor was convinced of the importance of these TBAs who understood their community and were respected more than were the younger hospital midwives who often had not given birth themselves.

Undoubtedly Gladys had learned her skills from her mother but it was less obvious that the latter used dangerous herbs after undertaking the training course in which the danger of this is explained. Queenie may just have been more wary of me but I learned later that Gladys hid some activities from her mother. In many ways Gladys seemed naïve and told me things despite knowing I could cause trouble. She said:

> We give them medicine when sick – when she has backache we give her painkillers but when she is healthy we advise her to eat balanced meals. When she is experiencing oedema we give her medicine to stop it and if she is anaemic we also give her the traditional medicine to bring back the blood to her body.

Gladys also reported giving medicine to relieve pain in labour. I thought this referred to a natural analgesic, perhaps the one used for backache in the statement above. Later I learned more. But for the time being I was happy, assured there had been no maternal deaths in this area in living memory and that they were quick to transfer women to hospital when needed. Gladys, maybe Queenie too, was indeed using the herbal oxytocin to 'help' some labouring women and was proud of her ability. However, her supervisor knew about this so there was no need for me to face a decision about breaking confidentiality or risk my relationship. I returned to the UK for a time, blissfully ignorant of the fact that my illusions were to be shattered on my return.

Gladys and her 'accident'

Gladys had been responsible for an 'accident'. I learned of this from the supervisor while driving past her baby clinic. Gladys had kept a labouring woman too long in the village and had given her several doses of oxytocic medicine. When the woman was unconscious and bleeding heavily, her brother-in-law finally took her to hospital in a friend's car. The baby was dead and so, nearly, had been the woman. With a badly torn uterus, a hysterectomy plus blood transfusions from relatives had been needed to save her. Gladys was summoned and threatened with withdrawal of her 'instruments', a punishment of great symbolic meaning. (The importance of these badges of office can be deduced from her photograph taken in front of the ornamented placenta pit.) A meeting of all *azamba* was called to remind them of the rules; everyone in the locality had found out – except me. For days Gladys avoided me. I was dying of curiosity; this was a magnificent opportunity to explore her knowledge and concepts of risk – an important focus of my research. I was told women like Gladys believed what they learned both from training courses and from their elders. (I was reluctant to ask so held back and tried to continue as normal, relying on Jane to be discreet and help me be alert for opportunities.) I wrote in my notes:

> I have to find a way of investigating the thinking behind Gladys's actions – she knows very well what the rules are. Why did she not follow them this time? Or has she been sailing close to the wind – and got away with it until now? However she has not told me about the incident herself yet and I don't think it's appropriate to ask her questions outright. I also would like to talk to the woman and her family and I need her help to gain access. At the same time Gladys often surprises me and maybe will just tell me if I'm open. Whatever, it is an ideal opportunity to investigate the dissonance between bio-medical and indigenous ideas about birth and what governs action.

For me it was a gift that I was unsure how to unwrap. I tried on several occasions to provide opportunities for Gladys to bring the topic up. Maybe each of us was trying to outwit the other, and my notes start one day with the triumphant phrase 'hook, line and sinker, I caught her at last'. The opportunity came in the car with no tape recorder running or notebook to hand. Perhaps she allowed herself to be cornered; she had not needed to escort us. We started discussing women who feared being 'cut' at the hospital. Did women she was very worried about ever refuse to go? Yes she had one who had been first to another midwife. She, Gladys, had been very worried but the woman refused to go to hospital until she started bleeding heavily and could not walk; her husband then took the woman to hospital by car. The baby was born dead by operation and they had to take away the uterus. She was fine now.

After dropping Gladys off to walk home (she seemed in rather a hurry to get away from me), I learned unexpectedly that the woman concerned was related to my interpreter's friend and it could be arranged for me to talk with her. Such are the opportunities of fieldwork.

This all relates to access to hidden knowledge only, but the dilemma 'to tell or not to tell' soon arose.

Gladys had told me she could relieve the pain of women in labour by using herbs. Earlier I had not been alert to the potential significance of this information. Was this the same medicine as the one used to stimulate labour contractions, I asked later, or was it a different one? 'Oh it's the same, it just helps pain rather than altering contractions, then women have less problems because they are not in so much pain', was the reply. 'That is how it helps.' I could believe the principle about pain relief, but selective action of a potent natural chemical depending on what the user wanted of it – that was too much to believe. Mulling over the day's events by the light of my hurricane lamp, that night I wrote:

> At first I thought that as long as the supervisor knows it is being given it doesn't matter too much and I would need to say nothing. However it has occurred to me that Gladys may start to give it more often if she really has got it into her head that the stuff relieves pain – so my dilemma is that from a midwifery viewpoint I ought to speak to her supervisor. Yet from a research ethics viewpoint I have privileged information that I should not disclose and it may well ruin my relationship with Gladys, as she will probably find out. On the other hand – she may assume I will tell her. I suppose in the end the safety of mothers has to be paramount and I'm quite sure I am justified in putting 'scientific' knowledge before traditional here.

It was becoming apparent that I would need to 'tell' even if it spoiled the field for me, and I resolved to find a way of doing so when next I saw the supervisor. But I did not see her again. My last meeting was cancelled because of illness and she could not attend my farewell party. Writing a letter was too formal. It has never happened.

There is a postscript to this. I received the detailed transcription of my interview from the translator some time after my final return to the UK. This clearly indicates the contradictory nature of Gladys' statements. It reads:

Me: You mention pain medicine today; another day you mentioned
         medicine for making the baby come faster. What do you mean?
Gladys: –The medicine stops the pain. There is no medicine to make the baby
         come faster.
Me: Does the medicine make the uterus work harder?
Gladys: It has nothing to do with the uterus – the medicine is to release the
         pain only.

Unable to work out what Gladys really believed, what was merely said on
the spur of the moment, and which medicine she was really describing, I
dropped the subject. I had to be content with the knowledge that many
like Gladys accept explanations from both worlds, and they work with
parallel and intertwined, though different paradigms of childbearing, or
perhaps more correctly, do not differentiate and categorise in the manner in
which I do.

The anthropologist's dilemma: The politics and ethics of whistle-blowing

Anthropologists live their research. It must be the supreme example of
embodied knowledge, and dilemmas cannot be switched off at the end of the
day. For me a dilemma existed because of competing paradigms of practice,
not so much between anthropology and midwifery as I expected, but more
because I believed that no one form of childbirth knowledge had all the
answers. The obvious choice from a medical professional's viewpoint was to
report what had happened. But my position in the community revealed to me
wider consequences of such an action, both for women in the locality and for
the midwives who were my main informants and collaborators.

   It was important to get it right but codes of practice are designed to guide
and alert the reader to the issues at stake; they are ethical principles that
express the articulated norms for specific groups. Codes express expectation
rather than direction. As Fryer (1995), Whyte (1984) and many others
comment, they facilitate ethical reasoning rather than providing moral
judgements or definitive answers to dilemmas. Decisions have to be made in
the light of the unfolding situation and with hindsight one may wish to have
handled a dilemma differently. In the end, attitude is all-important: 'ethical
conduct derives from a way of seeing and interpreting relationships'
(Kellehear 1989: 71). Codes can do little but indicate a profession's view of
desirable attributes, especially when, as in anthropology, there is no universal
sanction available except perhaps withdrawal of sponsorship, dismissal and
public disgrace. This is a major difference from midwifery in the UK and
many other places where practitioners may be called to account under threat
of withdrawal of registration, which makes continuing to practice illegal.

Even in such professions where the issue of accountability may be finely honed, codes of practice have no statutory authority, acting as a normative guide backed up in the case of British midwifery by a more powerful set of rules.

There is a long history of the anthropologist as advocate and it may inevitably be a very political activity, although seen as an option rather than a requirement (AAA 1998). Promoting the role of the traditional midwife is a form of advocacy. In effect their status as focal points for my fieldwork was a form of advocacy too within the wider community, my presence as a researcher inevitably acting as a legitimising factor for them. Advocacy is a form of intervention. Nevertheless the more active intervention that I might have undertaken, perhaps to try to deal with Gladys myself and tell her what I thought of her actions, was, I felt at that time, outside my authority and presumptive of my relationship with her. Teaching comes naturally to me but I tried deliberately to leave the teacher part of my self at the airport and adopt the reciprocal stance to my enquiries commended by Oakley (1981) and Anderson (1991). Furthermore, I deliberately cultivated an element of exchange and only shared my practice as they shared theirs and asked about mine. It had taken some effort to convince the community that I was not there to teach; I was reluctant to change direction. Clearly then, there was an element of protecting my position in my decision not to criticise Gladys, both to preserve my access and to retain trust.

There were more altruistic motivations to which I make claim. The big issue was to tell or not to tell. The consequences of not telling the supervisor might be continuing dangerous practice, while the consequences of doing so could lead to a complete lack of experienced care for women. The more probable scenario of excess publicity was that Gladys might be removed from recognition and continue to practice unsupervised and unchecked, and her supervisor shared this understanding. No means existed of enforcing a cessation of her practice. It was my belief that in other ways her care was far preferable to that of the completely untrained women of the village, and that the usually inaudible voices of women could be heard confirming this in my interviews. Women were indeed continuing to seek Gladys's help despite the widespread local knowledge of the incident.

Leaving aside such consequential reckoning, the matter of confidentiality and anonymity remains. I was given information in a private setting, but with the tape recorder running, pen in hand and with no promise for them of anonymity. For villagers interviewed I had promised anonymity, and had guaranteed that it would not be possible to identify what individuals had said in anything I wrote. I had made no such promise to the *azamba*, knowing how much more identifiable they were. Indeed the expectation was that Gladys, Queenie and Sissie would feature clearly in the written word; it was hardly a confidential setting and at the time they did not expect the locality to remain unidentified. They gave me information for a specific purpose, however, and that did not include reporting on them for disciplinary reasons. Gladys' activities had nevertheless entered the public domain without my intervention, and most importantly, the authorities were conversant with her activities even before she went too far. I nevertheless would continue with the intention to limit their identification to the best of my ability.

It can be seen then that ethical decision-making in anthropology is a dynamic process that has to be taken forward in the context of guidance from those who have been before, but with one eye on the consequences for a variety of actors in the specific scenario. To some extent researchers have to act as agents for these actors and perhaps make decisions themselves that can affect others' lives. It is not as simple as the 'do good and do no harm' of the health care professional, if that can indeed be called straightforward. Certainly it complicates matters when the anthropologist carries another label such as 'midwife' with all the self-imposed and public expectations of doing good, not harm, that go with it. For the anthropologist, however, an added responsibility exists of considering consequences not anticipated by informants.

The issue of secret knowledge and confidentiality is more complicated, then, when informants have limited insight into the potential for trouble inherent in their openness. I moved in from another world, experienced in both one-to-one and group encounters, made friends, and with the help of a local interpreter succeeded in getting people talking in ways they would never normally do. At times I wanted to warn Gladys, 'You shouldn't be telling me this', but I never did. Did she realise how much trouble I could cause for her? With Sissie things were different and she gave me no cause for concern. Sissie appeared to be highly conscious of women's safety and to be conforming to what the authorities wanted of her even to the detriment of her own income. She may, of course, have had more insight into my potential. At the same time am I guilty of paternalism in thinking Gladys may not have known what she was doing? Did she in fact relish the element of confession mixed with showmanship in the way she shared her practice with me? Such a dilemma is indeed anticipated in the *Ethical Guidelines* (ASA 1999), which acknowledge this imbalance in awareness of consequences.

There is another item too on my personal agenda regarding disclosure of information. I believe firmly in the importance of 'traditional' midwives in the context of limited resources and the unreality of expecting rapid change to universal provision of professional skilled attendants for birth. I remain unconvinced by the sceptics' views of problems in educating and supervising them adequately. I also believe that these women will continue to provide a valuable service alongside professional midwives even once the system is fully staffed with such 'skilled' carers, a far-distant situation in environments such as Malawi. Could my revelations about Gladys, a well-supervised 'trained TBA', just serve to reinforce negative attitudes among policy-makers and deprive women of these trusted companions? The international maternal

GILL BARBER

health community, however, knows already of their limitations and my continued access permitted additional insights into the beliefs and knowledge that underlie the actions of traditional midwives. I can thus bear witness to the care these women provided in circumstances of great deprivation to women who would otherwise give birth alone or with attendants of significantly more uncertain skills. As the *Statements on Ethics* of the American Anthropological Association (AAA 1986) suggested, I have a responsibility to speak out what I know and believe from the vantage point of my professional expertise.

In conclusion

Planning my fieldwork led me to expect dilemmas around access to secret information. I sidestepped the issue of the 'secret' knowledge of women – I deliberately did not pursue it further than a minimum on the basis of 'not needing to know'. Such an expedient decision would have to be reviewed if another purpose and more opportunities arose, and women's views on the revelation of their knowledge would have to be sought, understood and accommodated.

I glimpsed the herbal knowledge of the *azamba*, substances commonly used and hardly secret knowledge. I now regret having curbed my curiosity when information was there for the asking. Some information learned was, however, too personal to be revealed and no one knows what this is. Such is confidentiality. Anonymity has, nevertheless, to be actively pursued and demands constant safeguarding.

I finally return to whistle-blowing. I have analysed the background to why I was uncertain how to act, considered the guidance available and described what happened in the field. The codes and literature do not feature specific guidance about the ethics of intervention or about secret knowledge. Case studies (AAA 1998) and examples from the past, enjoinders to consider the public good (UKCC 1992) and the overall emphasis on confidentiality, provide clear principles for the practitioner, whether of anthropology or of midwifery. In the end Gladys was really doing nothing very different from her usual activities and her supervisor was aware of the need to watch and educate her, which got me off the hook. Gladys herself broadcast her skills and knowledge with no fear of retribution until the incident when she went too far; her knowledge was hardly secret. It would have been a different story if I had learned of activities that were not known about already, or witnessed practices of immediate danger to a woman; then my decision-making would have inevitably reached a different conclusion.

As a final assessment, the ethics of anthropology and midwifery turned out to be not so different after all, concentrating as they do on preserving the rights and the good of those who are involved. The dilemmas I encountered were, moreover, less serious than in my imaginings, and within my capacity to manage from my dual stance as anthropologist and midwife.

Bibliography

American Anthropological Association (1986) (amended) *Statements on Ethics*, Online. Available HTTP: <http://www.aaanet.org/committees/ethics.htm> (accessed 13 January 1998 and 22 January 2002).

American Anthropological Association (1998) *Code of Ethics of the American Anthropological Association*, Online. Available HTTP: <:http:// www..aaanet.org/committees/ethics/ethcode:html> (accessed 2 February 2001).

Anderson, J.M. (1991) 'Reflexivity in fieldwork: toward a feminist methodology', *IMAGE Journal of Nursing Scholarship*, 23.2 Summer: 115–18.

Association of Social Anthropologists of the UK and the Commonwealth (1999) *Ethical Guidelines for Good Research Practice*, Online. Available HTTP: <:http://les1net.man.ac.uk/sa/ASA/ethics.htm> (accessed 2 February 2001).

Bullough, C.H.W. (1980) 'Traditional birth attendants in Malawi', unpublished thesis, University of Glasgow.

Cassell, J. and Jacobs, S. (1987) *Handbook on Ethical Issues in Anthropology*, American Anthropological Association, Online. Available HTTP: <http://www.aaanet.org/committees/ethics/toc.htm> (accessed 2 February 2001).

Corey, G., Schneider Corey, M. and Callanan, P. (1988) *Issues and Ethics in the Helping Professions*, 3rd edn, Pacific Grove, CA: Brooks/Cole Publishing Company.

Forster, P.G. (1998) 'Religion, magic, witchcraft, and AIDS in Malawi', *Anthropos*, 93: 537–45.

Fryer, N. (1995) 'How useful is a knowledge of ethics?' *British Journal of Midwifery*, June, 3.6: 341–6.

Gennaro, S., Kamwendo, L.A., Mbweza, E. and Kershbaumer, R. (1998) 'Childbearing in Malawi, Africa', *Journal of Obstetrical and Gynacological Nursing*, March/April: 191–6.

Hicks, C. (1996) 'Ethics in midwifery research', in L. Frith (ed.) *Ethics and Midwifery: Issues in contemporary practice*, Hale: Books for Midwives Press.

Homans, R. (1991) *The Ethics of Social Research*, London: Longman.

International Confederation of Midwives (2000) *International Code of Ethics for Midwives*, Online. Available HTTP: <http://www.rcm.org.uk/files/info/documents/230401124908-43-1.doc> (accessed 11 Feb 2001).

Kamwendo, L. (1996) 'Birth rituals: the Malawian perspective', paper presented at International Confederation of Midwives, 24th Triennial Congress Proceedings, Oslo, 26–31 May.

Kellehear, A. (1989) 'Ethics and social research', in J. Perry (ed.) *Doing Fieldwork. Eight personal accounts of social research*, Geelong, Victoria, Australia: Deakin University Press.

Lewis, G. (2000) *A Failure of Therapy*, Oxford: Oxford University Press.

Morris, B. (1998) *The Power of Animals: an ethnography*, Oxford: Berg.

Ministry of Health and Population, Malawi (1995) *The Malawi National Safe Motherhood Programme: Malawi National Strategic Plan for Safe Motherhood*, Lilongwe: MOHP.

Nkata, M. (1996) 'Rupture of the uterus: a review of 32 cases in a general hospital in Zambia', *British Medical Journal*, 312, 11 May: 1204–5.

Oakley, A. (1981) 'Interviewing women: a contradiction in terms', in H. Roberts (ed.) *Doing Feminist Research*, London: Routledge.

Plummer, K. (1983) *Documents of Life: an introduction to the problems and literature of a humanistic method*, London: Unwin Hyman.

Royal College of Nursing (1993) *Ethics Related to Nursing Research*, London: Scutari Press for the RCN.

Singleton, J. and McLaren, S. (eds) (1995) *Ethical Foundations of Health Care. Responsibilities in decision making*, London: Mosby.

Strathern, M. (2000) 'Accountability and ethnography' in M. Strathern (ed.) *Audit Cultures: anthropological studies in accountability, ethics and the academy*, London: Routledge.

United Kingdom Central Council for Nurses, Midwives and Health Visitors (1992) *Code of Professional Conduct*, London: UKCC.

United Kingdom Central Council for Nurses, Midwives and Health Visitors (1998) *Midwives Rules and Code of Practice,* London: UKCC.

Whyte, W.F. (1984) *Learning from the Field. A guide from experience*, Newbury Park: Sage.

8

THE CONSTRUCTION OF OTHERNESS IN MODERN GREECE

The state, the church and the study of a religious minority

Vasiliki Kravva

Introduction

This chapter is an exploration of two important processes involved in the production of anthropological knowledge, namely interpretation and textualisation. The analysis of the constraints and strategies involved in the process of knowledge production is an attempt to deconstruct the anthropological representation of 'others'. In what follows I refer to some critiques concerning the scientific validity of social anthropology and also discuss the advantages and limitations of a 'native' approach. My research, which deals with the formation of Jewish identities in the Greek city of Thessaloniki, will be used as an example of how ethical considerations relating to the study of the 'other' are inevitably revealed in the process of interpretation and analysis.

The chapter argues that Jewish identities do not exist in a cultural vacuum and that the formation of such identities must be placed within a meaningful context. In the case of Greece the construction of any religious minority inevitably raises the discussion of the pivotal position of the Orthodox Christian Church. In the explorations of the devices by which social exclusion is constructed, the study of the local press acquires a significant position reflecting some of the current issues that concern Greece. By contextualising the 'making of otherness' in modern Greece, in this case the non-Orthodox, my aim is to provide an intepretive framework that takes into account some ethical issues. The first part of this chapter includes the presentation and assessment of the relationship between the State and the Church and in particular the initiatives of the current archbishop as indications of a nationalist rhetoric in modern Greece. The second part is a discussion with Thessalonikan Jews about the role of the Orthodox Church in Greece.

The crisis of representation revisited

From an epistemological and ethical point of view the deconstruction of conventional representation suggests greater reflexivity, multivocality, plurality and the recognition of partiality. Several critiques have proposed dialogism and polyphony as ways of deconstructing monophonic authority and enhancing the reflexivity of textual accounts (Clifford 1986, 1988). Some anthropologists have also suggested that the figure of the 'indigenous ethnographer' could significantly enrich our understanding of a culture (Clifford 1986) and could provide a more reflexive, 'thick' description by taking into account 'the native's point of view' (Geertz 1984: 13).

Although responses to the figure of the native ethnographer have been varied, the exercise has provided useful insights. The divisions between insiders and outsiders have been viewed as 'slippery relativities' and a 'user-friendly' ethnography, incorporating the kind of reflexive ethnography that avoids privileging either natives or non-natives,[1] has been proposed. But what does the term 'native' really imply? A number of scholars have problematised the notion of 'doing anthropology at home' and have produced accounts of the tensions between the native and the professional self, the multiplicity of the native condition, and the diffracted self involved in the process of doing fieldwork at home (Mascarenhas-Keyes 1987, Cheater 1987). Nowadays there are numerous anthropologists who have been trained outside their country and return 'home' to do fieldwork. Yet 'home' itself becomes a relative concept since this is not a homogeneous entity: it consists of several known and unknown fields of social interaction.

My research and the question of nativeness

Being a 'native' who was partly educated abroad I returned in 1998 to my native city, Thessaloniki, in order to carry out field research. The fact that I was a 'native' did not render my status as a researcher less problematic. However, returning after some years to my native city to research a religious minority I knew little about rendered my nativeness both distant and complex at the same time. Gefou-Madianou, a Greek anthropologist who was trained in the United States, writes as follows on the native condition:

> I am therefore continually forced to realize that I am not only caught between two discourses, an intellectual anthropological discourse and the indigenous social discourse of the people I study, but that I have to take into account my position within Greek society as well: I have therefore become a native with multiple identities sometimes marginalising myself in my own country.
>
> (Gefou-Madianou 1993: 169)

My field research was carried out among Thessalonikan Jews, who now constitute a small religious minority in northern Greece. Yet throughout the nineteenth and early twentieth centuries the Jews in Thessaloniki represented a significant proportion of the city's population and at certain periods even formed the majority. According to the census of 1913, the year when Thessaloniki was incorporated into the Greek nation-state, the city's population was almost 160,000 and the Jewish population constituted the largest part of this with almost 62,000 people. After the annexation of Macedonia – and Thessaloniki – into Greece at the end of the Balkan wars in 1913, there was a noticeable endeavour on the part of the newly born Greek state to build a 'homogeneous' Greek Macedonia. Thus a process of the Hellenisation of Greek Macedonia – with a number of different groups in it – gradually took place. The role of education in this process was significant: through the imposition of the Greek language in schools all the local vernaculars, including the Thessalonikan-Jewish, Judaeo-Spanish language, were gradually marginalised. Further, the mixture of the population of Thessaloniki changed drastically after the Asia Minor disaster in 1922. The refugees from Asia Minor who found shelter in the city were not only Orthodox Christians but also Greek speakers. With the arrival of these refugees the Jews instantly became a minority group and Thessaloniki was transformed from a multi-cultural to a largely Christian city in northern Greece. The Second World War completed the changes: from the 70,000 Jewish people who were sent to the concentration camps only 2,000 escaped death, and while some of these returned to Thessaloniki, others migrated to Israel. Today the Jewish community numbers just under 1,000, and it is a minority whose 'Greekness' is often questioned.

For Jews themselves, the basis of citizenship, of being 'a Salonikan' and belonging to a distinct community seem to be central issues. The Jewish people of Thessaloniki rework and in certain cases even resist their sense of belonging to a 'community'. Thus during my fieldwork I was constantly witnessing opposed and contested views about 'belonging'. Some Thessalonikan Jews claimed that they had 'nothing to do with the community's activities', others claimed a 'perfect consciousness of Jewishness' while yet others replied that they did 'not want to be different'. The identities within this 'group' are neither fixed nor given but subject to negotiation, transformation and change. It should be noted here that identities do not exist in a vacuum but are the product of various contextual relations. The Jews of Thessaloniki, who at the beginning of the century constituted a viable and economically powerful part of the city's population, today find themselves belonging to a marginalised minority.

The shift that their identities have experienced must be placed within the wider context of the building of the Greek nation-state along with the particular history of the city of Thessaloniki. Special attention should also be given to the role of the Orthodox Christian faith and the institution of the church.

Since groups and collectivities are always constructed relatively, the cultural images created by others shape and reshape membership as a responsive device. What we are faced with is a dynamic situation of multiple interrelations. Hylland-Eriksen has stressed that a group's identity is 'an aspect of a relationship not a property of a group' (Hylland-Eriksen 1993: 9). According to this principle Thessalonikan-Jewish identity does not exist in a metaphysical vacuum but is a product of the mutuality of at least two discourses: being Greek and not being Greek. Significantly enough not only are the overwhelming majority of Greeks Orthodox Christians but for a significant section of Greek society members of minority groups are perceived as 'imperfect' Greeks who 'lack' a basic ingredient of Greekness. Accordingly, for some, 'Jewishness' seems to exclude 'Greekness' and vice versa. The role of the Orthodox faith and the church are of major importance since to a great extent they shape the notion of Greek citizenship. By deconstructing the context in which such identities are formulated my aim is to produce an anthropological account that is sensitive to local conditions. Maryon McDonald, when talking about the politics of her fieldwork among the Bretons, argued:

An anthropological approach to ethnicity cannot now, I think, join this pursuit of identity through the construction of an autonomous minority history, any more that we can search for the 'true' meaning of a word in, say, its earliest attestation of etymology. Rather, the history becomes part of the ethnography and, like the ethnic identity it describes assumes its meaning from the contemporary context.

(McDonald 1987: 129)

While carrying out fieldwork I always thought that I was divided between two discourses. On the one hand I had the responsibility of producing a fair and realistic account of the Jewish people in Thessaloniki. On the other – because of contacts with Greek academics – I was constantly made aware of the need to depict the wider Greek society as objectively as I could. This was a double ethical dilemma that covered not only the period of my research but also that of the writing of the thesis. In January 2000 I was invited by the Organisation for the Study of Greek Jewry to give a paper about the Jewish community of Thessaloniki. I was terrified by the thought that I had to present 'them' as 'other' in front of 'them'. The presentation went well despite my hesitations. My informants identified their own narratives in my quotations and this enabled them to participate in the discussion that followed. They seemed satisfied because they felt I had made good use of their words.

The second aspect of the ethical dilemmas that my research raises is directly connected with Greek academia. I am still struggling to present a fair and realistic picture of the Greek reality but it is not straightforward. The paper, which refers to the relation between the church and the state, was also given to four Greek academics. Only two of them accepted it as a partial explanation of the current situation in Greece. According to the other two it was 'aggressive' but I was excused 'as a young, inexperienced scientist'. In particular one of them commented: 'Well, it is fine, you have lots of information and to be honest it helped me remember the initiatives of the new Archbishop that I had forgotten. But I don't think Greeks care much about the issues he raised. It is just the media, which gave him publicity. Greeks are like that. They are governed by the media. And anyway I don't think that your thesis on Salonikan Jews has anything to do with the initiatives of the church.' After the above conversation the phrase 'marginalising myself from my own country' no longer sounded like an abstract aphorism to me but an inevitable reality for which I had to prepare myself.

The relationship between the Greek state and the church

During fieldwork I had the opportunity to discuss with many Orthodox Christian Greeks – friends, relatives and students – from various age groups and different educational backgrounds the role of Orthodoxy for them and the way they viewed Greek-Jewish identity. Of course the responses they gave varied to a great extent. Some problematised the notion of 'being Greek' providing me with sensitive accounts such as that of Giorghos, a former colleague from the University:

> It is interesting that they do not teach us anything at school, I mean about the history of Macedonia or this city. You know when I go to the gym I hear many young men saying that the Jews are to be blamed for the war in ex-Yugoslavia. There is still much prejudice in Greece. We attribute many bad things to them. Maybe this is because the Greeks are very obsessed with Orthodoxy.

For the majority, including educated people, Jewishness excluded Greekness and vice versa. This was the case for Andreas, an educated man in his late forties: 'The topic you have chosen is good but I expected you to choose something more Greek ... We can never find out the feelings that Jews have for Greece.' Later during my fieldwork when I repeated this comment to David, a Thessalonikan Jew, he replied: 'You know this comment could be an excellent way to begin your thesis. It is very indicative of people's mentality here.'

Therefore I argue that in the Greek case there seems to be a strong relation between the church and the state and that Orthodoxy exercises significant power in defining Greek national identity. A careful reading of the Greek press is extremely revealing about the relationship between the state and the church in modern Greece; in some cases they appear to be almost inseparable. By presenting some articles from the press that refer to this relation I am not arguing that Orthodoxy per se is responsible for nationalist discourses or expressions. Yet the discourses that are employed and especially those of 'genos',5 'homeland' and 'cultural continuity' support the exclusion of the non-Orthodox from Greek society. The centrality of the Orthodox faith and its penetration into crucial areas such as education and political life leaves room for the construction of neo-nationalist ideologies. Recently, Alivizatos has argued: 'The Greek Orthodox religion and the Greek language have been the fundamental pillars of its modern identity.3 Any approach to current Greek reality that fails to take these factors seriously into account will no doubt lead to false interpretations' (1999: 33).

At this point I would like to discuss an extract from the newspaper *Eleftherotipia* in the edition of 20 December 1998. According to this a foreigner cannot obtain Greek citizenship if she/he: 'does not obtain Greek consciousness and is not able to adjust to the Greek reality, to its customs, to national and religious traditions and ignores or avoids the learning and the use of the Greek language'. Hence he will not be given Greek citizenship 'if he shows strict devotion to his religion and tries to influence members of his family [to do likewise]'.4 Rather, the following qualities are considered necessary for obtaining the privilege of Greek citizenship: 'perfect adjustment to Greek reality by obtaining a Greek consciousness, good knowledge of the Greek language and daily use of it, conversion to Christianity, quiet and *ellinoprepis*5 behaviour, participation in public events and organised activities of a national and religious character'. Every foreigner who wishes to become a citizen must complete a questionnaire and is interviewed on relevant issues by members of the police force. In each individual case the police station in charge must send its report – whether positive or negative – for examination by the Ministry of Foreign Affairs.

This extract indicates the apparently inseparable link between 'being Greek' and being an Orthodox Christian, in other words between Greek citizenship and the institution of the church. In fact, Orthodox religion is present in all aspects of Greek national life: the third article of the Constitution declares that Orthodox Christianity is the sovereign religion of Greece,6 the identity card includes a reference to the religious faith of the person it identifies,7 the church blesses all the political parties that come into power, education and religion come together under one government, that of the Ministry of Education and Religion,8 and Greek constitutional Law prohibits proselytism.9 As a result, if a religious minority wishes to establish a house of worship, permission must be obtained from the Ministry of Education and Religion (Pollis 1992).

Stavros notes that 'A law which enables a minister to review the necessity of the establishment of a place of worship is highly incompatible with freedom of religion as guaranteed in international human rights law' (Stavros 1995: 11). One example clearly illustrates his point. The proposed construction in 1999 of a mosque on the outskirts of Athens generated a strong reaction from the local religious leader. Accordingly he wrote the following proclamation and distributed it all over Athens:

> Do you know what a mosque means? All the surrounding area will be inhabited by Muslims and their children are going to be born here. After a few years they are going to claim that they were born here because their place of worship is here and their homes are here. A new Thrace, or even worse a new Kossovo will be created. The Serbs, although Kossovo was always a Serbian territory, lost it in exactly the same way. We will find ourselves in a similar situation after a few years. Greeks! Resist before it is too late. Do not allow the building of this mosque.

The religious leader who gathered signatures to prevent the building of the mosque asked people to sign as 'Greek citizens'. In the Sunday newspaper *Kathimerini* the debate about the construction of the mosque continued in the form of correspondence. In one letter a well-known Greek politician asserted:

> This issue must be examined contextually. In Saudi Arabia everything Christian, whether a church, a mass or a cross, is forbidden. In Turkey the ecumenical patriarch is restricted by the internal laws of a state with an intolerant religion ... The sacred places of Greece – those which survived the disastrous madness of the Ottomans and neo-Turks – belong and must be attributed to their natural and historical conveyor, the Patriarch. Where do you think the irrational is in all these thoughts and why don't you ask the two countries (Saudi Arabia, Turkey) for the same privileges that you are going to give? Why do you always have to give without taking?
>
> (*Kiriakatiki Kathimerini*, 11 June 2000)

Although the role of the church in the 'awakening' of Greek nationalism is a debatable topic,[10] many scholars[11] agree that the building process of the Greek nation-state and the institution of the church have formed integral parts of the same symbolic discourse.[12] Thus, being Greek has become almost synonymous with being an Orthodox Christian. This nationalisation of the church and the association of the Greek nation with Orthodoxy remains even today very powerful. Thus the Greek *ethnos* and the church are closely identified and appear almost equivalent (Stewart 1998). Pollis takes the argument a step further by arguing that:

> Since Eastern Orthodoxy is a defining and central part of Greekness it is not surprising that it was and remains a state-established religion ... Despite the claims of Greek Orthodoxy to universality, the church has assumed another mission: to preserve the superior spiritual ethos of Greekness by forging a symbiotic relationship between the church and state, a task simplified by the fact that the overwhelming majority of Greeks are Orthodox. The church's self-proclaimed duty to preserve this transcendent ethnos (along with financial privileges for itself and its clergy[13]) has strengthened a longstanding church–state interdependence.
>
> (Pollis 1992: 179)

The era of the new Archbishop of Greece as reflected in the press

On 28 April 1998 Christodoulos was elected by the Synod as the new Archbishop of Greece, an event which initiated many discussions about the church's power in influencing and shaping modern Greek society. The new archbishop is a very popular figure who plays an active role in the mass media, a factor leading many analysts[14] to argue about the new role that the church is seeking to play. As many as 60.9 per cent of the people in a survey thought it was right that he should be interested in issues outside the church.[15] As Alivizatos notes: 'Owing to [his] almost daily public appearances and statements covering topics ranging from foreign policy and European integration to cloning and premarital sex, Archbishop Christodoulos has become a point of reference in all aspects of public debate' (1999: 24).

The Greek archbishop has indeed proved to be a very dynamic religious leader. Since he took charge of the church establishment he has created a radio channel and an Internet page and has also tried to start a television channel. All his initiatives have been characterised by a tendency to modernise the image and the profile of the Orthodox Christian church in Greece. Apart from these modernising endeavours, Christodoulos has proved very keen to express his views on recent political issues such as the Greek–Turkish conflict over the island of Imia in 1996 or the war that broke out in Yugoslavia in 1999.[16] The day on which the Imia incident took place was declared a national holy day and Christodoulos commented: 'Three years ago we went through a national humiliation that we are not willing to let happen again.' According to him, the death of three Greek soldiers in that incident 'justified the expectations of a betrayed people for its national dignity' (*Eleftherotipia*, 5 February 1999).

From the inception of his leadership the initiatives of Greece's new archbishop generated strong and often opposed judgements. While a significant number of Greek citizens seemed to approve of his actions, the scientific and political world was divided into two opposite camps: one of them enthusiastically approved his stance whereas for others Christodoulos went far beyond the limits of religious authority. The newspaper *To Vima* published a number of articles supporting the archbishop's policy. In these articles he was presented as a modernist and a warm supporter of the European Union: 'Not only is he not a nationalist – since he rejects national confrontations – as many wanted to present him, but he is favourable to the dream of European unity ... I think what bothers [some people] most is his undeniably Christian *logos*'[17] (*Kiriakatiko Vima*, 21 March 1999).

Those who were against him expressed the attitude that his *logos* was purely political and not religious and that 'the archbishop showed from the first his wish to obtain secular power and to take political initiatives in non-religious matters' (*Kiriakatiko Vima*, 21 March 1999). Nevertheless, until 1999 the Greek government adopted a positive stance towards him and was very keen to maintain a good relationship between the church and the state. On his election in 1999, the present Prime Minister and leader of the socialist party PASOK, Costas Simitis, declared that: 'We are going to continue this close cooperation at many levels in order to produce some common solutions ... There are many issues that we can face together very effectively.' He concluded, 'Orthodoxy has always played a very important role for the ethnos' (*Kiriakatiko Vima*, 10 January 1999).

Yet the relation between the church and the modern Greek state cannot be characterised as a harmonious one; indeed the boundaries between them have experienced shifts and recently even serious tensions. The government's proposal to exclude any personal information – such as religion – from the new identity cards and to abolish examinations of *Thriskeutika* (religious education) in secondary schools generated a range of reactions which reflect the endeavour of the state to emancipate itself from the supervision of the church. From the early summer of 2000 the Greek press was mainly preoccupied with these issues. The strength of reactions to this policy reflects the central role that the decisions of the church play in people's lives and the formative power this institution exercises over them.

The archbishop and the majority of the Greek clergy – with only a very few exceptions – objected very strongly to the government's initiatives. Several bishops talked about the religious disorientation of Greek society and characterised these measures as an attempt to diminish and damage the prestige of the church: 'In 1981 they abolished the accents in our [written] language. Now they are ready to abolish a historical inscription 176 years old, which is inseparably connected with the emancipation of our ethnos ... I wonder what is next?' According to the same press source another representative noted that: 'The school text-books have no references to our

Orthodox faith, to Hagia Sofia, Poli,[18] or the Greek flag.' He added that: 'They have removed the shrine from the buses and no cross can be found in the new ambulances' (*Kiriakatiki Eleftherotipia*, 6 August 2000). As far as the issue of *Thriskeutika* was concerned another bishop claimed that: 'Those people do not want the presence of the church in the public profile of this country. They feel annoyed either by the power of the church or its presence' (*Eleftherotipia*, 25 August 2000).

The archbishop initiated a 'holy war' between the church and the government which went through a number of phases. At first Christodoulos used strong language and tried to turn public opinion in his favour and then he organised mass demonstrations in Athens and Thessaloniki. Finally the church decided – regardless of the government's opinion – to organise a referendum on whether Greeks agreed with the mention of religion on the new identity cards. The proclamations of Christodoulos clearly identified Orthodoxy with the history of the Greek ethnos and frequently implied that the Greek state and Orthodox Christianity are almost indistinguishable: 'They thought that it is possible to marginalise and render our blessed country to be without Christianity, without religion, without demonstrations for Christ and without our Hellene-Orthodox tradition' (*To Vima*, 9 June 2000). He also talked about the endeavour to de-Christianise the state as a phenomenon that has already occurred in some European countries but 'it is not going to happen in Greece ... As in previous difficult historical periods Jesus Christ is going to win in this place' (*Eleftherotipia*, 9 June 2000).

On 14 June Christodoulos and the church organised a mass demonstration in Thessaloniki to protest against the government's decision in relation to the new identity cards. This demonstration had a significant appeal to Thessalonikans. Some of the slogans heard were: 'Yes to our historical continuity', 'Yes to Orthodoxy', 'Yes to *Romiossini*',[19] 'No to mimicry of Europe', 'I am Orthodox and proud of it', 'They cannot bend our faith even if they give us millions'. The demonstration was massive and the participants carried Greek flags and flags with the emblem of the Byzantine Empire. The Mayor of Thessaloniki not only allowed the demonstration to take place in the most central square of the city but also decided to support it openly.

The socialist government of Costas Simitis was obviously against the church's power and thought it should be limited to religious and not political ends. Yet the political world seemed sceptical and divided. One Deputy and Member of Parliament belonging to the present government argued that he would not like to discuss such issues with journalists. Nevertheless he stressed that the Constitution refers to the Holy Trinity and that this is 'a matter of historical memory' (*To Vima*, June 2000). A representative of the conservative opposition declared, 'I will be on the side of the people who demonstrate against the politics of the government' (*Eleftherotipia*, 9 June 2000) while another Deputy of the same party objected to the fact that 'the morning prayer and the National Anthem had been dropped from the programmes of the public radio'. The Deputy asserted that such measures 'try to hurt the religious faith of the Greek people' (*Eleftherotipia*, 13 June 2000). Another independent Mayor argued that: 'Nobody can prevent the clergy from talking politically since their intention is not to seize secular power but to help the people and the ethnos' (*Eleftherotipia*, 2 September 2000).

Nonetheless, the government remained steadfast in its decision, as did the church. During a Synod the clergy took the initiative of holding a referendum on the issue of the new identity cards. Between 14 September 2000 and 25 March 2001 people were invited to vote in the local churches. The Synod asserted that:

> The participation of so many Greek citizens, especially of young people, in the demonstrations proves that the foundation of Greek democracy according to the Constitution, the citizens themselves, decided that they have the right of declaring their religion on identity cards. Identity cards are considered as a medium for recognising someone's persona and carry his/her signature. The free citizen of a free state who signs them has also the undeniable right of declaring his faith. All these multiply the responsibilities of the Holy Synod. So it assures the chosen people that it will never let down their hopes and expectations. All these scenarios against the church, which are worked by evil forces in order to hurt and divide our ethnos cannot be tolerated.
>
> (*Eleftherotipia*, 8 August 2000)

The voices of Thessalonikan Jews

How have Thessalonikan Jews responded to the current religious and political situation in Greece? Many of my discussions with them pointed to the central role that faith plays in the formation of modern Greek citizenship. I recall phrases such as 'The church here is very much into politics' or 'your faith is after you everywhere', but their overall evaluation of the state's attitude towards minorities was that it was not particularly negative. According to the older generation of Thessalonikan Jews, the state is not responsible for the creation of anti-Semitic feelings because prejudiced conceptions inevitably arise in everyday life. Thus Lina, a woman in her eighties, stated, 'It would be unfair to say that the Greek state is not tolerant towards minorities. Nowadays things are beginning to change. We have been given the same rights. On the surface (*fainomenika*) things seem to be very good. It is in everyday life that prejudice is being reproduced by people themselves.' Yet this woman – like many other Thessalonikan Jews – held an ambivalent view of the current situation in Greece. While she thought that the Greek state was tolerant she also thought that this tolerance was superficial and ephemeral. Hesitation and reluctance were the major characteristics of the discussions I had with people from this generation.

Middle-aged Salonican Jews had more definite views about the state's policy and the centrality of the Orthodox church in shaping modern Greek culture. Moris, a married man in his fifties, commented as follows:

> As far as prejudice against the Jews is concerned your church should be the first to to be blamed. Generally it creates a very negative climate. I remember that before the war here in Thessaloniki many streets had Jewish names. But not any more. We are even afraid to state our Jewishness openly. The other day I went to a grocery shop. A priest was chatting with a housewife. You can't imagine the things I heard. They both more or less agreed that Jewish people are responsible for all the bad things happening on this planet. The grocer knew that I am Jewish and he felt really uncomfortable. When the priest left I said to that lady, 'Look, I don't have horns. I might be Jewish but I am a normal human being like you are.'

Moris' words reveal his awareness of 'not being a full Greek citizen'. It is interesting that he declared his Jewishness only after the priest had gone.

Renee, a middle-aged working woman, stated openly that Greece's attitude towards minorities was intolerant: 'Unfortunately the basic premise of the Greek state is *patris, thriskia, oikogeneia* (homeland, religion, family), a relic that goes back to the days of the military dictatorship. In order to be Greek you have to be an Orthodox Christian. We often face prejudice, for example with our surname. Well, it doesn't sound very Greek to them.' For Renee the Orthodox Christian faith was the cornerstone of the Greek state. The exclusion of all other faiths generated intolerance and distance and such feelings were responsible for prejudiced behaviour. Hence for Renee non-Orthodox Greeks were treated as 'impure' Greeks, lacking an important quality. People of this generation repeatedly argued: 'After all in order to be a real Greek you have to be or become an Orthodox Christian.'

Miriam, a woman in her late thirties who was a schoolteacher, had views similar to those of Renee. She also believed that the centrality of Orthodox Christianity was a remnant of the military dictatorship: 'The military dictatorship left one heritage, the slogan that Greece is the homeland of Christian Greeks.' Miriam took the argument further by commenting on the recent bombings in the former Yugoslavia by NATO. She believed that the role of the Greek Archbishop Christodoulos was very dangerous and harmful. His emphasis on Orthodoxy could be perceived as sanctioning ethnic intolerance and ethnic cleansing: 'The Greek archbishop declared that the Westerners are trying to harm not only the Orthodox countries but Orthodoxy per se. I have the feeling that he expresses very dangerous ideas.

Don't you think so?' Her views were shared by the majority of middle-aged Thessalonikan Jews who also commented that the new archbishop was 'a dangerous and over-ambitious religious leader' whose words were 'examples of extreme nationalism'. All these rendered the future of Greece and of minority rights in it 'unsafe' and 'insecure'.

Conclusion

In this chapter I have tried to assess the centrality of the Orthodox Christian faith and the church in defining Greek national identity and citizenship. I suggest that the Greek church perpetuates an ethnocentric *logos* and thus leaves ample room for the construction of nationalist discourses. Of course Orthodoxy per se is not totally responsible for nationalist ideologies but the discourses it perpetuates, particularly those of *genos* and 'enslaved homelands', are often employed as vehicles for the expression of extreme ethnocentrism and xenophobia.

We must bear in mind that Greece is not the sole arena for the expression of such discourses: throughout Europe during the last few years there has been a rise of extreme nationalist ideologies, sometimes with the tolerance of the state. The feelings of xenophobia and hatred for what is different led to disastrous consequences, including the projection of solutions such as 'ethnic cleansing'. In general, Greece is considered a democratic, liberal country in which personal freedoms and freedom of expression are protected by the law. Thus extreme nationalistic ideologies are not widely accepted. The actions of fascist and neo-Nazi organisations are condemned not only by the state but also by the church[20] and Greek civil society. Yet there are some striking similarities between the discourses of extreme nationalists and those of church representatives.

The presence of any religious minority in Greece, such as the Jewish people, must be analysed within this context. Thus by placing the matrix of relations and interdependencies within a meaningful context anthropological analysis can claim to have approached some social truths. Only then does the problem of representation become a search for 'relevance' and a definition of relevance is closely associated with the 'moral significance' of the discipline (Ahmed and Shore 1995). This chapter does not claim to cover the topic of ethical reading and writing in anthropology. However, it does argue that there can be no neutral descriptions of 'others' since other people's identities do not exist in a cultural, or for that matter a moral, vacuum, but are often responses or reactions to wider political issues. By taking into consideration such dimensions, anthropological analysis gives voice to those conditions which construct the other and thus produces a more holistic picture. Such an analysis inevitably touches on ethical issues and can make serious claims to reflexivity and sensitivity to local conditions.

As far as my own research is concerned the fact that I am 'a native' seems rather complicated and bewildering. It constantly generates ethical dilemmas and reminds me of the multiple selves I have to deal with: I am an anthropologist, a Greek citizen, a Thessalonikan, an Orthodox Christian and a religious person. Yet at the same time I sympathise with minority groups and am a warm supporter of personal and religious freedom. This list encompasses a whole range of identities which raise all sorts of ethical, political and methodological issues. But above all I try to situate myself politically not only in my everyday life but also in relation to the discipline I have chosen to pursue. I make this effort because I believe that the production of academic knowledge, if it wishes to be called moral knowledge, should not overlook past and present political conditions.

Notes

1 Both terms are used by Loizos: 'It seems reasonable to suggest that all observer statuses carry specific strengths and weaknesses; perhaps our most serious problem is to become aware of them. There can be no such thing as the ideal participant–observer status, and neither "outsiders" nor "insiders" study cultures from a perfect vantage-point' (Loizos 1992: 170).

2 The notion of *genos* is actually translated as patriline and the word genealogy is derived from the same root, the verb *gennao* which means 'to give birth'. According to Anderson nationalist ideologies always use a vocabulary of kinship and family relations when referring to the nation-state. (Anderson 1983: 7).

3 This view is shared by non-Greeks as well: 'Orthodoxy has played a central role in the Greeks' image of themselves, aggressively defended against the Catholics to the west and the Muslims to the east. Conservative governments and regimes through the twentieth century reinforced the church as a pillar of social order' (*The Times*, 24 November 2000).

4 This extract is also indicative of the gendered issues which are revealed in the Greek reality: the women are absent from the language that is used by some officials, and in Ardener's words they constitute a 'muted group', 1975.

5 If there is any translation of this term at all it should be 'hellenic-orientated'!

6 Very few non-Orthodox Christians are employed in the public sector.

7 Although I discuss below the recent attempts of the Greek government to abolish this.

8 This has further implications for relations between state education and the church. For example before entering the classroom students have to attend morning prayers and are taken regularly – at least while in primary school – to attend mass. Such visits used to take place on Saturdays but now also occur during the week at the expense of some teaching lessons. Lessons on religion are compulsory until the final years of school. A non-Orthodox Christian is not entitled to teach in either primary or secondary school because he/she is considered unable to transmit to children the values of Orthodoxy.

9 Constitutional Law of 1975, article 13, paragraph 2. As Stavros observes: 'In the area of the rights of religious minorities the judgements of the European Court of Human Rights have so far given a rather narrow response. Thus, despite the finding of a violation in the Kokkinakis case, Greece has not repealed its much-criticised law on proselytism' (Stavros 1999: 15).

10 For an interesting discussion see Kitromilides 1989. According to Anderson the 'awakening' of European nationalisms, in the first half of the nineteenth century, was mainly promoted via the local 'cultivated middle classes' and the expansion of print capitalism (Anderson 1983).

11 Kitromilides 1989, Pollis 1992, Carabott 1993, Stewart 1994, 1998.

12 This reminds us that nationalism is not a homogeneous process that is the same everywhere. For example Greek nationalism has incorporated totally different elements from French or English nationalism. This is a matter of different historical conditions and different immediate or remote ends. Thus we can only talk about various nationalisms.

13 According to the Ministry of Agriculture the church holds more than 422 million square metres of land (*Kiriakatiki Eleftherotipia*, 2 July 2000).

14 *The Times* of London published a series of articles about modern Greece, one of which was concerned with the new archbishop, Christodoulos: 'In fact, this year a good many Greeks are saying that the leader of the opposition is not Karamanlis but a far less likely and more formidable figure, Archbishop Christodoulos, primate of the Orthodox Church of Greece' (*The Times*, 24 November 2000).

15 The research was carried out by MRB and the results were published in *Agelioforos*, 9 December 1988.

16 For a sensitive account of the various interpretations of local histories and the relevance of the past in everyday life see Sutton 1998.

17 I prefer the Greek term *logos* in place of 'speech' or 'discourse' because *logos* actually refers to speech with some inner logic and coherent arguments.

18 *Poli* literally means 'city' and refers to Constantinople. Hagia Sofia was the most important church in Constantinople before it was incorporated into Turkey in 1453. Until 1932 Hagia Sofia operated as a mosque. In 1934 it was renovated and since then it has functioned as a museum.

19 According to Herzfeld there is a cultural *disemia* in Greece which is encapsulated in the tension between the glorious and ancient notion of *Hellenism* and the Turkish notion of *Romiossini* (Herzfeld 1987). I believe that nowadays in modern Greece this tension has changed drastically: there is a wide recognition of *Romiossini* as an innate and positive quality of all Greeks.

20 For example, during the summer of 2000 members of *Chrissi Avgi*, the most widespread fascist organisation in Greece, destroyed part of the third cemetery in Athens in which Jewish tombs are to be found. Some members also vandalised the Synagogue of Monastiriotes and the Square of Jewish Martyrs in Thessaloniki. The vandals wrote in black paint: '*Erhomaste*' meaning 'We are coming', 'Yuden raus' and signed themselves 'SS members of *Chrissi Avgi*'. These acts of vandalism were condemned by Archbishop Christodoulos and by most of the Greek political world.

Bibliography

Ahmed, A. S. and Shore, C. (1995) 'Is Anthropology Relevant to the Contemporary World?' in A. S. Ahmed and C. Shore (eds) *The Future of Anthropology: Its Relevance to the Contemporary World*. London: Athlone Press.

Alivizatos, N. C. (1999) 'A New Role for the Greek Church?', *Journal of Modern Greek Studies* (17): 23–40.

Anderson, B. (1983) *Imagined Communities: Reflections on the Origin and Spread of Nationalism*. London: Verso.

Ardener, E. (1975) 'Belief and the Problem of Women' in S. Ardener (ed) *Perceiving Women*. London: Dent.

Birth, K. K. (1990) 'Reading and the Righting of Writing Ethnographies', *American Ethnologist* (17): 549–57.

Carabott, P. (1993) 'Politics, Orthodoxy and the Language Question in Greece: The Gospel Riots of November 1901', *Journal of Mediterranean Studies* (3): 117–38.

Cheater, A. P. (1987) 'The Anthropologist as Citizen: The Diffracted Self?' in Anthony Jackson (ed.) *Anthropology at Home*. London: Tavistock Publications.

Clifford, J. (1986) 'Partial Truths' in James Clifford and George E. Marcus (eds) *Writing Culture: The Poetics and Politics of Ethnography*. Berkeley: University of California Press.

—— (1988) 'On Ethnographic Authority' in *The Predicament of Culture*. Cambridge, MA: Harvard University Press.

Danforth, L. M. (1984) 'The Ideological Context of the Search for Continuities in Greek Culture', *Journal of Modern Greek Studies* (2): 53–85.

Geertz, C. (1984) 'From the Native's Point of View: On the Nature of Anthropological Understanding' in R. Shweder and R. LeVine (eds) *Culture Theory: Essays on Mind, Self and Emotion*. Cambridge: Cambridge University Press.

Gefou-Madianou, D. (1993) 'Mirroring Ourselves Through Western Texts: The Limits of an Indigenous Anthropology' in H. Driessen (ed.) *The Politics of Ethnographic Reading and Writing: Confrontations of Western and Indigenous Views*. Saarbrucken and Fort Lauderdale: Verlag Breitenbach Publishers.

Hastrup, K. (1995) 'The Native Voice: On Taking Responsibility' in her book *A Passage to Anthropology: Between Experience and Theory*. London: Routledge.

Herzfeld, M. (1982) *Ours Once More: Folklore, Ideology, and the Making of Modern Greece*. Austin: University of Texas Press.

—— (1985) '"Law" and "Custom": Ethnography *of* and *in* Greek National Identity', *Journal of Modern Greek Studies* (3): 167–85.

—— (1987) *Anthropology through the Looking-glass: Critical Ethnography in the Margins of Europe*. Cambridge: Cambridge University Press.

—— (1992) 'Segmentation and Politics in the European Nation-state: Making Sense of Political Events' in K. Hastrup (ed.) *Other Histories*. London: Routledge.

Hylland-Eriksen, T. (1993) *Ethnicity and Nationalism: Anthropological Perspectives*. London: Pluto Press.

Just, R. (1989) 'Triumph of the Ethnos' in E. Tonkin, M. McDonald and M. Chapman (eds) *History and Ethnicity*. London: Routledge.

Karakasidou, A. (1993) 'Politicizing Culture: Negating Ethnic Identity in Greek Macedonia', *Journal of Modern Greek Studies* (11): 1–28.

Kitromilides, P. (1989) 'Imagined Communities and the Origins of the National Question in the Balkans', *European History Quarterly* (19): 149–94.

Loizos, P. (1992) 'User-friendly Ethnography?' in Joao de Pina-Cabral and John Campbell (eds) *Europe Observed*. London: Macmillan.

Mascarenhas-Keyes, S. (1987) 'The Native Anthropologist. Constraints and Strategies in Research' in Anthony Jackson (ed.) *Anthropology at Home*. London: Tavistock Publications.

McDonald, M. (1986) 'Celtic Ethnic Kinship and the Problem of Being English', *Current Anthropology* (27): 333–47.

—— (1987) 'The Politics of Fieldwork in Brittany' in Anthony Jackson (ed.) *Anthropology at Home*. London: Tavistock Publications.

Pollis, A. (1992) 'Greek National Identity: Religious Minorities, Rights, and European Norms', *Journal of Modern Greek Studies* (10): 171–93.

Sangren, P. S. (1988) 'Rhetoric and the Authority of Ethnography', *Current Anthropology* (29): 405–35.

Sperber, D. (1985) 'Interpretive Ethnography and Theoretical Anthropology' in *On Anthropological Knowledge*. Cambridge: Cambridge University Press.

Stavros, S. (1995) 'The Legal Status of Minorities in Greece Today: The Adequacy of their Protection in the Light of Current Human Rights Perceptions', *Journal of Modern Greek Studies*: (13): 1–32.

—— (1999) 'Human Rights in Greece: Twelve Years of Supervision from Strasbourg', *Journal of Modern Greek Studies* (17): 3–21.

Stewart, C. (1994) 'Syncretism as a Dimension of Nationalist Discourse in Modern Greece' in Charles Stewart and Rosalind Shaw (eds) *Syncretism – Anti Syncretism: The Politics of Religious Synthesis*. London: Routledge.

—— (1998) 'Who Owns the Rotonda? Church vs. State in Greece', *Anthropology Today* (14): 3–9.

Sutton, E. D. (1998) *Memories Cast in Stone: The Relevance of the Past in Everyday Life*. Oxford: Berg.

9

AN APPROPRIATE QUESTION?

The propriety of anthropological analysis in the Australian political arena

Veronica Strang

Appropriate: *v.t.* to take to oneself as one's own, to filch ...
adj. set apart for a purpose, suitable ... [Fr. *propre* – L. *proprius*, own]
Proper: *adj.* own: appropriate ... befitting, decorous, goodly.
Propriety: *n.* ownership; rightness ... seemliness, decency,
conformity with good manners ... [Fr. *propriété* – L. *proprietas*, -atis,
proprius, own]

(Geddie 1964: 49)

Introduction

This chapter is concerned with some central issues for anthropology: the potential – or lack of it – for the universal application of professional codes of ethics, and the relationship between discourses about ethics and current debates about the extent to which theoretical models may also be applied cross-culturally. It takes the position that the potential for universality in ethics hinges upon the feasibility of generalising, cross-cultural comparisons. This leads us straight into a long-running argument as to whether anthropology should be treated as a science – capable of some degree of objectivity – or as a culturally relativist, interpretative endeavour. Implicitly, a model of anthropology as scientific endeavour tends to assume some degree of universality in human thought and behaviour, while postmodern models have tended to promulgate the opposite.

I would like to approach these questions reflexively, through a case study based on recent experiences of conducting fieldwork in northern Australia and, subsequently, constructing a representation of the research findings for a major conference in Perth. The particular ethical questions that this raised are whether anthropologists have a right to represent 'the other' at all, and whether, in doing so, their representations should be controlled and directed by the people about whom they are writing, or by their own, independent judgements about the issues that should be raised, and the processes or problems that should be elucidated. Obviously there is a balance to be attained here, but the process by which this is reached is entangled in the ethical and theoretical questions which I set out initially, as well as in the complex politics of race relations in Australia.

The political arena

To understand why representation is such a very sensitive question in Australia, it is necessary to sketch in some background about the political arena in which anthropological research is conducted. The Aboriginal minority in Australia represents about 2 per cent of the population as a whole. Colonisation of the country by Europeans has taken place over 200 years, with the major dispossession of the indigenous people occurring primarily in the first century of colonisation, but with some areas not fully 'settled' until early in the twentieth century. In some regions well into that century, the colonisation of land was accompanied by considerable violence and sometimes by outright genocide (see Plate 9.1).

Aboriginal groups largely had to choose between working for the European pastoralists who appropriated their land – which often entailed enforced concubinage for the women, and unpaid labour for the men and women alike – or fleeing to the protection of mission reserves, in which children were routinely separated from their families and traditional practices

Plate 9.1 Kunjen elder Paddy Yam points out the site of a massacre in his grandparents' generation

were firmly repressed. In the latter half of the twentieth century, the paternalistic dominance of the church was replaced by that of the state, with indigenous people in many parts of the country receiving neither wages for their work, nor the vote, until the 1960s.

The majority of Aboriginal people now live either in ex-mission reserve areas, or in ghettos on the fringes of urban areas. They are rarely employed on the cattle stations, and when they are, their families and homes remain elsewhere. Australia's indigenous communities are beset by social problems well beyond those experienced by the rest of the population. Aboriginal incomes are less than two-thirds of the national average; unemployment is three times the national average; rates of arrest, conviction and incarceration are also significantly higher (one prisoner in seven is Aboriginal), and deaths in custody are about 26 times the rate for other Australians. Suicide rates in Aboriginal communities, particularly by teenage males, are soaring, infant deaths are twice as common as in the wider population, and Aboriginal life expectancies are 20 years less than the national average. As Beckett says:

> Many people live in what journalists call 'third world conditions', wherein even so basic a need as clean water cannot be guaranteed, drunkenness is a long-standing apparently ineradicable problem, young men often ruin their health by sniffing petrol or glue, and there is a disproportionate incidence of many diseases that barely register among white Australians.
>
> (1987: 9)

As Bennett points out (1999), the situation of Aboriginal people does not meet Oppenheim's (1968) fundamental criteria of equality which include legal, political and economic equality, equality of opportunities, and equal satisfaction of basic needs. As Bennett puts it:

> Despite the existence of well-established democratic forms in Australia, there is no doubt that a disproportionate number of Aboriginal people do not enjoy all the basic advantages of living in this nation, due to the social and political inequality which is part and parcel of their existence.
>
> (1999: 2)

Throughout the two centuries of colonisation, Aboriginal people, though vastly outnumbered, have done their best to resist European dominance: they fought to defend their land and, even under the enforced control of settlers, missionaries and the state, continued to lead subversive 'double lives' in which they tried to maintain their own cultural practices. They have struggled for greater social, economic and political equality, and they have tried desperately to reclaim their land, or at least regain some measure of control over it. Because, without exception, land is central to Aboriginal cultural forms, this last battle is regarded as the most crucial, land rights being seen as the major – perhaps only – hope for the future.

The land rights issue – though not always called by this name – has always been the major conflict in relations between European Australians and indigenous groups, but it gained much greater impetus when Aboriginal communities began, in the 1960s, to regain some degree of self-determination. The 1970s brought the first Land Rights acts,[1] and the subsequent decades have been characterised by one legal battle after another, and a steady intensification of conflicts, culminating in the highly controversial Mabo case of 1992[2] in which the High Court ruled that Aboriginal people did have a system of land ownership prior to colonisation, and so established a concept of Native Title – something which had been fervently denied by non-Aboriginal Australians for 200 years. The Federal Government promptly produced the 1993 Native Title Bill, enabling further land claims. This was greeted with hope by some as a significant step towards justice and reconciliation, and with dismay by others as a national disaster which threatened the tenure – and thus the economic survival – of other non-Aboriginal land-holding groups. The hysteria grew, encouraged by the pastoralist and mining industries, and there was a sharp upsurge in support for extreme right-wing parties such as One Nation, led by the notorious Pauline Hanson. This brought right to the surface the racism which has always dogged the relationship between black and white Australians, and, in a violent backlash, a conservative-dominated Coalition government was elected in 1996, with a mandate to dismantle, or at least ameliorate the reformist efforts of the previous liberal regime.[3]

This conflict exposes a deep divide in the wider Australian population. It is partly an urban–rural divide, but is based more on the different interests and political views of those closely involved in land use and primary production and those in urban service industries. Primary resources remain an important part of Australia's economy: although the farming industry has declined greatly, mining is still a 'mainstay of the economy' in several states. The attitude of these sectors to Aboriginal groups has often been deeply hostile, presenting them as parasitic land grabbers, and framing Native Title as a threat to national stability. The imagery used to portray Aboriginal interests is at times extreme: for example, a few years ago the mining association in Western Australia commissioned a television advertisement showing a black hand coming down to grab the land, and another in which a wall was being built to keep white Australians off the land. Overt racism is largely tolerated – indeed normalised – in many parts of Australia, most particularly in Western Australia and Queensland, which have had particularly conservative state governments and are the areas most dependent on primary industries. Racism is common even in urban areas, although this is where one also finds the liberal groups – the intellectuals, the environmentalists, the socialists, the professionals – who consider such racism to be deeply shameful, and who now represent significant support for Aboriginal people and their rights, marching to protest on their behalf, organising petitions, and of course voting for more liberal governance.

The role of anthropology

Anthropology has played an unusually important and visible part in this equation. With an indigenous population so recently living as hunter-gatherers, Australia has long been an area of great interest to anthropologists. Our discipline's own ancestral heroes were utterly fascinated by the opportunity to study theirs. This led to very early involvement with Aboriginal groups – in some instances ahead of the settlers who claimed their land – which raises an interesting question about who led the way in imposing colonial dominance.

However, I think it is also fair to say that Australia is one part of the world in which anthropologists have been able to make themselves genuinely useful to indigenous groups. For many decades now, they have been instrumental in assisting Aboriginal people in recording cultural knowledge and using this to support their claims to land and resources and their efforts to regain self-determination. They have acted as advocates and expert witnesses in every land claim, they have advised at every stage of legislative development, they have provided insights into Aboriginal culture for policy makers. As a result Australian legislation has now made room for some of the basic tenets of Aboriginal Law: for example, the concept of inalienable collective rights to land determined by ancestral clan membership has effectively been translated via anthropological models (see Strang 2000a).

More generally, anthropologists have acted as interpreters, elucidating Aboriginal culture for the mainstream population, and adding to a crucial educative effort which has undoubtedly contributed to the rise in understanding and sympathy demonstrated by the liberal groups mentioned previously. With anthropological support, Aboriginal art has moved from being 'primitive and worthless' to being one of the most highly sought-after art forms in the world, bringing economic independence to a number of communities. Aboriginal relations with land have entered wider environmental and spiritual discourses, often very romantically, but this has still been productive in enlisting support for indigenous rights. There is now significant support for Aboriginal interests, and for reconciliation between Aboriginal and non-Aboriginal Australians.

Relatively speaking, if one considers other parts of the world – such as Southern Africa and South America – in which tiny minorities of hunter-gatherers have also been dispossessed by European colonial settlement, Aboriginal Australian efforts to regain land title and autonomy have been at least partially successful. Clearly there is some way to go, but nevertheless, without the presence of the large tribal groups which have assisted Native American and Maori claimants,[4] Aboriginal Australians have made significant progress towards their goals.

However, what this has meant for anthropologists is that they are commonly described by the extreme elements in groups opposed to these interests as 'traitors', 'troublemakers' or 'bloody interfering do-gooders'. Seen as being aligned with Aboriginal interests, they are co-recipients of the same racist hostilities, and are regularly subjected, in the field and in the media, to attacks upon their professional competence, their integrity and their supposed objectivity. (This resonates with the experiences related by Kravva in Chapter 8 of this volume, of Orthodox Greek responses to anthropological research on Jewish groups in Thessaloniki.) In the outback, the pastoralist community is rarely shy about expressing its feelings on these issues, and thus conducting ethnographic research in places such as North Queensland can be quite lively. One has, quite routinely, to deal with hostile responses to involvement with Aboriginal communities along the lines of 'Why on earth do you want to work with those people?' – though not always framed in such polite terms.

The latest development in Australia is for those opposed to land claims to spend very large sums of money suing anthropologists for millions of dollars, as in the Hindmarsh case, in which anthropologist Deane Fergie was forced to defend her evidence to the land tribunal, and her professional reputation. The Hindmarsh case began in 1994, and hinged upon the claim by a group of Ngarrindjeri women, assisted by Fergie, a feminist (who was appointed by the Aboriginal Legal Rights Movement), that the construction of a bridge across from the mainland to Hindmarsh Island would damage their sacred sites. In mid-1995 a different group of Ngarrindjeri women disputed this claim, opening up a violently contentious debate about the 'fabrication' of evidence and resulting in a virulent attack upon anthropology and – most specifically – feminist anthropology. As Gelder and Jacobs point out, in this argument:

> the Right is sceptical ('rational', 'commonsensical', 'masculine'), while the Left is gullible ('indulgent', 'feminine', 'too accommodating').
>
> (1997: 6)

Clearly the issue of anthropology as a 'science' is central to this case, and it demonstrates precisely why the concept of professional objectivity is vital in the legal arena. It also opens up another way of considering how the feminisation of anthropology has set it politically at odds with fundamentally patriarchal institutions – but this is a time-consuming tangent which we might leave to another occasion.

These legal issues were discussed extensively at a recent conference on Native Title in Perth, which brought together lawyers, historians, linguists and anthropologists, as well as leading Aboriginal academics and activists. Much concern was expressed about the lack of legal protection afforded to anthropologists. Deane Fergie is fortunate (depending on how you look at it) in that her university carries some insurance and is supporting her legal battle, but many anthropologists in Australia work independently, and, although there is a professional Association similar to that in the UK, it does not have a licensing system or professional insurance to provide any kind of protective umbrella.

In this difficult context, anthropologists are, not surprisingly, heavily bogged down in legal technicalities, either compiling evidence for land claims, or defending their data in a rather fraught legal and political arena. Reflexive discussions about ethics are something of a luxury under such circumstances, yet also – perhaps because of the political exigencies – have become increasingly important. There have been some major developments in the relationship between anthropologists and the people who are – more often than not – both their clients and the objects of anthropological research.

Negotiating the (mine)field

Early encounters were characterised by a fairly typical colonial dynamic, in which anthropologists were at least overtly in control of the interaction, although it is equally clear that Aboriginal communities have always directed the engagement in many subtle ways. Nevertheless, anthropologists produced their representations of Aboriginal culture untroubled by reflexive angst, and with little opposition. At the same time, even in the earliest days, they often made real efforts to assist the Aboriginal groups with whom they worked, mediating and interceding with colonial authorities to protect and support Aboriginal interests. In subsequent decades it was a relatively natural shift to become involved as advocates and advisers in the land rights movement and other emergent struggles for Aboriginal autonomy.

Some of the changes in the relationship have been initiated by developments within anthropology itself: its own rejection of colonialism; the critique of its power relations with informants by feminist anthropologists and the postmodernists who followed their lead towards polyvocality and equality. The move towards new power dynamics has been further encouraged by reflexive theoretical questioning of the potential for objectivity – and thus of anthropology as a science – and by cultural relativism and the implied impossibility of an 'outsider' offering an emic perspective.

Meanwhile, with rising self-determination, Aboriginal Australians have become steadily more experienced in the process of engagement with legal and political institutions, learning the language of political discourse and tapping into the debates independently. There are now leading Aboriginal academics and lawyers, a number of urban and rural activist groups, and even in Aboriginal communities still living on or near their land in remote areas, much greater engagement with discourses about rights, power relations and representation. Aboriginal leaders such as Noel Pearson have made explicit statements about the need for 'a moral society which keeps the mechanisms of justice functioning' and for new institutions which disavow colonialism (Pearson and Sanders 1995: 1, 3).

This has created a considerable diversity of attitudes to anthropology. On the one hand, many – possibly most – anthropologists who work in Australia enjoy close, long-term relationships with specific Aboriginal groups. This is carefully managed by the communities, who typically demand that all anthropologists now seek permission to conduct research, that the relationship should be reciprocal and that its benefits to the community should be made clear. More often than not, anthropologists 'exchange' work or expertise in order to do 'their own' research. For example, whenever I make a trip to the community I work with in North Queensland, I usually spend a significant amount of time doing cultural mapping – collecting information that the elders want to see recorded in some concrete form. This work is largely unpublished, being held by the community for its own uses: usually educational purposes and land claim evidence. I also send research proposals to the community prior to starting the project, and outline any broader benefits which I hope will result from the work.

Modern relationships with Aboriginal groups require very careful negotiation: there are delicate questions about access to, ownership of, and publication of Aboriginal cultural knowledge. These questions can have major legal implications, since most communities are now embroiled in battles over land. There are tricky social issues: generational differences in attitudes to anthropologists and envisaged power relations. Thus one can find, on the one hand, elders who offer anthropologists (often unwanted) decision-making powers and authority, while on the other hand middle-aged Local Council members may be attempting to assert the community's independence and create very different forms of interaction with outsiders. Relations between the anthropologist and adoptive Aboriginal families may be quite different from those with their more distant kin or members of other language groups. Further complications can be produced by the influence of European Australian gatekeepers and community employees, who may have their own views of what the relationship should entail. Pastoralists on surrounding cattle stations, worried that the Native Title legislation will threaten their tenure and control over the land, often introduce another source of tension into the equation.

It is therefore something of a minefield, and outsiders must necessarily make considerable efforts to negotiate its complexities without causing offence to one party or another. With such diversity of views, this is far from straightforward, and occasionally researchers are rudely ejected from communities for having taken a wrong step. For example, a few years ago when I was in Kowanyama, a linguist who had spent 20 years working with one of the language groups wrote something deemed patronising by a long-term gatekeeper, and, despite the protests of his adoptive family, found himself expelled from the community and forbidden to return. I last saw him sitting under a tree, crying because of this sudden rejection, and the severing of 20 years of academic endeavour and personal friendships.

Thus Aboriginal communities have been able to rebalance the relationship between themselves and anthropologists quite considerably, although it is obvious that professional academics, despite an awkward political position and savage funding cuts, are still educationally, socially and economically advantaged in comparison with most Aboriginal people. Nevertheless, the relationship is now probably as near equal as can be achieved without parity in all of these areas. It is therefore feasible, in such a context, to practice anthropology with some confidence that there is a genuinely reciprocal role built into research practices. Unless one is unlucky, the contentious issues can usually be negotiated within the context of long-term relationships in which the anthropologist is incorporated into the community as a trusted supporter of Aboriginal aspirations.

Providing such support is rarely a source of conflict for anthropologists: being privy to an understanding of Aboriginal relations with land, the majority of researchers have little doubt as to the validity of Native Title, and as witnesses of the social difficulties challenging many Aboriginal communities, are obviously sympathetic to calls for social justice. Even those of us who also work with other non-Aboriginal Australian groups, and can empathise with their concerns, have to situate these alongside the compelling evidence of Aboriginal groups' need for the wider society to change. Nevertheless, there is a need for keen reflexive awareness that the personal sympathies that might be engendered by such intimate knowledge have to be placed alongside – rather than muddled with – the process of ethnographic analysis. It is also clear that there are sometimes conflicting demands in the roles of ethnographer and advocate.

Representing 'the other'

The ethical dilemmas faced by anthropologists are perhaps more visible when anthropologists publish their work in a wider arena. The small but growing number of Aboriginal academics, lawyers and political activists already referred to, are closely engaged in debating the ethics and practice of anthropology. At a larger, more abstract level, without the trust engendered by long-term relationships, and with some political gain to be made from asserting Aboriginal autonomy in intellectual as well as practical matters, anthropologists find themselves increasingly questioned, not only by the groups most hostile to Aboriginal interests, but by Aboriginal leaders themselves. Although this suggests a further welcome equalisation of relations, it also poses some challenging questions which go right to the heart of anthropologists' own debates about professional ethics.

Let us return, for example, to the issue of representing the other, and the open question as to the propriety of doing this. I use the word 'propriety' deliberately, because, like the words 'appropriate' and 'proper', it has a double meaning, referring on the one hand to 'good conduct' and 'suitability' and on the other to concepts of 'ownership' and 'appropriation'. The propriety or ethical 'suitability' of anthropological representation cannot be detached from questions about who owns such representation, and who has the right to decide how – or indeed whether or not – it will be constructed.

This is an issue which has exercised anthropological consciences for some time and which is intertwined with the shift away from a view of anthropology as a science. Science – doubtless far more than it deserves – is still considered to contain the potential for objective analysis and 'laws' or 'rules' which can be generalised. Anthropology, meanwhile, has undergone an intense critique of this supposed 'objectivity' by feminist anthropologists and writers keen to expose colonial hegemony.[5] The postmodern theories which emerged from this critique have further pushed the discipline towards the humanities, and have continued to encourage a highly reflexive approach.[6]

In the last few decades anthropologists, in an attempt to leave behind their colonial baggage, have embraced an increasingly liberal political stance, characterised by a growing discourse about ethics and real efforts to attain more equal and reciprocal relationships with informants. However, at the same time many scholars have become concerned that a professional willingness to admit to being subjective, fallible, and hampered by north–south inequalities in economic and political power, coupled with a marked shift towards cultural relativism, is in danger of undermining the very foundations of anthropology: its ability to make valid cross-cultural comparisons. Sperber, for example, maintained that:

> the huge mass of data collected by ethnographers is twice devoid of scientific usefulness: today because there are hardly any anthropological hypotheses to confirm or disconfirm; forever because the interpretative character of these data is not compatible with the required level of reliability.
>
> (1985: 11)

'Yet' he went on to say, 'without ethnographic evidence, no science of culture is conceivable' (*ibid.*).

Clifford, while taking a shot at what he calls 'the myth of fieldwork', notes that:

The actual experience, hedged around with contingencies, rarely lives up to the ideal; but as a means for producing knowledge from an intense, intersubjective engagement, the practice of ethnography retains a certain exemplary status.

(1988: 24)

And Peacock, though commenting that all so-called 'science' is interpretative, comes out in support of ethnography as a basis for analysis:

Ethnography is also a way of generalising about humanity. Like the novel, poem and parable, but also like the scientific experiment, ethnography ... must imply and teach general significances through presentation of particular experiences and patterns ... A great ethnographic work is both scientific and literary, attaining a marked degree of objective precision, yet translating patterns discerned in the alien group into a form comprehensible to the reader at home.

(1986: 90)

Modern anthropology is therefore often described as suffering from a crisis of identity, an internal angst which vacillates between an anxious desire to conduct research without taking an authoritative role, and a staunch defence of precisely such 'authority'. At the same time, anthropology has tumbled down the pecking order of disciplinary status from being a leading intellectual profession in the first half of the twentieth century, to being a more dubious activity in the second. It is interesting to note that this change has been accompanied by a demographic 'feminisation' of anthropology, and in a sense, one might describe this internal divide as a conflict between the *anima* and the *animus* of the profession expressing the sometimes gendered values of its practitioners.

What are the implications of this '*crise*' for the ethical practice of anthropology? And how does it affect relationships between anthropologists and indigenous groups and the issue of anthropological representation? In the Australian political arena a large proportion of the work that anthropologists do is applied: people are either professionally involved in the land claim process, assisting Aboriginal groups in their efforts to regain traditional land, or working as advisers in the development of policies aimed at dealing with economic and social inequities. It is extremely rare for anthropologists to act for the groups opposed to Aboriginal interests. In this sense, practitioners are fulfilling both meanings of 'representation': acting as authors of particular depictions of Aboriginal lives and also as petitioners on behalf of Aboriginal rights.

In this context, representation and advocacy are not readily detached from one another, and it is clear that the question as to whether or not anthropology is a science has crucial political implications. If it has no ability to offer 'objective' analysis or specialist 'expertise' its potential to carry legal weight is seriously undermined. In effect, a successful land claim depends upon the court's acceptance of empirical ethnographic data as evidence – i.e. as proof – of land tenure. Thus, the opponents of Aboriginal rights, as I mentioned previously, have gone to considerable lengths to foreground the subjective, interpretative nature of anthropology, and its 'unreliable narration'.[7] In a country where people are often proud of their lack of respect for intellectual achievement and scholarly endeavour, such groups have been quite successful in devaluing the representations offered by anthropologists and promulgating the view that, rather than being accurate, impartial analysts, anthropologists are merely bleeding-heart liberal do-gooders, or left-wing subversives, identifying emotionally with indigenous groups, and anxious to preserve them in traditional aspic so as to have a suitably 'authentic' object of study.

The political tensions about representation in the legal arena have also made it difficult for anthropologists to 'represent' Aboriginal culture in a wider sense. As well as being involved in land claims, most also undertake what could be called 'pure' anthropological research, although in reality this – more often than not – takes place alongside more applied roles, or at least within the frame of a professional relationship characterised by these. Because all aspects of Aboriginal life are traditionally mediated by the land, there are few, if any, areas of research in which land issues are irrelevant. Even work apparently unrelated to land claims is regularly used by the courts, who are also empowered to *sub poena* any unpublished material, field notes, or data of any kind. For example, when I organised an Oxford seminar given by the President of the National Native Title Tribunal, he mentioned casually that my book, *Uncommon Ground*, had turned up on his desk labelled as 'Exhibit Number 11'.

In effect, then, no ethnographic research relating to Aboriginal life is free of political implication and potential conflict. For example, because of the difficulties experienced by Aboriginal communities in gaining the support and respect of many Australians, it is extremely contentious to write about some social problems such as the levels of violence in indigenous communities, or their related problems with drugs and alcohol. In this context Bell, writing about rape in indigenous communities, critiqued the cultural relativism applied in the courts, and found that her efforts to explore the ethical dilemmas were suppressed:

> I was commissioned by several journals to write about the ethical dilemmas confronting anthropologists in the courts ... but found that the lawyers on the case had approached the journals and requested that in 'best interests' of Aborigines, the piece did not

appear. Although one was already typeset, the editor withdrew the piece.

(1993: 38–9)[8]

Although practitioners who have well-established relationships with communities are now beginning to write about these issues, for a long time it has seemed that there is an expectation for anthropologists to be uncritical cultural relativists or complicit in a denial of these problems, rather than to provide fuel for the often simplistic and negative portrayal of Aboriginal life in the general media. At the same time, the causes of such social problems are complex, and the solutions highly elusive. If they are to be solved at all, they require precisely the kinds of in-depth analysis that anthropology is most able to provide.

There are other, more subtle problems experienced by Aboriginal people, which may also benefit from anthropological forms of analysis. For example, there are some representational issues which, with the intense focus on legal nitty-gritty, have so far been largely ignored. In attempting to consider these at the Perth conference, I ran into precisely the ethical question raised at the outset: the propriety of an 'outsider' making representations of Aboriginal culture.

The conference was concerned with the issues of Native Title, and it was attended by lawyers, anthropologists, historians, linguists and a small number of Aboriginal writers and activists. The paper I presented (Strang, in press) considered the recursive effects of Aboriginal involvement in the Native Title process. To be successful in a land claim, Aboriginal groups have to prove several things. There is no need here to go into the complexities of the legislative criteria but, basically, they have to establish that they had prior ownership of the land, that they were dispossessed, and that they retain customary – social and religious – ties to the land – i.e. clan estates based on totemic ancestry.

In practice, what this means is that the legal process – which often takes many years (for example the Mabo case took 10), requires that they display themselves – to their advocates and protagonists alike – as victims of colonial violence and subsequent subjugation and as a people still living according to 'authentic' traditions and 'Ancestral Law'. It therefore requires Aboriginal people to construct a self-representation of identity based heavily on the past, and most specifically on the negative events in the past: it is often a lengthy account of massacres, murders, poisoning, abductions, rape, the separation of families, dispersal and dispossession.

Because many groups have been moved a long way from their traditional land their opportunities to visit it may be very limited. Quite often expeditions to traditional country will take place with outsiders, and will be for the purpose of communicating these messages to them within a legislative context (see Strang 2000b). Such representations can therefore form a

184

significant proportion of the interactions that people have with their traditional land. The focus is on sites at which these events took place, creating, in effect, a representational tour of past traumas, rather than a more normal, holistic interaction with the land (see Plate 9.2).

Involvement in Native Title can therefore have a narrowing, reductive effect. Like most such communities, since achieving self-governance in 1987 the Aboriginal groups in Kowanyama have developed a broad range of ways to interact with other local land users and interest groups in debates about land management and control. As a community adviser commented:

> 'Raising the dead', as you have put it, is just one of the many tools that many people – including indigenous [peoples] – use in their interaction with others, and often in negotiations.
>
> (Viv Sinnamon, personal communication)

However, the demanding endeavour of embarking upon a Native Title claim tends to give precedence to the legislative requirements. More reductive and contentious issues are brought to the foreground and can often come to dominate the proceedings, sometimes superseding – and even damaging – the more sophisticated and delicate negotiations with other groups that Aboriginal communities have developed over a number of years.

Plate 9.2 Kunjen elder Colin Lawrence describes the history of a large grave site

Native Title legislation is generally presented as a process of Aboriginal empowerment; there is no doubt that it has significantly improved the possibilities for Aboriginal groups to reclaim their land or at least to regain some access to it, and some control. It has also had some important effects in bringing together dispersed communities and re-establishing the transmission of traditional knowledge. However, the question I raised at the Perth conference was about the recursive psychological effects of the Native Title process: the way in which it requires a continual revisiting of sites of trauma, and demands that – in order to prove dispossession – Aboriginal groups identify themselves, over and over, as the victims of colonial events. I suggested that, in the light of some of the social issues endemic in Aboriginal communities, there is a need to examine the Native Title process reflexively, to consider its effects on the well-being of Aboriginal communities, and to ask whether, in enforcing this kind of identification, it is fundamentally disempowering.

In general, the paper was well received. However, the very first response came from a leading Aboriginal academic, and it was expressed with considerable force. Was this question, she asked, an appropriate one? Was it, in other words, appropriate for a non-Aboriginal person to comment on this issue?

A good question, albeit a challenging one, in front of a large and politically very diverse audience.

I suggested that the heavy focus on legal issues should not preclude a more reflexive analysis of the Native Title process itself, and that such questions ought to be considered. She was more concerned, however, with the political dimension of a non-Aboriginal commentary on what is clearly a highly sensitive issue.

'Imagine if you were Jewish', she said.

'I am Jewish', I answered.

'Well, imagine that you had lost all your family in the Holocaust!', she continued.

I replied that this question was very close to home, as my father, a refugee from Prague, had indeed lost all his family in the Holocaust. 'But,' I said, 'this is a very good comparison, because clearly this issue is also one that many Jewish groups have had to consider: whether to revisit and represent the past continually, in order that people do not forget it, or whether to deny it, in order to try to put it behind them.'

We ended up having what I felt was a productive discussion about the problem for all 'victim' groups, in choosing whether or how to identify with a traumatic past, and the psychological effects of doing so. After the session we had a much longer, and very amiable talk about the complex issues involved. I was asked subsequently by the conference organisers to enlarge the paper for publication, and hope that this Aboriginal academic will be chosen as one of the referees, because her input would undoubtedly be very useful.

All the same, her question remains a challenging one. I have been visiting Kowanyama for nearly 20 years. I did all my doctoral research there; I have close relationships with quite a few people in the community; I have an adoptive family and thus a 'bush name' and a place in the kinship structure of the Kunjen people. I have always been made welcome there; accommodation has been provided for me for each visit, and my research has been supported by the Community Council and the Office which manages land and resources. Although there is a keen and sometimes interrogative interest in my research from the community advisers and leaders, no-one in Kowanyama has ever questioned its 'propriety'. I send them anything I have written about the community so that they can comment on it, but only once have they ever asked me to omit anything (some maps which had some potential to be significant in legal terms). If they have concerns, the concerns are generally in this area – to do with the publication of material which may be used in evidence at a land claim. Otherwise, the only feedback I have had is positive – usually in the form of alternative views and useful additional information.

All the same, I would not at any time classify myself as an 'insider', and I am keenly aware that in the context of research with the community, proprietary rights or ownership of the knowledge generated is always a potentially problematic issue. Much of the information would never be generated without the application of anthropological theoretical models, but it is nonetheless based on empirical data which are Aboriginal at source, and the acquisition of this knowledge is empowering – not just according to Foucault (1972, 1984) but also in Aboriginal cultural terms in which the gaining of restricted knowledge is the basis for social and political authority. At the same time, it is impossible to do anthropology at all without to some extent 'appropriating' cultural knowledge for the purposes of analysis, and the question remains whether, in an unequal power relationship, it is 'appropriate' to do this, or whether it constitutes what, in an obvious reference to Said's work (1979, 1993), Attwood and Arnold have called 'Aboriginalism'. One of the criteria for this, they say, are Aboriginal studies by 'experts' who claim that Aboriginal people cannot represent themselves, and must therefore be represented by experts who know more about them than they do themselves (Attwood and Arnold 1992: i).

In attempting to answer the Aboriginal professor's question, I pointed to the potential for cross-cultural comparison, and the validity of common experience. Although this was not at all calculated – her question was actually quite unnerving in such a public and politically charged forum – I am aware that for my Aboriginal friends in Queensland this would probably be regarded as the most valid of potential responses. It is, essentially, an identification with their experiences, and so suggestive, if not of 'insider' status, at least of some important areas of common ground which, as Josephides notes in Chapter 3 of this volume, provides the basis for empathy. Over the years, although I have had little reason to discuss my family history with people in Kowanyama, it has occasionally entered discussions about – and comparison with – colonial activities and dispossession in other parts of the world, and I recall one friend expressing surprise and relief that this is not something that happens just to Aboriginal people.

Other anthropologists have commented upon the value of shared experience. As Clifford says:

> 'Experience' has served as an effective guarantee of ethnographic authority ... [it] evokes a participatory presence, a sensitive contact with the world to be understood, a rapport with its people, a concreteness of perception. It also suggests a cumulative, deepening knowledge.
>
> (1988: 37)

Dwyer (1982) has suggested that our ability to understand and describe 'the other' depends upon 'identifying with' the communities with which we work, and Rosaldo indicates that it was only his own experiences of bereavement that enabled him to understand grief among the head-hunting Ilongots of the Philippines. As he put it:

> The ethnographer, as a positioned subject, grasps certain human phenomena better than others ... life experiences both enable and inhibit particular kinds of insight ... nothing in my own experience equipped me even to imagine the anger possible in bereavement until after Michelle Rosaldo's death in 1981. Only then was I in a position to grasp the force of what Ilongots had repeatedly told me about grief, rage and headhunting.
>
> (Rosaldo 1993: 19)

However, an open identification with the experiences of 'the other', although it may be seen by 'the other' as a positive expression of empathy and as a political statement of equality, also makes the anthropologist vulnerable to accusations of subjectivity or 'appropriation' which most of us seek to avoid. It also raises a major question as to whether such identification can be reconciled with the apparently opposite pole of impartial, scientific objectivity demanded not only by some elements within the profession, but also by the realities of involvement in the political arena.

As Hsu has suggested, the problem of 'who has a right to represent a culture' could be avoided – at least to some degree[9] – by concentrating on conducting anthropological research 'at home', 'making the systematic study of the ethnographer's own culture ... the first order of business' (1979: 526), and by leaving Aboriginal studies to be done by Aboriginal people. However, this removes what some regard as a vital potential for cross-cultural comparison, and it also presents some practical problems.

In working with Aboriginal communities, it is sometimes difficult for 'outsiders', including anthropologists, to tackle sensitive social issues. At the same time, it is perhaps even more difficult for Aboriginal people, as 'insiders', to adopt an analytic 'outsider' role. Anthropology is, essentially, a discipline whose theoretical frameworks and discourses have been formed in individuated mobile western societies in which it is much more feasible for people to detach themselves from particular communities, and take the stance of an 'outsider' in order to do anthropology 'at home'. Having taught anthropology and archaeology to Aboriginal people, as part of a Ranger Training programme, and observed subsequent do-it-yourself efforts to collect ethnographic evidence for land claims, I would contend that this task is much more difficult for Aboriginal 'insiders'. This is not because of any lack of ability – although there are some educational and literacy-related obstacles to collecting data in a non-Aboriginal and highly specialised form – but largely because in such closely integrated long-term communities, it is very hard for people to accept that individuals can step 'outside' their long-standing social identity and collect information impartially. In the case of land claim data this has considerable potential to create internal divisions, and where data have been collected by people with a direct interest in the land there is also a real danger that in the tribunals subsequently assessing this evidence, opponents of the claim will be better placed to cast doubts on its impartiality and scientific objectivity.

Such a contention obviously leaves the door open to accusations of Aboriginalism: the idea that Aboriginal people cannot represent themselves. Clearly they can and do represent themselves, in many ways, in many fora, and often highly effectively, but there are both cultural and political reasons why in some contexts self-representation is more difficult and less useful than making use of the particular skills and outsider status of anthropology. Attwood and Arnold imply that no outside 'expert' can know more about a culture than its members know about themselves. At one level this is obviously irrefutable. However, one might also ask whether, if anthropology provides no meta-discourse about culture, no special 'expertise' in cultural analysis, it has any value at all, either at home or in relation to 'other' cultural groups.

Anthropologists in Australia have to deal with a reality in which if they genuinely want to assist the groups with whom they work, they must – at least in the public arena – subsume the subjective aspects of their research and sometimes the agency of the groups they 'represent'. If, instead of taking a scientifically authoritative position, they choose to wear a veil of false modesty, and frame their activities as unreliable or purely interpretative, or present their research as an anthropologically 'P.C.' collaboration with the groups with whom they work, they may actually undercut a vital role in support of indigenous communities, leaving legislative processes and social policies to be decided by groups whose understanding of Aboriginal culture is rarely more than superficial.

In such circumstances, an abdication of professional 'authority' may also become an abdication of responsibility – a denial of the political realities which attend anthropological research, and a failure to use its potential to solve problems or enable moves towards social justice.[10]

Ethics in theory

This brings us back to the relationship between ethics and theory. Writing in the 1980s Sperber maintained that:

> Anthropologists have neither the authority nor the competence to act as spokesmen for the people who have tolerated their presence, and even less to give the world professional guidance in moral or political matters.

> (1985: 5)

However, as David Mills comments in Chapter 2 of this volume, the implied separation of moral or ethical issues from intellectual endeavour is artificial. To suggest either that anthropological practice is so subjective and culturally relative as to be politically impotent, or that it is so perfectly objective as to offer value-free impartiality is to deny its very real involvement in political discourses. As Attwood and Arnold put it:

> All knowledge is political, that is, constructed by relationships of power – of domination and subordination – it is inseparable from these.

> (1992: ii)

Conclusion

Although anthropologists are by no means homogenous in their political beliefs and values, the profession's long involvement with indigenous peoples, and most particularly with minority groups, has led to a general awareness of – and concern about – human rights issues such as safety and security, social equality, land and resource distribution and cultural autonomy. It is by no means coincidental that discourses about ethics and the development of codes of ethics, has arrived alongside ideologies which reject colonialism.

As David Mills points out, our professional codes of ethics draw upon basic conventions of human rights as enshrined, for example, in the Nuremberg Convention. There are unavoidable political connotations: the very idea of rights is founded on basic principles of equality. In anthropological practice, as well as incorporating basic human rights, this extends to ideas about equality in the relationship between the anthropologist and 'the other'. Our various ethical codes are founded, implicitly, on an assumption that anthropologists should construct relationships with the groups with which they work on a basis of equality, and that – as guests – they should prioritise the needs of their host communities.

In defining general rights and responsibilities such codes are also bound up with theory, being dependent upon an assumption that there is some potential for universality, some level of commonality in human experience. Without the potential for cross-cultural comparison there is little foundation for 'universal rights' of any kind. In this sense, absolute cultural relativity – while it can sound more tolerant – may be far more devoid of moral content than the most appropriative of 'scientific' models. As Nugent suggests in Chapter 4 of this volume, a widespread commitment to cultural relativism makes ethical codes redundant.

Nevertheless, ethical codes, if they are not to be merely a further imposition of western colonial authority, do need to accommodate culturally diverse values 'up to a point' – and this point is where universal rights take precedence. There is thus considerable congruence between the need to balance models of cultural diversity with concepts of common humanity. At a theoretical level, we need to accommodate modest subjective interpretations as well as the comparative potential of anthropology's more 'authoritative' meta-discourses about culture. In neither case are the extremes mutually exclusive: it is more a matter of reconciling the *anima* and the *animus* of anthropology, and enabling them to live together harmoniously. As Harvey says:

> the universality condition can never be avoided, and those who seek to do so (as is the case in many post-modern and post-structuralist formulations) only end up hiding rather than eliminating the condition. But universality must be construed in dialectical relation with particularity. Each defines the other in such a way as to make the universality criterion always open to negotiation through the particularities of difference.
>
> (1993: 63)

On the ground, in political battlefields such as the Australian conflicts over land rights, anthropologists need to incorporate this balance into the positioning of their profession, on the one hand being willing to identify and empathise with their host communities, but on the other maintaining a level of scientific detachment which allows them to construct useful representations of Aboriginal life, both intellectually and in the legal arena. They don't necessarily have to do these things simultaneously: in reality, fieldwork is characterised by a back-and-forth motion between participation and observation, and different contexts require different foregrounding of these modes of being. In the modern relationship between anthropologists and Aboriginal communities, there is no doubt that scientific detachment and analysis is the more contentious part of the equation. However, it may also be true to say that, however comfortable close empathy and identification may be, it is the theoretical, analytic aspects of the discipline that are most valuable in assisting communities to consider their social issues reflexively and in representing Aboriginal culture in a legal arena which demands impartiality. These hard-earned skills are the real gift that anthropologists can 'exchange' reciprocally with communities, and it is these skills which, in partnership with Aboriginal communities, enable them to ask – and perhaps help to answer – 'appropriate questions'.

Notes

1 The Woodward Commission's attempts to formalise a translation of Aboriginal Law into European terms resulted in the first Aboriginal Land Rights (NT) Act of 1976, described by McCorquodale as 'one of the most far-reaching advances in vesting title to land in corporate bodies representing Aborigines' (1987: 13).

2 In 1992, the High Court of Australia ruled that an Aboriginal form of property in land had existed before the colonial invasion. This finding established the reality of Native Title, reversing the fallacy of *terra nullius* that had permitted the Crown to assume title to the land.

> 'Aboriginal and Torres Strait Islander rights of ownership existed before non-Aboriginal settlement, and may still exist where the connection with the land has been maintained and title has not been extinguished.'
>
> (Council for Aboriginal Reconciliation 1993: 5)

3 The new government devised a '10-point plan' which a leading Aboriginal activist, Noel Pearson (usually regarded as a moderate), described as 'absolutely obscene'. He went on to characterise the new government as 'racist scum' (Attwood and Markus 1999: 323).

4 A further difference is the early acknowledgement of Native Title encapsulated in such accords as the 1840 Treaty of Waitangi in New Zealand.

5 The critiques of Said (1979), Maquet (1961, 1973) and Asad (1970) have forcefully repudiated colonial representations of 'the other', and Foucault's work (1972, 1984) has made plain the inextricable relationships between power, knowledge and representation.

6 See for example Rabinow 1977, Dumont 1978, Clifford and Marcus 1986, Peacock 1986, Caplan 1988, Clifford 1988, Geertz 1988.

7 This is not, as a rule, because they have engaged with the internal debates within anthropology, but arises from a more general view of the discipline as an Arts or Humanities subject rather than a Science. No doubt this is partly due to anthropology's own self-representations, but it is also entangled in broader ideas about the relative reliability of qualitative 'interpretation' and quantitative 'science'.

8 See also Bell 1986, 1991.

9 This would not, of course, remove representational questions about the ethnographer's social or economic class, gender or other issues of relative power within her or his 'own' society.

10 Susan Greenwood makes a similar point elsewhere in this volume. In previous work on the occult she has also noted the conflict between 'academic anthropological discourses and an internal examination of the process and philosophy of magical practice ... so-called "rational" and "irrational" worlds' (2000: 18–19).

Bibliography

Asad, T. (1970) *The Kababish Arabs: power, authority and consent in a nomadic tribe*, London: C. Hurst.

Attwood, B. and Arnold, J. (eds) (1992) *Power, Knowledge and Aborigines, special edition of the Journal of Australian Studies*, Clayton, Victoria: La Trobe University Press in association with the National Centre for Australian Studies.

Attwood, B. and Markus, A. (1999) *The Struggle for Aboriginal Rights: a documentary history*, NSW: Allen and Unwin.

Beckett, J. (1987) *Torres Strait Islanders: custom and colonialism*, Cambridge: Cambridge University Press.

Bell, D. (1986) 'In the case of the anthropologists and the lawyers', *Legal Services Bulletin*, 11 (5): 202–6.

—— (1991) 'Intra-racial rape revisited: on forging a feminist future beyond factions and frightening politics', *Women's Studies International Forum*, 14 (5): 385–412; 507–13.

—— (1993) 'Yes Virginia, there is a feminist ethnography: reflections from three Australian fields', in D. Bell, P. Caplan and W. Karim (eds) *Gendered Fields: women, men and ethnography*, London: Routledge.

Bell, D., Caplan, P. and Karim, W. (eds) (1993) *Gendered Fields: women, men and ethnography*, London: Routledge.

Bennett, S. (1999) *White Politics and Black Australians*, St Leonards, NSW: Allen and Unwin.

Caplan, P. (1988) 'Engendering knowledge: the politics of anthropology', *Anthropology Today*, 4 (5): 8–12, and 4 (6): 14–17.

Clifford, J. (1988) *The Predicament of Culture: twentieth century ethnography, literature and art*, Cambridge, MA and London: Harvard University Press.

Clifford J. and Marcus, G. (1986) *Writing Culture: the poetics and the politics of ethnography*, Berkeley: University of California Press.

Council for Aboriginal Reconciliation (1993) *Making Things Right: reconciliation after the High Court's decision on Native Title*, Canberra: Council for Aboriginal Reconciliation.

Dumont, J-P. (1978) *The Headman and I: ambiguity and ambivalence in the fieldworking experience*, Austin and London: University of Texas Press.

Dwyer, K. (1982) *Moroccan Dialogues: anthropology in question*, Baltimore, MD: Johns Hopkins University Press.

Foucault, M. (1972) *The Archaeology of Knowledge*, London: Tavistock.

—— (1984) *The History of Sexuality*, Vol 1. Harmondsworth: Penguin.

Geertz, C. (1988) *Works and Lives: the anthropologist as author*, Cambridge: Polity Press.

—— (1993) *The Interpretation of Cultures*, New York: Fontana Press.

Geddie, W. (ed.) (1964) *Chambers Twentieth Century Dictionary*, Edinburgh, London: W. and R. Chambers Ltd.

Gelder, K. and Jacobs, J. (1997) 'Promiscuous sacred sites: reflections on secrecy and scepticism in the Hindmarsh Island affair', *Australian Humanities Review*, http://www.lib.latrobe.edu.au/AHR/archive/Issue-June 1997/gelder.html

Greenwood, S. (2000) *Magic, Witchcraft and the Otherworld: an anthropology*, Oxford, New York: Berg.

Harvey, D. (1993) 'Class relations, social justice and the politics of difference', in M. Keith and S. Pile (eds) *Place and the Politics of Identity*, London and New York: Routledge.

Hsu, F. (1979) 'The cultural problem of the cultural anthropologist', *American Anthropologist*, 81: 517–32.

Maquet, J. (1961) *The Premise of Inequality in Ruanda: a study of political relations in a Central African kingdom*, London: Oxford University Press.

—— (1973) *The Sociology of Knowledge, its Structure and its Relation to the Philosophy of Knowledge: a critical analysis of the systems of Karl Mannheim and Pitirim A. Sorokin*; transl. J. Locke, Westport, CN: Greenwood Press.

McCorquodale, J. (1987) *Aborigines and the Law: a digest*, Canberra: Aboriginal Studies Press.

Oppenheim, F. (1968) 'The concept of equality', *The International Encylopedia of the Social Sciences*, New York: Macmillan.

Peacock, J. (1986) *The Anthropological Lens: harsh light, soft focus*, Cambridge, London, New York: Cambridge University Press.

Pearson, N. and Sanders, W. (1995) *Indigenous Peoples and Reshaping Australian Institutions: two perspectives*, Discussion paper No. 102/1995, Canberra: Centre for Aboriginal Economic Policy Research.

Rabinow, P. (1977) *Reflections on Fieldwork in Morocco*, Berkeley: University of California Press.

Rosaldo, R. (1993) *Culture and Truth: the remaking of social analysis*, London: Routledge.

Said, E. (1979) *Orientalism*, New York: Random House.

—— (1993) *Culture and Imperialism*, London: Chatto and Windus.

Sperber, D. (1985) *On Anthropological Knowledge: three essays*, Cambridge and Paris: Cambridge University Press.

Strang, V. (2000a) 'Not so black and white: the effects of aboriginal law on Australian legislation', in A. Abramson and D. Theodossopoulos (eds) *Mythical Lands, Legal Boundaries: rites and rights in historical and cultural context*, London: Pluto Press.

—— (2000b) 'Showing and telling: Australian land rights and material moralities', *Journal of Material Culture*, 5 (3): 275–99.

—— (in press) 'Raising the dead: reflecting on engagement in the Native Title process', in S. Toussaint (ed.) *Crossing Boundaries: cultural, legal and historical issues in Native Title*, Melbourne: Melbourne University Press.

10

BRITISH PAGANISM, MORALITY AND THE POLITICS OF KNOWLEDGE

Susan Greenwood

Introduction

A growing number of people in (post)modern western societies are practising magic as a form of spirituality; they are often collectively termed Pagans. Paganism is an umbrella term for various alternative spiritual 'traditions' – such as high or ceremonial magic, druidry, witchcraft or 'wicca', heathenism, and shamanism – most of which, with the exception of high or ceremonial magic (which espouses an esoteric Christianity), attempt to create what their practitioners see as a pre-Christian magical worldview. Although certain fantasy aspects of magic have been incorporated and accepted into mainstream society – through fiction for example, the most recent being J.K. Rowling's enormously popular Harry Potter children's books – practising magic as a form of spirituality is still largely regarded as countercultural and morally suspect. 'The occult' is commonly seen by mainstream British society to be concerned with a hidden power of evil that can be harnessed and used against God and 'the good'. Consequently, in the West debates on magic are frequently framed in terms of magic being inherently morally questionable.

My aim in this chapter is to examine how morality is viewed in British Paganism and to set this within the context of a discussion of some ethical issues that have arisen both from my anthropological research on Paganism, and also from my work as an anthropologist representing Paganism to the wider society. A central focus of the debate concerns the politics of the construction and use of knowledge.

While contemporary British society is multicultural, ideas about morality are largely shaped by Christianity, being framed in terms of a dualism of good and evil, the latter viewed as a malign force in the world capable of being manipulated by certain individuals, especially those who practise magic. In the past the Christian Church perpetuated notions of heresy in the construction of the witch as a follower of Satan, a force of evil set in a dualistic opposition to God, and then proceeded from the fifteenth century to the eighteenth to persecute ordinary people in the name of crimes that were largely of its own imagining (Cohn 1993). Such notions associating witchcraft with evil still have currency. More recently, in the twentieth century, there have been moral panics associated with so-called satanic abuse (Richardson *et al.* 1991). Ideas about Satan and his supposed apostate followers are thus deeply embedded in British cultural history and psychic memory; they profoundly affect how morality and magic are viewed.

Pagans tend to incorporate what are seen as the less socially acceptable aspects of magic, which they usually term 'the dark'. This generally refers to aspects of life that are, in their opinion, repressed or denied by the wider society in general and by Christianity in particular, which they often stereotype as having a focus on transcendent spirit and 'the light'. The dark may incorporate repressed aspects of the self, sexuality, and death as part of the material process of life which is seen to be intrinsically divine. Within this magical worldview there are *dualities* – such as between positive and negative, and light and dark – but no *dualism* because an underlying commonality and continuity is also recognised: there is both unity and diversity within the cosmos. The majority of Pagans claim they work with all the forces of the cosmos, which frequently involves confronting the psychological dark in the form of 'demons' or repressed aspects of the self. Many Pagans claim to be able to harness magical forces and direct them to a given aim or goal through ritual. All of this is problematic for Christianity which focuses more on the veneration of divinity, and sees the channelling of magical forces as occult manipulation.

Many Pagans tend to see their magical practice in moral terms: the idea that they are handling 'dark' and powerful forces lends weight to the notion that the power to heal, curse or employ the 'black arts' is available to those who know how to do so. Most Pagans say they make a conscious ethical choice about how to use these powers. The idea of moral choice enhances a person's identity and status and lends to it an aura of mystery, enchantment, and fantasy – the image of a powerful magician which is often a compelling motive for people to start practising magic. Indeed, some may be attracted to magic because they themselves lack power as a consequence of having suffered psychological and/or sexual trauma. Thus morality is central to magical practices, but it is an ambiguous area. Notions of morality in contemporary British magic are complex and pose many issues concerning identity and power or, more specifically, the lack of power, for the anthropological researcher (see Greenwood 2000). In this chapter I focus on three aspects of morality related to my research: first, the practices of a witchcraft coven with whose members I shared various rituals; secondly, the 'public face' of anthropology, and the morality and ethics involved in what has become known as 'auto-anthropology' or the practice of doing research within one's own culture; and thirdly, some ethical issues that have arisen through my work as an anthropologist in communicating ideas about magic in the media and to the social services. What is at issue is the problem of conveying a magical worldview to the wider culture, which, although incorporating many magical ideas, is still largely suspicious of magic when it comes to issues of morality. Before turning to these matters it is important to consider the western occult tradition in general and what is meant by a magical worldview in particular.

The western occult tradition and its magical worldview

A resurgence of interest in magic is due to a de-traditionalisation of mainstream religions and the rise of New Age and alternative spiritualities. Paganism is largely viewed as a subculture, but there is no clear dividing line between subculture and mainstream (just as there is no clear demarcation between magic and religion). Historically, ever since Christianity became the dominant religion, there has always been a partly hidden and fragmented presence of a subculture of magic in western society existing in tension with a largely Christian-influenced wider culture. The boundaries between the two have been blurred by a sustained western occult tradition dating from the Renaissance when certain magicians were influenced by the *Corpus Hermetica*, a body of first- to third-century Greek texts with strong neoplatonic influences aimed at bringing the individual closer to the deity (Yates 1991). Since that time there has been a fluctuating substratum of magico-religious ideas, cosmologies and ontologies incorporating Rosicrucianism, Freemasonry, Theosophy and Liberal Catholicism.

The occult tradition has been expressed in romantic creations of Celticity used in regional power confrontations against English nationalism. One obvious example is the political campaign of the poet W.B.Yeats which invoked an Irish nationalist Celtic spirituality, but others include fairy stories and, more recently, films (*The Blair Witch Project* and its sequel; *Harry Potter and the Philosopher's Stone*; *The Lord of the Rings*) and television programmes (*Xena the Warrior Princess*; *Buffy the Vampire Slayer*; *Charm*, an American series about teenage witches). In addition, mainstream bookshops are full of books on magic ranging from historical studies of medieval grimoires and examination of the literature on the Faust legends, to practical manuals on working magic aimed at the popular market. There are the Harry Potter books for children young and old, and for teenage witches there are titles such as *How to Turn Your Ex-boyfriend into a Toad*, and *Sabrina*, a magazine advertised on television giving the usual girlie advice on fashion and make-up but with a 'witchy' glamour. There are also the perennially popular classics of J.R.R. Tolkien, which are currently undergoing a huge new interest with the release of the films, and the humorous novels of Terry Pratchet.

The western occult tradition has had élite aspects to its varied history. It has been associated with the upper classes and political leaders of the time. For example, Cosimo de' Medici employed the Renaissance magician Marsilio Ficino to translate the *Corpus Hermetica* from Greek into Latin; Elizabeth I relied on John Dee, her court astrologer and adviser; and during the twentieth century it was said that Nancy Reagan, wife of US President Ronald Reagan, and Princess Diana also consulted astrologers. Magic has also been taken up by the middle classes: a revival in the nineteenth century of the Hermetic Order of the Golden Dawn by leading Rosicrucians and Freemasons provided much of the impetus for the development of modern witchcraft, synthesised from various elements of high magic in the 1940s by Gerald Gardner, a retired civil servant. Modern witchcraft in the early days of the 1950s was a middle-class pursuit, broadening its appeal only in the 1980s. Druidry likewise has changed its image from an eighteenth century 'gentlemen's club' to a 'nature religion' allegedly open to all. Magic has reached its most working-class expression in 'chaos magick', a derivative of chaos theory and punk rock. Nonetheless, contemporary Pagans are often, although not exclusively, middle class; they frequently elect to opt out of the mainstream culture by placing themselves on the cultural margins of society through choice rather than circumstance. They are, for the most part, intelligent and well educated, perhaps opting out of a life which they consider to be alien and boring; others may be employed in well-paid jobs – especially in the computer industry (Luhrmann 1989). A significant number may be asserting their identities as 'native peoples', reflected in Celtic or heathen spiritualities.

The sociologist Max Weber observed that the 'fate of our times' was characterised by rationalisation, intellectualisation and, above all, by the 'disenchantment of the world' (in Gerth and Wright Mills 1974: 155). Through the use of Friedrich Schiller's phrase, he was referring to the degree to which rationalisation had displaced magical elements in modern societies (*ibid.*: 51). Many Pagans seek an alternative spirituality which involves a re-enchantment of the world by (re)learning to think magically, coming to see the world as alive rather than as an inanimate machine. This is a view that sees psychic and spiritual connections between phenomena – broadly in the terms of Frazer's 'sympathetic magic' – as a cognitive orientation formed by relationships between things. Ideologically, magicians have a dialectical relationship to the process of life. This means that all of Nature – perhaps symbolised as Gaia, or the Goddess – is viewed by many magicians as organismic, animate and having a vital force. It also means that good and evil – light and dark – are integral components of the world: they form a dialectical relationship to each other rather than an oppositional dualism as Christianity would have it. Practically, this means that most Pagans seek to include those aspects denied or suppressed by dualistic cosmologies under the heading of 'the dark'.

Thus re-enchantment means developing a different worldview whereby the world is viewed as composed of inherent energies – positive and negative – all of which may be tapped by persons so attuned. Michel Foucault, in his history of insanity, *Madness and Civilization* (1999), noted that Renaissance magic encompassed all aspects of the dark including the demons of madness that could lead to esoteric knowledge and wisdom about the meaning of life and death. Later, during the classical 'age of reason' in the eighteenth century, such notions came to be denied and projected onto the mad. He claimed that the invention of madness as a disease was peculiar to western civilisation; it served as a means of evading a penetrating vision into the depths of the self, combined with externalising this vision onto others who became 'the mad'.[1] Thus for contemporary Pagans contacting the dark concerns a certain amount of spiritual psychotherapy. Engaging with the dark may also be used for positive healing purposes, spiritual growth and self-understanding, as well as hexing and cursing in the form of rituals aimed at a specific purpose, such as retribution against an unreasonable employer. Inevitably, Pagans are much like other people in that sometimes what they say is different from what they do and their ideals may differ from their lived practice. Through a discussion of morality, and using a specific example of what I consider to be 'negative magic', I now turn to some ethical parameters and implications of my fieldwork.

Morality in witchcraft

Notions of morality are central to magic. The idea of choice – the ability to choose positive life-affirming magic over negative – is central to magicians' ideas of self identity. It is said by many practitioners that a magician must know how to handle the dark and be able to use those powers where necessary to facilitate healing, self-understanding, and the mysteries of transformation. Morality is personal, internal and determined ideologically by an individual's relationship with a spiritual otherworld. In practice, it is also determined by social context of witchcraft coven, magical group or magical lodge. In witchcraft the 'Wiccan Rede' – 'An it harm none, do as ye will' – is the main moral maxim, but it is vague and problematic when applied to practical social ethics. Morality is a 'grey area' where there are no formal codes of behaviour or practice. Everything ultimately rests on an individual's relationship with otherworldly spirits, and otherworldly spirits tend to reflect social power. In other words, those who are deemed more important socially have spiritual contacts which are more 'authentic', thus carrying more weight.

In Paganism there are no institutional checks and balances to pick up any abuse of power, unlike the situation in an established mainstream religion such as the Church of England, for example. However, it is worth noting that this is no guarantee of protection: the Catholic Church has not been very effective in this area, sometimes supporting its priests at the expense of those who have been abused. Each witchcraft coven is a small 'family-type' group traditionally said to have a maximum of 13 members, but frequently many fewer – perhaps half that number in my experience. Usually the high priestess and her high priest have overall charge of what happens in the group; when coveners reach the status of high priestess or high priest (typically after two or three initiations, depending on tradition) they 'hive off' to form a new coven. Instead of this happening, however, sometimes the high priestess and high priest may encourage dependency – with the high priestess and high priest meeting their own needs and acting as 'parents' – rather than fostering independence. Morality is mediated through the power flow within the group: the high priestess and high priest are in a powerful position to define what is ethically right or wrong and in this they are backed up by divine legitimation of the otherworldly forces. They also have the threat of hexing to ensure conformity by potentially recalcitrant members if things get too difficult. Thus while creating a magical worldview has its positive side and can be spiritually therapeutic and healing, it can also lead to paranoia: if you believe you have been cursed, and you believe in curses, then the curse is usually effective.

Magical practices attract a large number of people with various psycho-sexual problems who are drawn to magic as moths to a flame: the promise of power to the powerless. There is a strong sexual dynamic in witchcraft since sexuality is valued highly and seen as sacred. Magical knowledge is passed on in wicca from woman to man and vice versa and this adds a potent dimension to the cocktail of power relationships within a coven. Any abuse of power does usually get to be known within the wider Pagan community, but although it generates bad publicity, little or nothing is done because there is a reluctance to become involved in another coven's affairs. Paganism is an eclectic spiritual path, and it is ideologically, if not in practice, tolerant of difference; to interfere with the spiritual paths of others goes against the grain.

The popularisation of magic has made it a potential vehicle for powerful personal imaginative experiences, and this can be positively beneficial and healing. In some cases, however, things are less positive. Magical practices give people a framework for certain disassociative techniques that they have learnt in childhood as a response to physical, emotional or sexual abuse: withdrawal into an alternative fantasy world is a common survival technique for dealing with unbearable trauma. They may reproduce this behaviour in their coven relationships. Research suggests that a high number of Pagans are survivors of childhood abuse (Rabinovich 1992). There is a fine line between someone who is in control of mediating otherworlds – who knows exactly which world they are in and can act in each appropriately – and mental instability. I know of one feminist witchcraft network, loosely formed some 14 years ago, which follows a basic 'starhawkian' ideology of psycho-spiritual healing. Its members work for change within the self through the development of 'power within', combined with active protest against patriarchy and capitalism (Starhawk 1982), especially in anti-globalisation demonstrations. This coven is riven with internal strife caused by some members' psychological and emotional abuse of co-members. The actual practice of magic may compound such problems since magical practices can, in the worst cases, seriously affect physical and emotional health, thus compounding an existing mental fragility. It is for this reason that much high or ceremonial magic stresses the importance of psychotherapy and 'grounding' before starting the magical work of invoking otherworldly deities (Regardie 1981, 1991).

During my fieldwork, I was involved in a coven that was practising what I termed 'negative magic'. The high priestess had a background of having been physically and sexually abused by her father. I felt that she reproduced in the circle the power relations experienced between herself and her father, but this time she took the powerful position: instead of being a powerless child she wielded authority as high priestess. As a member of her coven, I felt totally disempowered and child-like as this high priestess manipulated the coven for her own ends. My first intuitive feeling on meeting her and her high priest was of unease, but I was not quite sure why. Before my first ritual with them, which was held in the middle of a wood at night, I experienced extreme anxiety: everything in me was telling me not to go. Ordinarily, I would not have considered joining any group feeling as I did, but I wanted to find out more about them for the research. In the event, I employed some magical techniques I had been taught and found that I could contain what I was experiencing as paralysing fear.[2]

It was a few months later that I discovered why I had been feeling so unsettled. During a surprise initiation ritual that the high priestess, in collaboration with the high priest, had sprung on the group, its dynamics suddenly became clear to me. Nobody present knew that the ritual was going to be an initiation ritual, and much was made of the fact that the coveners' participation was an act of trust in the high priestess. The high priestess set up a ritual circle in which she could play out a power confrontation – a re-enactment of a childhood abuse situation – but this time with the important difference that she emerged powerful rather than powerless. The high priest invoked the Goddess into the high priestess, who became radiant and charismatic – she spoke as the Goddess – and he expressed his allegiance to her. He performed a dramatic knife display, during which he flourished a sharp athame (a ritual knife, part of a witch's magical paraphernalia) while shouting and leaping around the room; eventually he placed the athame against a vein in his arm. With athame thus directed, he approached each woman present (apart from the high priestess, who was the Goddess) and demanded to know whether she would suffer pain for the Goddess. As one young woman, in a stunned voice, said that she wanted to learn, she was led to the altar to be initiated. The high priestess's this-worldly power having become divinely legitimated, she confirmed her own power through the initiation of the young woman and her own childhood powerlessness was (temporarily) overcome (for a fuller account see Greenwood 2000: 137–44).

Feeling as though at last I had the answer to my initial feelings of reluctance about joining this coven, I had to face the dilemma of whether or not to write about my findings. I spoke to the then President of the Pagan Federation, as well as other wiccans, about whether this surprise initiation ritual, with its threat of violence, was a legitimate wiccan practice. The general consensus was that it was not. The President pressed me for details of the high priest and high priestess, which I did not feel at liberty to give. However, I decided to write about my experience, changing personal details but keeping to the spirit of the actions, thus raising the issue of the abuse of power. As abuse is thought likely to be reproduced in families with members who have experienced abuse, I was undecided about whether I should inform social services about my anxieties about the ritual and about any possible effect on the high priestess' and high priest's children. In the event I decided not to do so, thinking that perhaps the witchcraft ritual offered a cathartic space for this woman to act out her powerlessness, thus perhaps sparing the children, if not the members of the coven.

At the time of writing the first draft of this chapter (January 2001), news has just broken of the case involving the death of Anna (later identified as Victoria) Climbié, an eight-year-old girl from Ivory Coast, thought by her great-aunt and her great-aunt's boyfriend to be possessed by demons. At the Old Bailey the aunt said that the 128 scars on the little girl's body, some of which were inflicted by knives, were caused by witchcraft. This is a different conception of witchcraft,[3] but it does demonstrate the power of magico-spiritual worldviews in legitimating abuse, and even death, in the eyes of its perpetrators. The media questioned why the social services and the medical profession did not pick up on the abuse in this case, and I reflected on whether I have done the right thing in remaining quiet about my own concerns about the witchcraft coven.

The public face of anthropology

The role of anthropologist is often an ambiguous one. There are many grey areas which may be difficult to deal with, and this may be especially so when studying within one's own country as cultural boundaries may be less clear. How does the anthropologist talk about and explain Paganism within the academic discipline of anthropology? How does she or he communicate to the wider society what has been learnt from his or her research?

In the wake of the Tierney affair, John Gledhill, in an article for the magazine *Anthropology Today*, puts out a clarion call for anthropologists to find a new public face for the discipline. Bemoaning the fact that anthropology has a low media profile and that the 'big message' about the scope of anthropology is not getting through into the public domain, he asks what is an appropriate postcolonial image of anthropology, and how should it be projected into the public sphere. Traditionally anthropologists have studied small-scale non-western societies and so surely one way of changing the image of anthropology is to develop auto-anthropology, defined by Marilyn Strathern as 'anthropology carried out in the social context which produced it' (Strathern 1987: 17); it generally concerns the study of one's own culture and one's self. The reason I chose to research contemporary western magic was that I, as a Westerner, was personally interested in magic. Although critical of much magical practice, I felt, and still feel, that it could offer an alternative view of the world. A magical worldview has potentially positive value: the physical world, women, the body, sexuality, and the environment – all of which have been denigrated by Christianity – are seen as being enspirited and are consequently valued. This could have important environmental implications.

When I started my PhD research in 1989 I was interested in examining magic 'from the inside', as a practitioner and as an anthropologist. These were, and to a certain extent still are, mutually incompatible positions. I considered myself as part of a bridge of communication between two worlds: the practitioners' world of magic and the academic discipline of anthropology. These two domains were for most of the period of my PhD fieldwork quite distinct, with little communication between them. This was largely due to the fact that the theoretical frameworks available to explain magic were still coming largely from a rationalist perspective which sees magic as lacking when compared with a positivistic view of science (for example, Luhrmann 1989). Magic has too often been understood mainly in social and cultural terms and very infrequently in terms of what it means to the individual. This has had moral and ethical consequences for the creation of a shared language to explain peoples' experiences of magic since the theoretical frameworks that exist are deeply offensive to practitioners' own understandings of what magic means to them. Indeed, for some anthropologists who take positivistic science as their model, the very idea of breaking down the boundaries between researcher and researched, as well as the theoretical dualisms between rationality and what is still perceived as 'irrationality', appear to be deeply threatening. Fortunately, other anthropologists are starting to use alternative models to think beyond rationalistic conceptions. They are reframing their theoretical metaphors and models to include multiple orderings of reality by dismantling western dualisms and looking for the connections between phenomena. Many are drawing on the pioneering work of the anthropologist, biologist and psychologist Gregory Bateson (1985, 2000) (for example, Samuel 1990, and Ingold 2000). Tim Ingold argues, in relation to studying ecology and the environment, that we need to descend from the imaginary heights of abstract reason to resituate ourselves in active and ongoing engagement with the environment to recover the reality of the life process itself (2000: 16). In effect, this is what Pagans are seeking to do, in theory if not always in practice. The implication for anthropology, and indeed for the social sciences more generally, is that the aspect of rationality is just one component of the theoretical whole; it is emphatically not a denial of rationality as such, rather a critique of rationalism.

I took a reflexive and experiential approach to my research which I felt to be morally and ethically appropriate. Thus if I was asking others to speak of intimate experiences outside the cultural norm and make them public, perhaps to a sceptical or hostile audience, then I should be prepared to do the same. The personal experience of magic is important as a way of learning about the self and what a magical worldview means; it is also vital as a basis for understanding what others are likely to be experiencing. I chose not to become formally initiated as I discovered that this was an ethically problematic area. Abusing the trust of initiation by allowing access to people, rituals and information would betray confidences and result in a breakdown of the relationship between researcher and informants, a situation I wanted to avoid. This did not mean that I was not interested in initiation and the social implications that this entailed, but I was more concerned with initiation into a magical enspirited worldview through personal experience, which I came to discover was the basis of magic. My approach, through the attempt at reducing the imbalance of power between anthropologist and informant, sought the much more mundane 'essence of magic' as ordinary, everyday practice. This did not mean that I was in the power of my informants. On the contrary, I regularly raised ethically problematic areas for the subculture as a whole on the misuse and abuse of power, and on power relationships. After I had spoken at one academic/practitioner conference about magical power and its misuse, a number of Pagans in the audience were extremely hostile to what I had to say, while some were in tears of agreement. A few approached me afterwards to thank me for raising issues which they felt they could not talk about. This was done from a position of trying to understand the dynamics of magic, and from a recognition of the centrality of the notion of an 'otherworld' as a realm of spirits or beings vital for the practice of magic but not considered important to a rationalist anthropological view.

Gledhill also asserts that anthropologists must engage with the public sphere, and that anthropological perspectives are more important than ever for society as a whole. There is a need to move from partisanship and advocacy in fieldwork to engaging with the public domain through writing:

> We need the courage to argue for and against alternatives, to challenge ethnocentrism and media stereotypes – which is sometimes a matter of revealing what is positive in the situations we study – and to contest the claims of vested interests and the politically powerful (where these claims are demonstrably false). It is

a matter of denouncing prejudice, discrimination, cynicism and hypocrisy more loudly and effectively than we can do through academic publishing alone.

(Gledhill 2000: 3)

As a British anthropologist conducting research in the West, I have been researching western magical culture, writing and talking to the media for over 10 years about magic, and consider that my work is part of the 'new public face of anthropology'. I concur with Gledhill that anthropologists need the courage to challenge ethnocentrism, vested power interests, discrimination and so on, but what about revealing what is less than positive in the situations we study? What about the abuse of power, an example of which I have already discussed? When should we 'blow the whistle' on those we study? These issues are less clear.

Engaging with the public sphere

Although I think that it is important to put across positive aspects of contemporary magical practice to counter the general distrust engendered by western cultural history, I have also had some reservations about advocating magical practice as a form of spirituality. This has given me cause for reflection on a number of occasions when my professional opinion was sought, and below I give four examples to demonstrate the type of issues with which I have had to contend. The first was when I was invited to write a book on magic and witchcraft for a popular audience; the second, when I acted as consultant for a children's book on witches and wizards; the third concerned a discussion in a church among Christians, one of whom was convinced she had satanic neighbours; and the fourth was when I had to give my considered opinion as Expert Witness in a child custody case.

Writing about witchcraft

With regard to writing about British Paganism in a non-academic context, the anthropological challenge has been to confront stereotypes of witches and magicians. I was invited to write a book on magic and witchcraft for a popular audience by a large publishing company with worldwide distribution. Feeling that it was important for anthropological work to be made more accessible, I accepted their proposal, and the work is now published as *The Encyclopedia of Magic and Witchcraft* (2001). It was an opportunity to put an anthropological and historical perspective on a misunderstood and sensationalised subject; I wanted to put across some positive aspects of magical practice – for example, its potentially positive attitude to the environment. I wrote chapters on witchcraft from around the world, early modern European witchcraft, and the witch trials.

However, the process was not unproblematic. There were no problems with writing what I wanted to regarding the historical sections, but when it came to the implications for contemporary social life and problems with established religions and child abuse, my text was altered to make it 'less political'. It was not possible for me to discuss how people might find it easier to blame scapegoats – such as satanists – for child abuse than to accept the hard reality that the perpetrator might in all probability be someone in their own family, or another known and trusted adult. This raises the issue of control, and how to deal with a popular press that is concerned with the profit from book sales and consequently does not want to be seen to be 'political'. The issue of power and its misuse can more easily be addressed in an academic format, whereas it is more difficult to raise and discuss such matters in a wider context without people reverting to stereotypes of evil magicians and witches, and 'black magic' for explanations.

Representing magic to children

As a consultant on a children's book for 7–12-year-olds on witches and wizards, I had occasion to reflect on how magic should be represented to children. How does one strike the right balance in weighing up the positive and negative aspects of contemporary witchcraft practice, for example? While I wanted to make sure that no popular stereotypical conceptions of evil witches were allowed into the author's text, I also considered what effect the book would have on young people, and whether it would encourage them to seek out a magical group when they were older (magical groups do not usually allow those under 18 to attend rituals). I feel ambivalent about some of the magical groups that I have known, but I feel equally ambivalent about some of my experiences within Christian churches. Many covens tend to reproduce social power rather than empower, but the same could be said of families as well as of other religious organisations. Morality in magical practices tends to be vague and individual, potentially encouraging a misuse of power because it is not clear-cut. However, on the plus side, thinking 'magically' – in terms of relationships between things – not only comes easily to children (Johnson 2000), but is an alternative worldview akin to that of many non-western peoples (Ingold 2000), and it is, in my opinion, the most positive aspect of western Paganism (see Greenwood, forthcoming). Tending to think animistically, children impute consciousness to things that are later learnt to be inanimate. There may be environmental implications for future generations if children are encouraged to relate to the living world around them, rather than to a lifeless 'out there'. On balance, I felt that children should be provided with as much accurate information as possible in the book to enable them to decide what they thought about magic.

Trying to provide unbiased information

Working as a consultant for INFORM (Information Focus On Religious Movements – a charity set up by the sociologist Eileen Barker of the London School of Economics to provide unbiased information on new religious movements), I have found myself in the rather frightening situation of being in the pulpit of a Christian church explaining Paganism to the congregation, one of whom was convinced that her neighbours were satanists and were sacrificing cats. How much of this is due to the stereotyped image of satanists and an active imagination fuelled by fear, and how much is true? Pagans are not satanists, and to my knowledge satanists do not usually sacrifice cats, but there are always people who will use the image of magic and satan to conduct their own form of abuse, as I have already outlined in the witchcraft ritual example. My aim in giving the talk was to try to establish communication and tolerance, and an understanding of difference. To my relief, the ensuing discussion in the church vestry was productive for all concerned and did, I felt, break down popular stereotypes and prejudices on both sides.

Acting as an Expert Witness in court

On another occasion I was called as an Expert Witness in a court case to explain a wiccan high priest's religious beliefs. He was applying for custody of his grandson, because his daughter, the mother of the boy, was unable to care for the child. She, however, did not want her father to have custody, claiming that he practised witchcraft. Her father, who had been involved in a number of different magical practices, had (deliberately, I suspect) been confusing the social workers who could not make head or tail of his beliefs. He was an extremely intelligent, self-taught man who seemed to me to take delight in creating a powerful image. He kept talking to me about 'blood rituals' and sacrifice. In the circumstances, this was not very sensible because I had to prepare a report for the Court about his Pagan practices. Contrary to my feelings about the high priestess in the abusive coven situation above, and despite his trying to impress me by his power, I felt that he was a decent person, unlikely to harm a child. This decision was based on informed intuition and it was a difficult one to make when a child's happiness and security potentially hung in the balance.

These examples demonstrate the enormous leap that a working anthropologist has to make from a theoretical and academic study of a chosen field to a practical engagement with the wider mainstream culture in providing explanations of fieldwork informants' beliefs, practices and behaviour. The anthropologist's opinion may often be sought and she or he will have to present a coherent and considered view in order to sum up concisely what may be a complex and ambiguous reality of lived experience.

Concluding reflections

For many Pagans, magic is associated with the dark as a dialectical process, not as an evil one, but practitioners frequently take on the identity of powerful magicians working with dark forces to bolster their own fragile identities, having been attracted to magic from positions of extreme powerlessness, sometimes through childhood abuse. Many do not want magic to become socially acceptable, since they enjoy the glamour of hexing and cursing and the aura of mystery, like the witch who talked to me about blood rites and sacrifice. Magical practices, for these practitioners, thus need, to a certain extent, to be morally unacceptable in the wider society precisely so that they can maintain their image of power. All these factors create a difficult situation for the anthropologist working as a mediator between mainstream society and the world of magic. In terms of morality, the baseline is, as one Pagan pointed out to me, a 'spectrum of grey'. While this may be a fundamental tenet of Pagan practice, it is sometimes hard to translate for the wider community in specific situations – such as in the court case above, or the concern over neighbours sacrificing cats – when there is a need for specific parameters with which to make judgements. In terms of morality, the magical subculture is a particularly difficult and problematic area because of its antinomian ideologies and lack of clear ethical guidelines.

While I am not advocating some universal notion of morality, the group dynamics and moral individualism in Paganism, coupled with the attraction of occult power to the powerless, makes it difficult to provide definite answers to difficult questions posed by a wider society which still largely mistrusts or misunderstands the moral relativism of magic. This is where more work needs to be done both in terms of the production of theories which explain the relativity of a magical worldview in the social sciences, and also by anthropologists and other social scientists engaging in discussion of such subjects in the non-academic press and other media. Challenging ethnocentrism on all counts includes challenging our theoretical tools of analysis. This means engaging in a much more critical relationship with the politics of knowledge in western, as well as non-western, societies. Such a step would not only help those studying and researching in the future, but would also make communication clearer between anthropologist and the wider public sphere, a situation which can only be beneficial.

Notes

1   Foucault points out that the dawn of madness was perceptible in the decay of Gothic symbolic images that had represented a metamorphosis between humans and animals. He

suggests that Hermetic esoteric learning had involved crossing forbidden limits, for example by animals revealing knowledge of esoteric truth. At this time, such symbolism was turned into images that expressed nightrnares (Foucault 1999: 19–22).

2   This involved visualising a powerful Egyptian goddess. For a fuller account see Greenwood 2000: 88.

3   Witchcraft in African societies is largely seen as immoral and anti-social (Evans-Pritchard 1985; Mair 1969).

Bibliography

Bateson, G. (1985) *Mind and Nature: a necessary unity*, London: Fontana.

—— (2000 *Steps to an Ecology of Mind*, Chicago: Chicago University Press.

Cohn, N. (1993) *Europe's Inner Demons*, London: Pimlico.

Evans-Pritchard, E.E. (1985 *Witchcraft, Oracles and Magic among the Azande*, Oxford: Clarendon.

Foucault, M. (1999) *Madness and Civilization*, London: Routledge.

Gerth, H.H. and Mills, C. Wright (1974) *From Max Weber: essays in sociology*, London: Routledge and Kegan Paul.

Gledhill, J. (2000) 'Finding a new public face for anthropology', *Anthropology Today*, 16 (6): 2–3.

Greenwood, S. (2000) *Magic, Witchcraft and the Otherworld: an anthropology*, Oxford: Berg.

—— (2001) *The Encyclopedia of Magic and Witchcraft*, London: Lorenz.

—— (forthcoming) *Nature Religion and Magical Consciousness*.

Ingold, T. (2000) *The Perception of the Environment: essays in livelihood, dwelling and skill*, London: Routledge.

Johnson, C. (2000) 'Putting different things together: the development of metaphysical thinking' in Rosengren, K., Johnson, C., and Matrfris P. (eds) *Imagining the Impossible: magical, scientific and religious thinking in children*, Cambridge: Cambridge University Press.

Luhrmann, T. (1989) *Persuasions of the Witch's Craft*, Oxford: Basil Blackwell.

Mair, L. (1969) *Witchcraft*, London: Weidenfeld and Nicolson.

Rabinovich, S. (1992) '"An ye harm none, do what ye will": neo-pagans and witches in Canada', unpublished MA thesis, Department of Sociology, New York University.

Regardie, I. (1981) *The Art of True Healing*, Jersey: SOL (private publication).

—— (1991) *The Middle Pillar*, St. Paul, MN: Llewellyn Publications.

Richardson, J., Best, J. and Bromley D. (eds) (1991) *The Satanism Scare*, New York: Aldine de Gruyter

Samuel, G. (1990) *Mind, Body and Culture: anthropology and the biological interface*, Cambridge: Cambridge University Press.

Starhawk, M.S. (1982) *Dreaming the Dark: magic, sex and politics*, Boston: Beacon.

Strathern, M. (1987) 'The limits of autoanthropology' in A. Jackson (ed.) *Anthropology at Home*, London: Routledge.

Yates, F. (1991) *Giordano Bruno and the Hermetic Tradition*, Chicago: University of Chicago Press.

11

REVEALING A POPULAR
SOUTH AFRICAN DECEIT

The ethical challenges of an etymological exercise

Andrew Spiegel

The theme in 2000 for a local high schools' entrepreneurship competition in northern KwaZulu-Natal province was tourism. Ideas submitted included 'decorative plates, a *spaza* shop, Zulu regalia, unusual candles and giftwrap, cheerful items made from recycled material, magnetic fridge notepads with ethnic borders and pens covered with fake animal fur' (*Sunday Tribune*, 22 July 2000; http://www./iol.co.za/index 18/01/02).

What is a *spaza* shop, and why should it be included in a list of tourism-related enterprises? What does *spaza* mean and whence does the word derive? Having begun to ask such questions, the answers they generated created various ethical challenges about the right of anthropologists to expose the meaning of a term which carries resistance connotations. Such challenges are exacerbated when significant popular culture personalities use it to resist the academic gaze, which, as Foucault (1979) argued, may be seen as part of the disciplinary processes of modernity. I return to those challenges after explaining how I came to discover various meanings of *spaza* and what those meanings are.[1]

I argue that perceiving uses of *spaza* simply as resistance misunderstands the nature of resistance, and, especially, hides the cultural creativity embedded in the meanings and uses of *spaza* as trope. I do so by drawing on ideas about the playfulness of subaltern discourse and recognising that the playfulness in the trope is the ethnographic focus of the article. Working from the perspective of an anthropologist in post-apartheid South Africa, I suggest that anthropologists need to prevent themselves from being trapped by the deadening pessimism that sees anthropology as just another agent of modernist control. Rather, I argue, the commitment that derives from living and working in a country that rejoices in change and transformation means that we have to look for ways to celebrate cultural creativity and imaginativeness. That is where the ethical challenge lies.

Spaza shops

Small house-shops are a feature of South Africa's contemporary inhabited landscape, particularly in black residential areas, described locally as townships. In most such areas previously designated for occupation by African people they are called *spaza* shops. *Spaza* shops are now so prevalent that they have come to be regarded as part of South Africa's contemporary African tradition and culture. Along with house-based retail liquor outlets also in the townships (shebeens),[2] they constitute a particular attraction for foreign tourists, especially those interested in the continuing legacies of apartheid planning on people's everyday lives: 'The highlight [of the Soweto township tour] is a visit to a shebeen or *spaza* (drinking place)' (http://www. traveltheplanet.co.za/html/ss_soweto.html 23/01/02).[3] The image of African traditionality that *spaza* shops have come to carry is captured in the name of Johannesburg's *Spaza* Art Gallery which displays 'work with a cultural and regional mix' including that of 'established artists such as … Eausibius Nawu, a former miner whose pictures depict his working experience … and products from community self-employment schemes' (*Mail & Guardian,* 27 April 2001; http://www.sn.apc.org/ wmail/issues 18/01/02).

The growing ubiquity of *spaza* shops has meant that the term has now entered everyday South African English, almost always as an adjective to describe a house-shop in an African-occupied residential area. This is revealed by a trawl through some 75 internet-accessible South African English-language newspaper articles published between mid-1997 and early 2002 in which there is reference to *spaza*. All but three refer to *spaza* shops (occasionally using the word *spaza* as a noun to describe such shops or an adjective to describe someone associated with a *spaza* shop).[4]

Association of the word *spaza* with house-shops is also revealed in local popular cultural productions, as in two episodes in the *Sgudi 'Snaysi* television sitcom where two neighbours set up such shops in competition with one another.[5] It is reinforced by use of the term *spaza* in the names of formal sector enterprises such as *Spaza*tainers, a company that distributes discarded sea-transport containers, and finances some for use as trading space by small-scale informal *spaza* shop traders (*The Star,* 5 December 2001; http://www.iol.co.za/index 18/01/02).

It was thus with some surprise that I listened in 1997 to Nontobeko Yose, then a graduate student working in the Marconi Beam shack area of Cape Town, telling me that all the houses there were *spaza* houses. She stilled my surprise when she explained that *spaza* can be used to describe something not contextually proper or normal, a simulacrum in the sense of an unsatisfactory alternative. The shacks in Marconi Beam, she explained, were *spaza* houses because they did not meet the standards accepted for urban living, just as an old broken bag would be *spaza* for a young aspirant student such as she, and just as a non-Christian celebrating a Christian-calendrical millennium is a *spaza* Christian.

With my anthropological curiosity in such polyvalency of meaning piqued, I immediately wondered about the derivation of the word *spaza*. But Ms Yose was unable to assist. She knew of its use to describe *spaza* shops and things not contextually right and proper – even, she added, artificial. But she was unable to say where it came from or why that word in particular was used to signify those meanings. And so I turned to other sources.

Spaza as resistance

As indicated, *spaza* shops are micro enterprises operated by black people, most commonly from within the confines of their residences. Yet, various respondents I consulted reminded me that there had been no *spaza* shops in the townships before the mid- to late 1970s. True, people had attempted to operate small retail outlets – particularly shebeens – from their township homes. But such outlets were not as common as they have become in the past 20 years or so. Why the growth? The explanations I received related to the nature of resistance to apartheid in the 1970s and 1980s.

The year 1976 saw the start of a major popular uprising against the injustices and inequities of apartheid. The uprising first sparked in Soweto with school children resisting the apartheid state's imposition of Afrikaans as a medium of school instruction for African students. But it was not simply against that one blunderous educational policy decision. The policy's propagation and implementation provided opportunity for expressions of deep-seated resistance that had long been welling up, but had been relatively submerged since the banning a decade and a half earlier of the African National Congress (ANC), Pan-Africanist Congress (PAC) and related resistance/liberation organisations.

A product of the uprising was widespread resistance to the institutions of apartheid oppression and exploitation. Such activism, suppressed and forced underground during the 1960s, had already become quite visible in the early 1970s. An increasingly powerful and vocal trade union movement arose and a new Black Consciousness movement developed. Activists managed, for a short while, to sidestep the bans that had been imposed early in the 1960s on the ANC and PAC, and on dissemination of their materials.

Among the methods of resistance adopted was a consumer boycott of certain formal economic retail outlets, particularly those associated with repressive actions against workers and their newly revived unions. But the principle of consumer boycott was not limited to worker and union support. It became a weapon against a range of political institutions and state agencies – local government in particular. When aimed at the private sector, it was often adopted with the intention that popular pressure on white-owned businesses might speed up the process whereby business leaders might feel coerced to demand reform (and hopefully eventual capitulation) by the apartheid regime.

Spaza shops, various respondents told me, developed as a feature of the township landscape, in the shadow of these boycotts. They arose in a context in which it was increasingly difficult to enforce apartheid legislation that had aimed to restrict African people's trading opportunities in the cities and their associated townships – allowing only select individuals a maximum of a single formal licence to trade in town (Southall 1980). The apartheid state's objective was that aspirant traders should remove to the Bantustans to trade – although restrictive regulations undermined opportunities for entrepreneurial growth there too and the objective was not often attained (e.g. Bank 1991, 1997).

While consumer boycotts of formal economic enterprises offered opportunity for informal trade to grow, of greater interest here is the nature of the new informal enterprises as part of a process of resistance. These enterprises provide a window onto some popular understandings of the origins of the idea of *spaza* and onto its etymology. I consider this next.

Etymology of *spaza*

The *Dictionary of South African English* (1996: 670) quotes various sources – all dating from the late 1980s – that reflect the idea that *spaza* shops grew from entrepreneurial efforts to engage in illicit informal trade. The *Dictionary* quotes Ngwenya's article in *Drum* magazine: 'The word [*spaza*] describes the way traders were forced to operate underground because they usually broke all rules and regulations' (1989). But it offers no etymology.

Why, I asked various respondents, were they called *spaza* shops? Where does the word come from? Among my first responses were those from Zulu first-language speakers who explained that it comes from the Zulu (and Xhosa) verb *ukuphazama* (or, more precisely, from its derivative noun *isiphazamisa* – see below for translations). The same respondents went on to explain why it came to be used in the late 1970s to refer to the retail outlets now widely described as *spaza* shops. The reasons were directly linked to the history of consumer boycotts outlined above.

Various respondents explained that, when small house-shops began to operate from people's homes in African townships (probably, they said, in the late 1970s), they were supported in part because they offered a way to purchase one's daily essentials without patronising formal white-owned shops. By engaging in such transactions, I was told, both the house-shop proprietors and their customers were said to be disturbing and hindering the operation of formal enterprises. Such a shop thus constituted an *isiphazamisa* (Zulu: 'clipped' to *spaza*; *isiphazamiso* in Xhosa), in other words a hindrance, impediment and disturbance to formal sector stores and implicitly to the whole formal economy (and political-economic system) that they were understood to represent. The element of resistance that *spaza* shops represented was thus constituted immediately in the original word used to describe them.

To be able to claim legitimacy for the above etymology requires establishing whether there are similar constructions in cognate languages. I have been able to find them in SiNdebele, Sesotho and Shona, although in the latter two instances one has to allow for sound shifts. SiNdebele, having only very recently branched off from what became Zulu, not surprisingly has almost identical words (with only the aspirating 'h' being absent in the dictionary (Elliot n.d.) I have consulted). For Sesotho the noun *sephatsamiso*, from the causative form of the verb (*ho-*) *phatsam*a, implies something annoying, bothering, disturbing etc. (Mabille *et al.* 1974: 371). Making allowance for further sound shifts, the equivalent noun in Shona is *chipatsaniso* or *zvipatsaniso* (Hannan 1974).

The very fact that there are equivalents in cognate languages suggests that there is strong reason to accept the etymology offered to me by my various sources. But, as we shall see below, the evidence about its direct link to 1970s political activism is much more difficult to demonstrate as compellingly. Popular understanding that *spaza* shops arose as institutions of resistance is indeed supported by the argument that, at least in one sense, the term *spaza* reflects precisely that resistance. In circumstances of increasing boycott and other forms of resistance to the apartheid state and the white-dominated institutions that supported it, forms of trade that had the effect of disrupting and disturbing formal economic enterprise were part of the struggle against apartheid. But the further fact that the word was already in use in the 1960s, as I soon came to discover, undermines the easy link between its use and political resistance in the 1970s.

Spaza as deceit: Resistance roots or not?

Seeking confirmation of the etymology I had been offered by my respondents, I turned for help to Cliff Dikeni, then a lecturer in African Languages at the University of Cape Town. He referred me to various sources that indeed confirmed my newly found understanding of the meaning and construction of the words *isiphazamisa* and *isiphazamiso*. But he surprised me when he explained that he remembered the word *spaza* being used as an adjective to mean 'imitation', in the Johannesburg of the 1960s (29 Feb. 2000, pers. comm.). At the time, he said, one could obtain copies of a popular brand of sneakers that went under the brand name 'Tenderfoot'. Those copies were described as *spaza tackies*[6] because they were not the real thing – a phrase that resonated immediately with Ms Yose's comment that first drew my interest. It also continues to be common today among some parents who, unable to afford the demands of their children for expensive footwear, buy cheap shoes to tide them over:

if your child's pair of shoes has just been worn out and you don't have sufficient money to buy the right thing, so you go to buy the R20.99[7] pair of tackies, and you call that a *spaza*. 'I've just bought this pair of *spaza*s until I've got the money to buy the Nikes that you want.' He can use them in the meantime so that he is not walking barefoot.

(Ntombizodumo Ngxabi, pers. comm., 26 October 2000)

Others too have since explained to me that one can describe various items of apparel as *spaza* when the item referred to is regarded as cheap and of poor quality. It is as if what some people described as South African street language (*Tsotsitaal*[8]) has developed its own word for ersatz: as leading poet, journalist and ex-Sophiatown[9] sage, Don Mattera, explained (pers. comm., 15 April 2000), 'If you ask me "Is that for real?" I will answer "That is no *spaza*" [i.e. it is indeed for real] … Something *spaza* is not the real McCoy. It is a deceit.' Similarly, others told me, actions can be described as *spaza*, so that one can say that a person walks *spaza* when one means that the person has a strange or unusual gait; yet others have explained the use of *spaza* as an adjective to describe a stupid and incompetent person.

Interestingly, despite its lack of etymology, the *Dictionary of South African English* recognises these same kinds of meanings. Its first entry against the word *spaza* is 'camouflaged', 'dummy' (1996: 670).

Continuing my enquiries, I entered discussions with a range of people, both men and women and ranging in age from their early thirties to their mid-sixties, in the Western Cape and Gauteng provinces. Most confirmed the use of the word *spaza* as imitation or deceit by offering explanations that something is *spaza* when it is unreal or artificial. Significantly, various respondents added to their explanations that the verb *ukuphazamisa* can be used to mean to tease, harass or even torment through offering a false or misleading picture or story that is then described as *spaza* – one that is not simply and only fake but also intended to dissemble and thereby to deceive confuse, discompose and bewilder.

Other experts to whom I turned for advice confirmed the above meanings of *spaza*. Sizwe Satyo (Professor of African Languages at the University of Cape Town, pers. comm., 17 April 2000), Aggrey Klaaste (editor-in-chief of *New Africa Publications*; pers. comm., 13 April 2000) and Don Mattera (poet, playright and writer; pers. comm., 15 April 2000) all indicated that the word *spaza* can be used in the form of a verb, to mean much the same as what I have above explained *ukuphazamisa* to mean. Satyo said that, as a verb, *spaza* means 'to show off; to be pretentious and not genuine'. In Klaaste's words, 'If I *spaza* you, I am making a fool of you; pulling the wool over your eyes' while in Mattera's much more richly flavoured version:

Spaza is a Sophiatown word; *Tsotsitaal* ... You are only playing the fool: *Ek spaza net* [I just *spaza*]. *Net 'n negro-in-die-tien.*[10] It's a form of speech. Beating about the bush. *[Ek] spaza maar net* [(I) am just kidding] ... *Ag man, die Boere* are giving us trouble, *maar 'snet die spaza* [Oh, man, the police are troubling us, but it's just a ploy]. *Hulle spaza maar net met die gaai* [They are simply fooling around with the guy]. You can also use *spaza* to mean 'eyeblind' the authorities. Think about Bezwoda:[11] *hy't 'n spaza geslaan met'ie Amerikans* (lit: he hit a *spaza* with the Americans; he pulled a fast one with the Americans).

The notion of *spaza* as something intended to bewilder or deceive ('eyeblind' in Mattera's terms) is evident in two other reports I gathered about its use. Both of their contexts again suggested that the term might have anti-apartheid political roots. But this time they date from the 1960s. Interestingly, however, in my interview with Mattera he followed his comment about 'eyeblinding the authorities' by insisting that *spaza* has no direct political connotations, a position for which he found support from his journalist colleague, Sidney Mahlangu, who was with him for some of the time during the interview. Yet Mattera's reference to the *Boere* (police) as the targets of efforts to dissemble, confuse and deceive suggests that it is indeed the police who were commonly so targeted, rather than friends, kin and neighbours engaged in banter and teasing.

A good example comes from my discussion with a small group of first-language Xhosa-speaking women in the Western Cape. Among them was Nomangesi Mbobosi Mzamo who, during that first discussion, was initially unable (or unwilling) to offer me any etymology of the term *spaza* (pers. comm., 14 March 2000). All she did, almost as if to put me off the track and *spaza* (or *phazamisa*) me, was to agree with another member of the group who said simply: '*spaza* comes from *Tsotsitaal*' – as if saying that meant it would have no further etymology because it derived from a language that itself was not 'proper' and that was certainly not her mother-tongue (Xhosa). Yet, when I suggested, in response, that I'd gathered from other sources that it might be an abbreviated version of the Xhosa word *isiphazamiso*, Ms Mzamo suddenly changed tack and, almost elatedly, confirmed that that was correct.

She then went on to explain that one could use the term to describe activities such as concerts and church services. For example, she explained, she had grown up in the Western Cape town of Wellington and, during 1964, had seen church-type gatherings held at the edges of wooded areas near the town. But these were not real church services. Rather they were gatherings called during times when meetings of the ANC and PAC, then necessarily underground because both organisations were officially banned, were held deep within those forests. Described locally as *spaza* services, the church-style gatherings were mere imitations of real church services deliberately called to provide decoys in order to deceive and confuse (*ukuphazamisa*) the police and put them off the scent.

Similarly, Steven Mosela, a first-language Sesotho-speaking worker in Johannesburg, born in Sophiatown in 1942 and relocated with his parents to Evaton near Vereeneging 10 years later, recalled decoy concerts being held outside people's Gauteng homes in which political meetings were held in the early 1960s. And, he added, they were described by the term *spaza* (pers. comm., 31 March 2000).

Spaza before the 1960s

But, tempting as it is to accept the simple argument that *spaza* is a term developed in the process of 1960s resistance to apartheid, evidence from those who grew up in and around Sophiatown, and from various others, obliged me to question it. For Khampe Khampe, a first-language Tswana speaker and now a member of the SA National Commission for UNESCO, 'it was something I learned on the soccer field in Rustenburg where I grew up' (pers. comm., 31 March 2000). Jim Buthelezi, a first-language Zulu-speaking worker born in Sophiatown in 1938 and bred in Pimville (now part of Soweto), explained: 'We used to rub a farthing against some silver paper to make a *spaza tickie*' (small silver threepenny coin – *Dictionary of South African English* 1996: 718–19). For him, the idea of *spaza* as fake, a copy, not the real thing, was something he learned as part of the process of being socialised in the world where he grew up. 'It just came to us from the old days' and did not arise only in the 1960s (pers. comm., 31 March 2000). Similarly, poet and writer Don Mattera, who was born in 1935 and whose earliest memories are from Sophiatown, places his first memory of the word in the early 1940s as meaning not real. Script writer, film director and popular sitcom actor, Joe Mafela, also born in Sophiatown, albeit somewhat later than Mattera and Buthelezi, also associates *spaza* with something ingenuous.

Were written vernacular sources available for earlier periods, we would, I suggest, be able to find those terms associated with a wide range of passive and hidden forms of resistance – detailed in the literature on resistance to colonialism in general, to segregation and apartheid in particular and to the exploitative nature of industrial labour – that were less directed towards upending the imposed status quo than towards disrupting its operations and confusing its agents (e.g. van Onselen 1976, 1982; Scott 1985). Gerald Stone, who is compiling a lexicon of prison and (Coloured) township gang slang, suggests (pers. comm., 4 October 2001) that the term *spaza* first came into use among members of the Regiment of the Hills, a gang of outlaw migrants during the last decade of the nineteenth century in and on the outskirts of the gold-mining centre that formed around what is now Johannesburg (van Onselen 1982). I have no further evidence to support such a claim or to be able to fix the moment (if there was one) when the clipped form *spaza* (or *sphaza*) began to prevail. Yet it seems more than likely that the terms *ukuphazamisa* and *isiphazamisa* have a long history of use with reference to those kinds of actions in southern African struggles against colonialism and apartheid, as well as against the constraints of industrial labour relations. I make the suggestion on the basis of the contemporary evidence about the use, described above, of both terms *ukuphazamisa* and *spaza* to suggest the intention to bewilder, both in everyday banter and in various contexts of a need to confuse, discompose, deceive and impede those who exercise power through the state. If that is indeed a persistent use of the terms *ukuphazamisa* and *isiphazamisa*, my arguments about both the epistemology and the struggle roots of *spaza* can hold, albeit without a neatly specified date of origin of the abbreviated (clipped) version, or of the context in which it was coined.

Politics and ethical challenges

How then to deal with both Don Mattera's and, later, Joe Mafela's adamant rejection of other respondents' suggestions that *spaza* derives from the Zulu *isiphazamisa*? Both men are recognised leaders of South African popular culture. Both have roots in and commitments to the memory of Sophiatown, an icon of the potential for African urban cultural creativity that was destroyed by the apartheid machine. What then are the ethics of appearing to write as if against them, particularly when Mattera (pers. comm., 15 April 2000) was equally adamant in refuting any link between *spaza* and political activism or resistance?

Of course one could explain black South African cultural leaders refuting a white South African academic's proposal about an African cultural issue as a legacy of apartheid. That system rendered black people suspicious of academic surveillance, particularly when the beneficiaries of recording subaltern culture were and continue to be academics (primarily white, but not always so) rather than its performers. Especially since the demise of apartheid, people – and particularly popular leaders – have felt empowered to question, often also to deny, those who assume the right to undertake social research exercises that do not clearly define developmental outcomes and benefits for those on the ground.

Moreover, as Ross (forthcoming) has indicated, when social research focuses, as did South Africa's Truth and Reconciliation Commission (TRC), on people's experiences of apartheid violence and their attempts to resist apartheid's structures, '[r]esearch subjects are perfectly aware of the ease with which research slips its ethical boundaries'. They may well therefore refuse access both to researchers and to institutions such as the TRC that aim to interrogate and publicise their pain and suffering. Or they express extreme anger – sometimes phrased in terms of racial stereotypes – when, having agreed access, they feel that the trust they have granted researchers (the TRC included) has been betrayed by, for example, publication of their stories in ways that undermine their dignity, appropriate their voices and then also fail to bring them benefits.[12]

Both Mattera and Mafela are, however, widely known public figures with far greater access today to the public cultural arena than a mere academic. The power differentials between researcher and respondent that pertain in the kinds of situations that Ross writes about are quite different from those in the context in which I have been working. Why then did two popular-culture leaders deny the Zulu origins of *spaza* that various other respondents had offered me? And have I been unethical in rejecting and exposing their argument?

Both took the position they did on the basis of a perceived clear distinction between the rural and the urban. As Mattera said: 'The word [*spaza*] has its origins in urban culture. It has no origins in rural things' (which 'things' implicitly include uses of the Zulu word *isiphazamisa*). Implicitly for Mattera, sustaining the idea of a distinctiveness to urban (township) life was more important than finding an etymological continuity between urban and rural. Yet, earlier in our conversation, and before any prompting from me, he had commented that *spaza* is not a Zulu word – almost as if he was wondering out loud about its likely Zulu (and therefore, for him, 'rural') origins. Mafela (pers. comm., 9 January 2002) concurred with Mattera's position by suggesting a clearly distinctive category of urban life as the source of what he called 'colloquial' terms such as *spaza*. As he said: 'It [*spaza*] is colloquial, and that's straightforward. It's not from anywhere except the townships.'

Professor Sizwe Satyo (pers. comm., 17 April 2000) has reminded me that the politics of language construction and definition is such that popular-culture leaders often claim ownership of words and their derivation that denies other possible etymologies. Both Mattera and Mafela are recognised sources of knowledge about *Tsotsitaal* and its Sophiatown (and 'colloquial') origins. For both that is an important personal ingredient of their professional reputations. In a sense, that very fact might explain their flat denial of an etymology that many others offered for *spaza*, an etymology that, in the eyes of these two popular-culture leaders, makes rural links to a word and practice they see as distinctively urban.

As elsewhere in the modernising world (see Williams 1973), it is common in South Africa to use tropes that construct a clear divide between what is thought to be rural and what is regarded as urban. The long-established phenomenon of oscillating rural–urban–rural migration (for many years enforced by the apartheid system) may be seen analytically to have created a single political-economic nexus of what is effectively a rural–urban continuum. Yet, precisely because of that apparent continuity, there is a popular insistence on maintaining a categorical distinction between its two poles, and between the types of behaviour and lifestyles regarded as normative in each.

The distinction is reinforced by a variety of popular tropes (Mayer and Mayer 1974; Comaroff and Comaroff 1987; James 1999). It underpinned Nontobeko Yose's explanation, spelled out at the start of this chapter, that all the houses in Marconi Beam were *spaza* houses because they were of a type that was popularly thought to be more suited to rural than to urban living (cf. Yose 1999). It is apparent in the work of Helen Meintjes (2000), another recent graduate student, who has shown how African people in various parts of Soweto deploy domestic appliances and items of modern material culture to signify their urban propriety, and thus distinguish their lifestyles from those of rural people. Is it not simply that same popular distinction, analytically discernible as socially constructed, to which Mattera and Mafela are appealing? And if it is, then is there really any ethical reason not to expose their denials for the urbanist prejudices they are?

Yet so neat an analytical sidestep fails to address the ethical problem underlying the contrast between the explicitly stated perspectives of cultural leaders on aspects of the popular culture that is their expert domain, and those of the anthropological analyst. It simply shifts the problem to another level.

This became apparent when Mattera, having just explained to me that to *spaza* is (simply) to fool around and tease or confound, immediately followed on by asking whether I was sure I had not been *spaza*-ed by those who had led me to believe the derives from the Zulu (pers. comm., 15 April 2000). I recognised that he was making fun of our discussion and simultaneously attempting to *spaza* me by deploying the irony in the trope. This helped me to realise that he was playing at bewildering me and my efforts to 'capture' and record the nature of the trickery and polyvalency that is *spaza*. The interchange also reminded me of Nomangesi Mbobosi Mzamo's initial unwillingness, some weeks earlier, to let me into the subterfuge of *spaza* until, I now realised, she was satisfied I had established my 'credentials' for being allowed into the secret by demonstrating some prior understanding.

Rosaldo (1989: 190ff.) has pointed to the fact that humour is often used as what he calls a 'weapon of subaltern consciousness'. He goes on (1989: 206ff.) to remind us that, when that occurs, we ethnographers are often blind to how that humour is being used by the subjects of our attentions to convey their perceptions of us as agents of the very processes that subordinate them. Such processes include our recording and codifying their practices and meanings.

Rosaldo's aim was to emphasise the importance of recognising, in ethnographic work, 'a relational form of understanding in which both parties actively engage in "the interpretation of cultures"'(1989: 206–7). My aim here is to indicate that, through methodologically recognising the relational nature of my efforts to establish an etymology of *spaza*, I seem to have fallen upon a kind of trickster trope in the word *spaza* that at least some of my informants – particularly those who are popular-culture leaders – used precisely to divert my interest and attention.

Dodging deceptions: Ethics of the anthropological gaze

Pursuing the meanings and the etymology of *spaza* has thus meant increasingly having to recognise that I too have been exposed to various exercises in deception, designed to divert my interest and attention, precisely because some informants wanted to prevent me recognising the subterfuge and deceptions that are *spaza*.[13] What in turn became clear was how the trope that constitutes *spaza* can be used as much to keep at bay the fundamental surveillance process that constitutes so much contemporary empirical social science – including much anthropology – as to confound agents of more direct oppressive intervention such as the police.

It is at that epistemological level, then, that the ethical challenge arises. If, among its various meanings, *spaza* involves a process of secreting itself from the prying scrutiny and gaze of social science, is it ethical to reveal that process as I have just done? If we must answer in the negative, then does that also mean that all social scientific research is unethical – particularly that which deals with resistance, defiance and popular processes of expressing disaffection, including those aimed at 'protecting tradition'?

Foucault (1979) argued that the expansion of modern institutions of administration and control depends, for its disciplinary functions, on sociological surveillance that is invasive by nature. Accepting that argument means that we need, in this case, to ask whether recording the meanings of *spaza*, and revealing how it works as a popular means to divert surveillance, can be turned into a means to intensify such surveillance and the disciplining processes of modern institutions. If they can be – and I believe that it is unlikely in this instance – then there is indeed a distinctly unethical component to creating such records.

Remaining with the Foucauldian argument, we need also to ask whether such popular diversionary tactics as constitute *spaza* are explicitly intended by those using them to constrain the disciplinary functions of modernising institutions, and whether they have the power to effect such constraints. In other words, was Mattera just playing, or was there a seriousness behind his playful taunt, a discursive consciousness, that derived from his determination to resist modernity and the standardisation and routinisation that it seems so often to impose? And, if he was serious, how effective could his efforts be?

Kaplan and Kelly remind us of the distinction between a Gramscian notion of resistance – passive reflections of unconscious subaltern discontent that must become conscious for agency to be able to effect revolutionary transformation – and one that 'take[s] conscious resistance as the most indisputable form of all resistance' (1994: 126). They argue that the notion of resistance has now been (over-)stretched 'to cover a vast range of practices' (*ibid.*) between the subaltern unconscious and revolutionary superconsciousness. They consequently refocus on 'a political terrain populated not only by unconscious resisters and alienated ideologues, but also by agents ... who challenge existing and permeable structures of domination, with varying scope of intention and facing varying modes of danger and levels of risk' (*ibid.*: 127).

Was Mattera such an agent? Are those who play *spaza* challenging structures of domination? And if they are, how consciously and to what end do they do so, and what risks are entailed? It is clear that conscious resistance of various forms continues in contemporary South Africa and that at least some of it has had, and continues to have, clear political and economic outcomes. It is equally clear (cf. Rosaldo 1989) that acts that challenge dominant structures are often playful. The *spaza* trope has, it seems, for the moment become so habituated that it has become more a playful performance that challenges only implicitly and with far less significant intent than an explicit act of political resistance. That may be the reason that Mattera denied that there are any political connotations to *spaza*.

For public figures such as Mattera and Mafela, irony such performances have become items of stock in their trade of playful challenge and creative cultural play. It is exemplified in Mafela's role as co-executive director and actor in a TV sitcom where a bogus diviner, playing the part for tourists, describes himself as 'a *spaza*'.[14] Yet it is also used by others, in contexts of a strongly embedded memory of the need to deceive, confuse and discompose those who are seen to represent exogenous institutions and their disciplinary processes. There too it is an habituated performance being played out, although, as always, the power play implicit in such practices means that an undercurrent of challenge (or resistance) remains.

If, however, it is primarily playful, then exposing it cannot be ethically questionable. Indeed, we should be seeking to celebrate such playfulness and the subaltern power it represents, precisely because it reveals the cultural moment of modernity where imagination and innovativeness is celebrated and where 'modernity is the transient, the fleeting, the contingent' (Baudelaire, quoted in Gaonkar 1999: 4). Particularly in the context of a post-apartheid South Africa, where the social and cultural flexibility that marks postcoloniality is one means of transforming the legacy of apartheid's deadening structures, such celebration of innovativeness and cultural creativity is crucial.

Gaonkar (1999) has argued that it is as important to recognise the creative cultural moment of modernity as it is to acknowledge the more commonly recognised social transformational one where Weberian disenchantment and meaninglessness, and Foucauldian routinisation and standardisation are seen to predominate. Accepting Gaonkar's argument creates scope for recording those culturally creative moments of playfulness: not as part of an exercise in surveillance to create a means of discipline, but as part of a celebration of cultural creativity and imaginativeness, and of forms of power that are exercised neither to control nor to resist. Using ethnographic methods to reveal the roots of a term such as *spaza* and, through doing so, to celebrate the creativeness that is marshalled to realise the polyvalency of the term, cannot then be unethical – even when its popular custodians deny those roots. If the denial is indeed meant to offer a challenge to the culturally deadening effect of the social transformational moment of modernity, surely a celebration of the spirit that lives in the term and its every use contributes to that challenge.

Extending the point more generally means, in addition, that as social analysts we must seek to recognise and realise spaces for a culturally creative type of social science. This is one that aims to rejoice rather than simply to record and that sets its sights on revelling in the transience and contingency of what it produces so that it can itself become part of the culturally creative and imaginative moment of modernity. The ethical challenge, then, is to find ways to work towards a distinctly imaginative and celebratory social science and to use anthropology to that end.

Notes

1 My thanks to Constance Nontobeko Yose who first alerted me to a meaning of *spaza* other than as the adjective in *spaza* shop. Also to Raj Mesthrie and Kay McCormick for their comments on my etymological efforts, to participants in a seminar in the Department of Social Anthropology, UCT, and to the various individuals cited as having contributed through their personal communications with me. Thanks also to Sally Frankental for her willingness, at short notice, to comment as insightfully as always. I, of course, accept sole responsibility for any errors or other shortcomings.

2 Shebeen (originally an Anglo-Irish word) describes an illegal (unlicensed) liquor outlet. Given the fact of legislated prohibition of sale (and indeed gifts too) of commercially produced alcohol to Africans in South Africa until 1962 (Rogerson 1992: 332), production and distribution of various home-brewed alcoholic beverages has long been a significant source of income for African women in South Africa's cities (cf. Hellmann 1948; van Onselen 1982). The description of illicit liquor outlets as shebeens dates back to at least 1900 (*Dictionary of South African English* 1996: 634).

3 Also see http://www.legendtours.co.za/Tours/TheTours_Pages/TownshipTours.html and Karen Rutter: 'the majority of registered township tours are aimed at foreign tourists (to be ticked off along with Big Five headcounts) ... [They offer] round trips through some of the poorer parts of the city [Cape Town] to experience "interactive experience in shebeens, spaza shops and people's homes"' (*Mail & Guardian*, 11 February 2000, 'Travelling and Grooving').

4 An internet search for items including the word *spaza* using the South African search engine (www.aardvark.co.za 24–29 January 2001) generated approximately 770 such items, and there too almost all referred to *spaza* shops.

5 Penguin Films, Cape Town. Produced by Roberta Durrant; directed by Joe Mafela. *Sgudi 'Snaysi* is a phonetic version of the phrase 'it's good it's nice' as pronounced by many local people.

6 *Tackies* (pl.; sing. = *tackie*) is a common word in South African English that is used to describe rubber-soled canvas shoes (sneakers; sandshoes) (*Dictionary of South African English* 1996: 705). One possible etymology for *tackies* is the Scottish–English dialect term 'tacky' to describe 'cheap, rubbishy' (*ibid.*). The idea of a cheap imitation of something rubbishy begins to beggar the imagination.

7 At the time of the interview, the South African Rand was worth about US$0.138.

8 *Tsotsitaal* is a patois used and developed differently across the country, and it derives from a mix of various African languages, Afrikaans and English (*Dictionary of South African English* 1996: 743). It has been said to have been a 'clever' language 'spoken first mainly by criminals, partly as a means of avoiding being understood by others within earshot' (*ibid*). Another description is *Flytaal*, 'An urban (especially township) argot', so described because it is a language (*taal* in Afrikaans) that is 'fly' (in the English sense of 'knowing; wide awake') (*Dictionary of South African English* 1996: 231).

9 A 'mixed-race' suburb in Johannesburg, demolished in the 1950s as part of the apartheid government's efforts to create racially segregated residential areas. Sophiatown was also very significant for being a locus of much interracial social activity – particularly around music – and is sometimes seen as the font of persistent urban African cultural forms.

10 Mattera carefully spelled this phrase out for me, but did not offer me a translation. I can only guess that it is another way of saying 'it's ersatz', though the derivation of the phrase itself cries out for explanation. Sally Frankental has wondered whether the phrase might be '*negro-in-die-tuin*' (rather than *tien*) which literally means Negro in the garden. Again, the implication is unclear.

11 A reference to Dr Werner Bezwoda, a Johannesburg oncologist who has allegedly faked breast-cancer chemotherapy trial results (*Mail & Guardian*, 14–20 April 2000).

12 Details of the government's final policy for reparations to victims of gross human rights abuses, as documented by the TRC, have still to be published. Nearly four years after the TRC's report on such violations was published and debated in parliament, finalisation of the reparations policy, and final payment of reparations, awaits completion of the TRC's final amnesty recommendations.

13 I have been told in passing on the street in Cape Town that *spaza* 'is a language for Coloured people, not a language for white people', again revealing the ways in which race continues so readily to be used as an overlay on many other social fission lines. To deal with this issue fully would require a quite different treatment. See, however, Spiegel 2000.

14 '*Ek is 'n spaza* (I am a *spaza*). I am a complete fraud.' *Going Up* series, episode entitled *Where Witchdoctor*, Penguin Films; broadcast on SABCTV1 Wed. 1 March 2000. My thanks to Pam Maseko for alerting me to this example.

Bibliography

Bank, Leslie (1991) 'A culture of violence: The migrant taxi trade in Qwaqwa 1980–90', in Eleanor Preston-Whyte and Christian Rogerson (eds) *South Africa's Informal Economy*, Cape Town: Oxford University Press.

—— (1997) 'Of livestock and deadstock: Entrepreneurship and tradition on the South African highveld', in Deborah Fahy Bryceson and Vali Jamal (eds) *Farewell to Farms: De-agrarianisation and employment in Africa*, Leiden: African Studies Centre.

Comaroff, John and Comaroff, Jean (1987) 'The madman and the migrant: Work and labour in the historical consciousness of a South African people', *American Ethnologist*, 14 (2): 191–209.

A Dictionary of South African English (1996), New York: Oxford University Press.

Doke, C. M. and Vilakazi, B. W. (1948) *Zulu–English Dictionary*, Johannesburg: Witwatersrand University Press.

Doke, C. M., Malcolm, D. M. and Sikakana, J. M. A. (1988) *English and Zulu Dictionary*, Johannesburg: Witwatersrand University Press.

Doke, C. M., Malcolm, D. M., Sikakana, J. M. A. and Vilakazi, B. W. (1990) *English–Zulu Zulu–English Dictionary*, Johannesburg: Witwatersrand University Press.

Elliot, W. A. (n.d.) *Notes for a Sindebele Dictionary and Grammar*, 2nd edn, Bristol: Sindebele Publishing Co.

Fischer, A. (1985) *English–Xhosa Dictionary*, Cape Town: Oxford University Press.

Foucault, Michel (1979) *Discipline and Punish: The birth of the prison*, Harmondsworth: Penguin.

Gaonkar, Dilip Parameshwar (1999) 'On alternative modernities', *Public Culture*, 11 (1): 1–18.

Hannan, M. (1974) *Standard Shona Dictionary*, 2nd edn, Salisbury and Bulawayo: Rhodesia Literature Bureau.

Hellmann, Ellen (1948) *Rooiyard: A sociological survey of a native slumyard*, Rhodes Livingstone Papers No. 30, Livingstone: Northern Rhodesia.

James, Deborah (1999) *Songs of the Women Migrants: Performance and identity in South Africa*, Johannesburg: Witwatersrand University Press.

Kaplan, Martha and Kelly, John D. (1994) 'Rethinking resistance: Dialogics of "disaffection" in colonial Fiji', *American Anthropologist*, 21 (1): 123–151.

Kropf, Albert and Godfrey, R. (1915) *Kafir–English Dictionary*, Lovedale: Lovedale Mission Press.

Mabille, A., Dieterlen, H. and Paroz, R. A. (1974) *Southern Sotho–English Dictionary*, Morija: Morija Sesuto Book Depot.

Mayer, Philip and Mayer, Iona (1974) *Townsmen or Tribesmen*, Cape Town: Oxford University Press.

Meintjes, Helen (2000) 'Poverty, possessions and proper living: Constructing and contesting propriety in Soweto and Lusaka City', unpublished MA dissertation, University of Cape Town.

Rogerson, Christian (1992) 'Drinking, apartheid and the removal of beerhalls in Johannesburg 1939–1962', in Jonathan Crush and Charles Ambler (eds) *Liquor and Labour in Southern Africa*, Athens: Ohio University Press.

Rosaldo, Renato (1989) *Culture and Truth: The remaking of social analysis*, London: Routledge.

Ross, Fiona (forthcoming) 'Ethics codes and dignity', in F. Nyamjoh (ed.) *Challenges and Responsibilities of Doing Social Research in Africa: Ethical responsibilities*.

Ross, Fiona and Spiegel, Andrew (2000) 'Diversity and fluidity amongst poor households in Cape Town and the heterogeneity of domestic consolidation practices', *Tanzanian Journal of Population Studies and Development*, 7 (2): 147–69.

Scott, James (1985) *Weapons of the Weak: Everyday forms of peasant resistance*, New Haven, CN: Yale University Press.

Silva, Penny (2002) 'South African English: Oppressor or liberator?', unpublished paper (http://www.ru.ac.za/affiliates/dsae/MAVEN.HTML 25/01/02).

Southall, Roger (1980) 'African capitalism in contemporary South Africa', *Journal of Southern African Studies*, 7.

Spiegel, Andrew (2002) 'Is it for real? Notes on the meanings and etymology of *spaza* in South African popular culture', in R. Gordon and D. Lebeau (eds) *Challenges for Anthropology in the African Renaissance,* Windhoek: University of Namibia Press.

van Onselen, Charles (1976) *Chibaro*, Johannesburg: Ravan.

—— (1982) *Studies in the Social and Economic History of the Witwatersrand* (2 vols), Harlow: Longman.

Via Afrika (n.d.) *English–Xhosa, Xhosa–English Dictionary*, Cape Town: Via Afrika Publishers.

Williams, Raymond (1973) *The Country and the City*, London: Chatto and Windus.

Yose, Constance Nontobeko (1999) 'From shacks to houses: Space usage and social change in a Western Cape shanty town', unpublished MA dissertation, University of Cape Town.

INDEX

presence 55–75; background 56–7; magic
and artifice 57–8; morality, theories of
58–67
Price, D. 40, 43, 49, 90
Principles 1971 49
Principles of Professional Responsibility 15,
20–1
professional guidelines 48–50
'proper' 181
'propriety' 181, 184, 187
Psychological Operations Headquarters 42
psychotherapy 201
public sphere, engagement with 205–7

Quigley, D. 3

Rabinovich, S. 200
Rabinow, P. 16
race relations 173
racism 175–6, 177
Radcliffe-Brown, R. 40
Ramazanoglu, C. 12
rapport 117–18, 127
Reagan, N. 198
Reagan, R. 82
'Reaganethics' 14–16, 49
reality 134–5
reciprocity 120–1, 122
Regardie, I. 201
Reiter, R. 11
relevance 5–7
religions, established 206
religious education examinations abolition
163–5
religious minority see Greece
Renaissance 197, 199
representation 23–6, 103–8, 124–7, 156,
173, 182–4; of magic to children 206; of
'other' 180–90
Research Assessment Exercise 22, 70–1, 91
research ethics 37–52; American
anthropology 39–44; Association of
Social Anthropologists 46–8; blinkered
science 38–9; British anthropology
44–6; ethical proliferation 50–1;
International Code of Ethics for
Midwives 139; professional guidelines
48–50
resistance 210, 214, 217, 221–2
respect 117, 127
responsibility 5–7
Rhodes-Livingstone Institute 46

Richards, A. 45
Richardson, J. 196
Ricoeur, P. 63
rights 117
rituals 206; see also initiation
Riviere, P. 46
Roberts, H. 12
Rohrlich-Leavitt, R. 11
Rosaldo, M. 11, 60
Rosaldo, R. 188, 220, 222
Rose, N.S. 51
Rosicrucianism 197, 198
Ross, A. 88
Ross, F. 218, 219
Rowling, J.K. 195
Royal Anthropological Institute 88
Royal College of Nursing 140
Rwandan genocide 21, 23, 24, 96–110; and
ethnicity 99–101; facts, objective 101–3;
legitimacy and historical narratives
98–9; representation 103–8
Rynkiewich, M.A. 14

Sahlins, M. 20, 42, 92, 121
Said, E. 11, 187
Samuel, G. 203
Sanders, W. 179
satanists 207
Satyo, S. 215, 219
Saudi Arabia 161
Schama, S. 99
Scheper-Hughes, N. 17–18
Schiller, F. 198
scholarship 84–8
Scholte, B. 8, 13–14
science 84–8, 91
Science Wars 87, 88, 92
Scott, J. 217
Second World War 40, 157
secrecy see Malawi
self identity 199
Seligman, D. 86–7
Senegal 137
Seremetakis, C.N. 68–9
sexual dynamic 200
shared experience 188
Sharpe, P. 13
Shell 2
Shore, C. 3, 19, 51, 167
Sicily 10
Siep, L. 4
Silverman, M. 21, 22, 24, 115–30